COME FOLLOW ME

To Father Raymond E. Brown, SS

For his witness of Priesthood

and Scholarship of the Sacred Scriptures

COME FOLLOW ME

DISCIPLESHIP REFLECTIONS ON THE SUNDAY GOSPEL READINGS FOR LITURGICAL YEAR A

DANIEL H. MUEGGENBORG

GRACEWING

First published in England in 2016

by

Gracewing
2 Southern Avenue
Leominster
Herefordshire HR6 0QF
United Kingdom

www.gracewing.co.uk

ISBN 978 085244 877 9

Typeset by Gracewing

Cover design by Bernardita Peña Hurtado,
incorporating *The Sermon on the Mount*
by Carl Heinrich Bloch (1834–1890)

CONTENTS

Introduction

There are moments in every disciple's life when the Word of God in sacred Scripture comes alive and the Christian's heart is filled with the fire of faith. For me this graced experience occurred in an extraordinary way during the fall of 1988 when the renowned American Scripture scholar Raymond Brown, SS, served as a visiting professor at the Pontifical Biblical Institute in Rome. While attending his class lectures on The Death of the Messiah provided valuable scholarly insights into the Passion Narratives of the Gospels, serving as his assistant provided insights into his personal character and priestly witness.

Brown's superior knowledge of the biblical texts and his mature reflection on the life of discipleship allowed him to be both an extraordinary professor and an exemplary spiritual guide. Every class was a challenge to take notes quickly enough lest any insight be lost or forgotten. His lectures were more than just studies of the biblical texts; they were living encounters with Jesus Christ Himself.

That moving experience of the Word of God in Sacred Scripture instilled within me a desire to help others experience Scripture as alive and powerful in their lives as well. Initially this desire was expressed in Gospel-based homilies that explored the biblical text. Next, it took the form of Scripture Studies in parishes. Eventually it led to the creation of distance learning programs throughout the Diocese of Tulsa. Most recently, it has been expressed in small faith groups that focus on a prayerful application of the Gospel message to everyday discipleship. This book, then, is the culmination of more than twenty-five years of reflection, study, and application of the Sunday Gospel passage.

This writing is a series of exegetical, in-depth, reflections based on the assigned Gospel reading for the Sundays of a given liturgical year. Each reflection contains a few insights that are explained and then applied to the lived experience of a Christian disciple.

I also wish to acknowledge the various excellent biblical commentaries from which the vast majority of insights were drawn

that are presented in these reflections. I strongly encourage anyone who wants to become a student of scripture to consult these
commentaries directly. In no way do I claim these biblical insights
to be my own. I am utterly dependent upon the research of gen-
erations of scholars. These reflections do not so much represent
an original work on my part as they do a composition of insights
gained from studying three essential biblical commentary series
and some online homily resources from a noted theologian.

The following biblical commentary series were used extensively
and repeatedly in the compilation of these reflections. Each of these
series has a separate volume for specific Gospels and other biblical
writings. The reader is encouraged to consult these commentary
series:

- *The Anchor Bible* (New York, Doubleday)
- *The New Interpreters Bible* (Nashville, Abingdon Press)
- *Sacra Pagina* ("A Michael Glazier Book." Collegeville: The
  Liturgical Press)

In addition to these three essential commentaries, I also gained
insights from the homilies given by the Most Rev. Robert Barron
from the Word on Fire website. Bishop Barron is one of the most
talented theologians and communicators in the Catholic Church
today. He is also a man of great humility, authenticity, and fidelity.
His homilies are an invaluable resource for all disciples and are
readily available as part of the "Resources" section of the Word on
Fire website (www.wordonfire.org). I researched the fifteen-year
collection of his homilies in preparation for each of the weekly
reflections contained in this book and used those insights, which
especially pertained to the biblical text. The reader is encouraged
to consult the Word on Fire website for further study of these
resources and for the other excellent evangelization resources available from that ministry.

The primary purpose of this writing is to promote a personal
discipleship-focused study of the Gospels and to facilitate small
group discussions. It is hoped that this book can be of benefit to
parishioners, homilists, and parish ministry staff.

As you read through these reflections in preparation for the
Sunday Mass, it is important to use a Bible so as to consult the many
scriptural references. The New American Bible Revised Edition is

referenced throughout the reflections. The abbreviation "cf." is used to indicate such opportunities to confer or compare other relevant biblical texts. The abbreviation "v." is used to identify corresponding scriptural quotes and/or passages.

There is no substitute for the Word of God in Scripture. These reflections may shed light on the biblical texts but should never replace those sacred texts in personal prayer and study.

When using these reflections for small group discussion, the following recommended process is simple and effective:

1. Start with an opening Prayer.
2. Read the relevant Biblical text.
3. Review one reflection at a time and focus the discussion on the application questions.
4. Proceed to review the next reflection and focus on those questions.
5. Continue this process until all the reflections for a given Gospel passage have been reviewed.
6. Conclude by praying for the members of the group and interceding for particular needs.

Acknowledgements

This book relies heavily on the scholarship and research of the essential sources that are listed in the bibliography. It also represents the cumulative effort of many people who assisted in the editing and composition process.

Most of all, I wish to acknowledge the following people who were involved in this publication:

Rev. Elkin José González, STD, who assisted in editing each reflection and provided references from the rich spiritual tradition of the Church to enhance and focus various topics.

Dr Henry Harder, PhD, for his assistance and expertise in proof-reading the text.

Sue Karol Roach, for her proof-reading of the final document.

A. J. Tierney, MFA, for her work in formatting and reviewing the text to ensure consistency and conformity.

First Sunday of Advent

Our Scripture passage for this Sunday comes from the Gospel of Matthew 24:37–44. It is one of the apocalyptic passages of the New Testament. The word "apocalypse" really means to "un-veil" or "reveal" and refers to writings that give us insights into the mystery of God's action and the divine will for our world. The Scripture passage for this week reveals the unknown nature of the timing of the coming of the Son of Man (also known as the Second Coming of Jesus). This weekend we celebrate the First Sunday of Advent and so begin a new year in the Church's cycle of time.

One of the most important points being addressed in this passage concerns the timing of Jesus' return. While the timing of our Lord's second coming cannot be known, the fact of His return remains certain. This reality creates a certain tension and temptation for disciples. The tension exists in the fact that people can sometimes become distracted by the desire to calculate the timing of the Lord's return. Such desires are intensified during milestone moments or traumatic events. This desire is fundamentally frustrating due to the impossibility for humans to know or decipher something the Father has reserved to Himself. The temptation can also be for disciples to procrastinate their growth in faith because of the false belief that they will always have time at the last minute to prepare themselves to meet Jesus. This reading tells us that those who wish to wait until the last minute to be prepared to greet the Lord will inevitably be unprepared to do so. Rather, it will catch them off guard like a thief in the night or like the people in the time of Noah who failed to use wisely the opportunities they had to prepare for the coming flood. "For, as in the days before the flood, they were eating and drinking (feasting and reveling without care or worry, 'sporting as though no evil would ever befall them' says Chrysostom)..."[1]

---

1. *The Great Commentary of Cornelius a Lapide: The Holy Gospel According to Saint Matthew Volume II*. Translated by Thomas W. Mossman; Revised and completed by Michael J. Miller (Fitzwilliam: Loreto Publications, 2008), pp. 455–456.

Advent is first and foremost a time of practical preparation to meet the Lord. We usually consider it to be a preparatory time for the celebration of Christmas, and so we tend to engage ourselves in the busy work of decorating, celebrating, and inviting family and friends to various events. That focus really misses the point. The Advent Time is really meant as a preparation for the coming of Jesus both personally and collectively. Every year we celebrate the first coming of our Lord as a babe in Bethlehem in order to remind us of God's fidelity and how He fulfilled His promise to send us a savior. Because of that fidelity, we can trust Jesus' promise to return again. Thus, we look to Jesus' first coming as a way of reaffirming our faith in, and preparing for, His second coming. When we properly understand the intended purpose of Advent, then we can consider the many timely and appropriate ways in which we can use these weeks to spiritually prepare to meet the Lord.

> *How prepared are you to greet the Lord?*
> *When in your life have you been the best prepared?*
> *If the Lord told you that He would come for you today, how would you live this day differently from every other day?*
> *Who is someone you know who lives prepared to meet the Lord every day?*
> *What might you and your family do during this Advent time to make it a more effective experience of spiritual preparation?*

Jesus also cautions us to be careful about focusing our attention on externals. Our Lord gives the specific examples of two situations in which people appeared to be very similar from all external observation but were actually quite different based on their interior dispositions of faith (see the story of the two men in the field and the two women grinding at the mill in Mt 24:40–41). What really distinguished those who were gathered to the Lord from those who were not gathered to the Lord was not so much what they were doing but rather the radical nature of their attachment to God. It is this interior and invisible quality of a person's faith commitment that drew them close to the Lord in this life and brought them into eternal communion with God in heaven. Our preparation to meet the Lord, then, is not primarily a matter of taking on particular practices, additional devotions, or other external changes of behavior. These things will mean nothing if they do not spring from an intense interior life of loving devotion to the Lord. In fact, if prudence is not exercised, sometimes these practices can be moved by a subtle yet harmful pride that distorts the meaning of the spiritual life.[2] For this reason, Jesus emphasizes the need for interior conversion and radical love for God from which a meaningful life of discipleship will naturally flow. Advent, then, is a time to draw close to the Lord in our daily prayer and to purify our hearts of the distractions and disordered affections that obstruct and impede our growth in holiness. This interior process of conversion can be far more difficult than merely changing our exterior actions for a few weeks, but it is also far more important. The interior change of life requires that we acknowledge our need for God because of our fallen and sinful state, see and recognize God's love for us in our Lord's saving and redeeming works—the greatest of which is the death and resurrection of Jesus—and pray for the gift of the Holy Spirit to fill our hearts so that we can love God even as God loves us.

> *What is the growth in prayer you desire during this Advent time?*
> *What are some of the obstacles or impediments you need to address so as to freely and deeply enter into communion with God?*
> *When are you most mindful of God's saving work in your life?*
> *From what situations do you most pray for God to save you now?*
> *How can you use this Advent time to foster that relationship with God in this life that you hope for in eternal life?*

It is interesting that Jesus uses the image of a thief to describe Himself in the final verses of today's passage. Our Lord's coming was similarly likened to that of a thief in other New Testament passages, which attests to the predominance of this image in the life of the early Church (1 Thes 5:2, 2 Pt 3:10, Rev 3:3, Rev

---

2.   St John of the Cross, *Dark Night*, Book 1, chap. 2, 1–2 (Washington, DC: ICS Publ., 1991), pp. 362–363.

16:15). Certainly we all identify with such a situation of pressing attentiveness. If we knew the hour then we would certainly be prepared lest disaster fall upon our household. Jesus used the image of a thief because sometimes people feel threatened by our Lord's promise to return. When some one is not living his or her life in radical commitment to God and selfless love for others, then the coming of the Lord is a threat to their independence, private kingdoms, and self-pursuits. But when someone is in a deeply committed relationship with God, the coming of the Lord is like welcoming a long-awaited friend. Jesus used the image of a thief because our Lord did not need to motivate those already living lives of preparedness. Rather, our Lord needed to motivate those who were not living such spiritual readiness. Each time we pray the Lord's Prayer we say, "Thy Kingdom come". One day God will answer that prayer with the coming of the Son of Man. Of course, Jesus is really the master of the house rather than a thief who breaks in. When we forget our role as disciples and stewards, it is easy to mistakenly believe ourselves to be the master of our own lives. That's when we perceive Jesus as a thief trying to take away what we falsely believe to be ours rather than the Lord of all creation simply laying claim to what has always belonged to Him.

> *How does this understanding of Christian identity change*
> *the way you perceive your responsibility as a disciple?*
> *Do you perceive the coming of Jesus with the image of wel-*
> *coming a longed-for friend or fearing a thief in the night?*
> *Will the Lord's coming be the hope-filled answer to your*
> *prayer or a surprise to your prayer?*

As we begin a new year in the life of the Church, this Sunday is always a good opportunity to stop and take inventory of our growth in faith this past year and to consider what growth we want to take place in the coming year. In short, it's time to make a "New Year's Resolution" for discipleship. Real growth happens when we intentionally look at where we are in our relationship with the Lord and identify the next steps to take so that we can dive more deeply into a life-giving relationship of loving faith. This would be a good subject for prayer during this week. Also, it is important to seek the counsel of others, especially spiritual mentors and ministry leaders, who can advise you on the best ways to pursue this spiritual growth. The Sacrament of Reconciliation is a wonderful way to remove the impediments and obstacles that are holding you back from freely continuing your journey of discipleship, and Advent is a timely opportunity to celebrate the grace of forgiveness. Along with the internal growth in faith, any discipleship resolution should also manifest itself in an external way. In short, we should always act as though the Son of Man were to come today. In the Gospel of Matthew, our Lord stresses the specific need to manifest mercy for those in need and forgiveness of our enemies and those who offend us. In Matthew, our Lord also asks us to be makers of peace who bring the light of Christ into a darkened world.

> *What would you like to be different about your faith life one year from now?*
> *What steps will you take to make it happen?*
> *What have been milestones of your growth in discipleship this past year?*
> *How has your growth in faith motivated a visible change in the way you live?*
> *What change of life do you pray for this next year?*

Although we await the full revelation of Jesus as the eternal King, we already experience His presence among us even now. There are various ways in which the eternal Son of God comes to us: in the incarnation of Jesus of Nazareth, in the Sacraments, in prayer, in the lives of faithful Christians, and in His Second Coming at the end of time. These are all His "Advent". The focus of our faith is not only on the past or the future but also on the present. One of the challenges of our Advent preparation is to have eyes that can see the presence of Jesus already with us in the present.

> *When are you most conscious of the presence of Jesus with you?*
> *What can you do to deepen your participation in the life of Christ during this Advent season?*
> *As you review the various ways that Jesus comes to us, in which one do you find it most difficult to see the presence of Jesus?*

What can you do this Advent to open your eyes so the presence of Jesus can be more clearly revealed to you?

Second Sunday Of Advent

Our Scripture passage for this Sunday comes from the Gospel of Matthew 3:1–12. In this passage we are introduced to the person of John the Baptist and his ministry of preparing the way for Jesus. Advent is a time of preparation, and the image of John the Baptist offers some insightful challenges for us as disciples who strive for preparedness of faith in our lives.

The first part of John's preaching calls on the crowds to repent. The word "repent" comes from the Greek word *metanoia* and literally means to "re-think" or "change one's mind". John preaches this message because our actions stem from our thoughts. If we want to change our lives, we have to change our thinking first. The call to repent is the invitation to see things from God's perspective and to take on the "mind of Christ" (as St Paul describes it in 1 Cor 2:16). When we see the situations of our lives from God's point of view, we will correctly prioritize our values and respond in a Christ-like way to the situations we face. Being a disciple is not a matter of following rules and regulations or just external observances. Rather, it is a matter of living in deep communion with God and expressing that communion in the way we act. Repentance is a good thing. There is both an inherent relationship and a difference between the moments of conversion and repentance in a person's life. Conversion means to "turn towards" the Lord and occurs in moments when a person's life is re-directed towards God. These moments can be born from a realization of God's presence, God's love, and God's forgiveness. Conversion occurs when we willingly refocus our lives on God. However, conversion must be lived out in practical actions so that our lives are, indeed, conformed to Christ Jesus and the Gospel. As we undertake each change, each step, we come closer to being conformed to the Lord. Repentance is the process of progressing in closeness to God through a life evermore conformed to the Gospel. The teachings of Jesus and our Lord's way of life are meant to inspire us so that we will follow wherever He leads us. Most people think of the term repentance in a penitential sense and so believe it to involve actions of self-denial, self-mortification, amendment of life, and so forth. While the process of repentance may involve these things, as well as other ascetic practices, it is a much more positive process. Its ultimate goal is to bring us to deeper communion with the Lord both in how we think and in what we do.

How does this teaching on repentance differ from your previous understanding of the term?

What values and priorities bring you closer to God, and what values and priorities lead you away from God in daily circumstances?

What is a situation you are facing now that you would like to see from God's perspective so as to respond with the mind of Christ?

Repentance is a life-long process for every disciple. What have been some of the significant experiences that have helped you to repent?

What have been some of the significant experiences that have helped you to redirect your life to God (conversion)?

The physical description of John the Baptist is interesting as we are told he wore a garment of camel's hair and a leather belt. This description correlates to that of the Prophet Elijah in 2 Kings 1:8 and suggests that John was clearly presenting himself as the new Elijah. That presentation was an important announcement because in Malachi 3:1, 4–5 we are told that Elijah would return to prepare for the Messiah. We are also told that John ate locusts and wild honey, which signifies much more than simply an odd diet. It is actually a statement that John was preserving himself in ritual purity even in the desert and was trusting in divine providence for his daily life. This description of John the Baptist may seem strange to us, but when we understand the statement he was making by his appearance and lifestyle then we better understand the message he was sending. As a disciple, John understood his responsibility to draw others to Christ with missionary outreach. John knew that attracting others to Jesus meant that he had to get their attention in a way that raised their curiosity. It was John's lifestyle and not just his words that attracted people to him and raised their awareness of the coming Messiah. Sometimes we, as disciples, don't like to stand out from the crowd in order to avoid being different from the rest. It is important to remember that our missionary outreach sometimes requires that we find ways to raise the curiosity of others. For John, this action involved his dress and diet. Regardless of the means, the challenge is the same. There should be something different about the way disciples live and that difference should intrigue and attract others to learn more about us. It is that curiosity that becomes the open door through which we can share with others the faith that guides and sustains our lives. As Saint Peter wrote in 1 Peter 3:15, "But in your hearts revere Christ as Lord. Always be prepared to give an answer to everyone who asks you to give the reason for the hope that you have." John attracted a crowd and John did not hesitate to inform that crowd of the reason for his hope—The Lord Jesus Christ.

> *What have you seen someone do that raised the curiosity of others and became an opportunity to share authentically, sincerely, and inspiringly the gift of faith?*
> *What do you do as a distinctive and overt expression of your discipleship so that others can be drawn to Jesus through you?*
> *What happens when disciples are just like everyone else in the crowd?*

Next, John warns the Pharisees and Sadducees to "Produce good fruits as evidence of your repentance." That's because these two groups were coming to be baptized for the sake of accumulating one more religious experience. John does not prevent them from being baptized but rather warns them that baptism must be lived out. If they fail to live out their action of repentance (baptism) then they cannot presume that their ritual action of faith alone will preserve them from God's wrath. There is an important analogy that is worth remembering in this regard: baptism is to the Christian life what a wedding is to a marriage. Once the ritual is celebrated, then comes the daily challenge of living it out. The Pharisees and Sadducees knew the fruit God expected of them since the Prophets often spoke about this theme (Hos 9:16, Is 27:6, Jer 12:2, 17, 8, and Ez 17:8–9, 23). As disciples, we can fall into the temptation to accumulate religious experiences as well, but if those experiences do not bear good fruit in the way we live then we have missed the point like the Pharisees and Sadducees. This failure to connect our religious actions and our daily lives occurs when we see someone in need and say, "I'll pray for you" but do nothing beyond that to help them. It happens when we go to church on Sunday because it's that time of the week but do not let our worship guide us throughout the week. It happens when we confess our sins but do not have a sincere desire for conversion. All the religious actions and good intentions we can muster really don't mean much if they don't lead to a practical change in the way we live. That's what makes the difference between religion as a means of entertainment and religion as a life-changing encounter with God.

> *What are the "Good fruits" the Lord expects us to produce every time we receive Communion?*
> *What are the "Good fruits" the Lord expects from us when we pray the Lord's Prayer?*
> *What are the "Good fruits" the Lord expects from you as a result of your study of the Sunday Gospel?*
> *What are the "Good fruits" the Lord expects from you through the blessings of your marriage and family?*
> *How are we tempted today to reduce our religious practice to entertainment rather than life-changing encounter?*

John then preaches that people should not rely on external relationships of faith. In particular, he says to the Pharisees and Sadducees, "Do not presume to say to yourselves, 'We have Abraham as our father.'" John knew that many people of his time thought they were automatically privileged in the eyes of God because of their relationship to Abraham. This message is an enduring caution to disciples of all time and reminds us we should not presume God's mercy or favor based upon a mere association with others or simply because of our religious affiliation. Rather, each person must make a personal and radical commitment to the person of Jesus in a life-changing relationship. No one else can do this for us. The example of others may lead us to this commitment and encourage us in it, but another's example is never a substitute for it. The good lives of our parents, relatives, friends, or fellow parishioners are not our lives. God wants us to respond to Him and not to excuse ourselves because of our association with others who have responded. If the Pharisees and Sadducees want to be children of Abraham then they have to imitate Abraham's fidelity and sacrificial love for God in their own lives. True children act like their father. Saint Paul reflects extensively on the example of Abraham in Galatians 3 and Romans 4 so that the early Christians of those communities would know how to imitate Abraham's faith in their own lives.

What are ways in which people can rely on superficial relationships of faith today?

When have you been tempted to think you automatically have a privileged relationship with God because of some external factor in your life (being Catholic or the family you belong to, as examples)?

How can external identifications of faith become helpful by informing and guiding our discipleship?

In Baptism we become the adopted sons and daughters of God. How would your day change if you were to live out that identity in a radical way?

Lastly, John turns the attention of the crowds away from him and towards the coming of Jesus. While many people were coming to him, he did not want them to be confused about who was really the Messiah. Rather, John clearly pointed out how much greater is Jesus. By doing so John is showing incredible humility in overcoming the temptation to pride and leading people to God rather than focusing people's attention and affection on himself. Just imagine how easy it would have been for John to make himself the focus of the people's admiration. We all like to be in the limelight in some way and to be respected and honored by those closest to us. John used his popularity and appeal to lead others to Jesus and so should we in order to preserve our inner freedom. In the XIV century the English Augustinian mystic Walter Hilton pointed out that if we want to know how much pride is inside of us, we need to observe wisely if flattery and praise are pleasing to us and turn into vain gladness and self-satisfaction. Also, we need to pay attention when others despise us with no reason and if we feel resentment against them with resistance against suffering and shame, then we need to look for repentance.[3]

> *What are the negative effects that occur when religious leaders focus people's attention on themselves rather than on Jesus? For whom are you the focus of attention?*
>
> *What talents or personality traits draw people to you and how could you use those talents and traits to lead people to Jesus?*
>
> *How can you channel others' attention and respect for you towards the Lord and so lead them to Him?*
>
> *John's most successful work was his preaching and baptism; he used both of those as the vehicles for his message of Jesus. What is your most successful work and how can it become the vehicle for you to communicate the message of Jesus?*
>
> *Sometimes we actually like it when other people see us as their savior. How do you think pride gets in the way of true discipleship and the message of the Gospel?*

---

3.   W. Hilton, *The Scale of Perfection*, Book 1, 63 (New York: Paulist Press, 1991), p. 134.

Third Sunday of Advent

Our Scripture passage for this Sunday comes from the Gospel of Matthew 11:2–11. In this passage we read about John the Baptist sending his messengers to ask whether or not Jesus is the Christ, "The One who is to come". While Jesus esteems John as being the greatest of the Prophets, He doesn't answer their question directly. Instead, Jesus tells them that they, and John, must make a personal decision of faith about Him. This reading offers several points of reflection for us during this third week of Advent.

Prophets are a very misunderstood group in the Scriptures. Oftentimes people think the prophets were those who foretold the future. Certainly that misunderstanding is exemplified by many of our secular tabloids. However, the role of a prophet like John the Baptist was to be God's spokesperson in the world. The prophets were people who interpreted the events of their times and called others to return to right relationship with God and neighbor. The prophets helped others to see things from God's perspective and to respond accordingly. Paul tells us in 1 Corinthians 12 that the gift of prophecy continued to be a ministry in the early Church. The charisms of the Holy Spirit are often intensified when significant movements are initiated. This intensification of charism was seen in the early Church that received the gift of the Holy Spirit in dramatic ways on Pentecost. Similar intensifications of the Spirit have also been manifested historically when religious orders and religious movements were being founded. Charisms can be manifested and recognized on a variety of levels including personal, communal (local parish and religious movements) and institutional. The institutionalization of a charism does not diminish in any way the effective gift of the Spirit to individuals but rather preserves it, incorporates it, and channels it into the formal life and ministry of the Church.

Who are the prophets in the Church today?
How do you tell the difference between an authentic prophet and an inauthentic one?

*When have you been a prophetic voice to someone else so
as to help them understand the events of their lives from
God's perspective and to respond accordingly?*
*To whom do you listen when you are seeking to understand
the events of our time or your life from God's perspective?*
*The prophets were often persecuted because of their mes-
sage. When have you been put down or rejected for communicating a message of faith?*

John prepared as best he could for the coming of Jesus. However,
John expected a Messiah who would bring punishment, destruction, and vengeance (cf. uses of "fire", "axe", "winnowing fork" in Mt
3:1–12). His preaching was a message of "fire and brimstone". Jesus,
however, came as someone who reconciled, converted, healed,
and redeemed. These were actions quite different from those of
John's expectations. This confused expectation helps us understand
why John sought clarification of Jesus' mission and identity. The
experience of John teaches us that the best we can do as disciples
is to be ready to welcome the Lord in the way He wishes to reveal
Himself. Even John's expectations were not completely accurate.
John thought the Messiah should punish the wicked and vindicate
the righteous, yet John remained unjustly imprisoned by Herod.
Perhaps John's personal situation of suffering made it difficult for
him to see how God's mercy could act in other people's lives (healing of the blind, lame, and so forth) while not in his own life. Part
of our Advent preparation as disciples is to examine the ways in
which we have allowed our own expectations of God to blind us
to the Lord's action in our world. It takes humility to let God be
God! That humility also requires that we study God's works in
salvation history so that we can better recognize how surprising
and unconventional is the Lord's action.

How have you seen God acting in unexpected ways?
*What are the dangers of insisting that God act according
to our expectations?*
*When do you find yourself frustrated in faith because God
doesn't act the way you think He should?*
*When has your personal suffering made it difficult for you
to rejoice in other people's blessings?*

How have you seen suffering become an obstacle to faith?
What is a way in which you can learn more about God's
actions in salvation history so as to better recognize the
Lord's works in the world today?
When do you find it difficult to let God be God?

When the disciples of John come to Jesus they seek clarification as to whether or not Jesus is the Messiah ("the One who is to come"). Jesus did not answer that question for them. Instead, He pointed to the works He had done and asked them to interpret for themselves what those signs mean. Jesus did heal the blind in Matthew 8:27–30, made the lame walk in Matthew 8:5–13 and Matthew 9:1–7, healed lepers in Matthew 8:1–4, made the deaf hear in Matthew 8:32–34, raised the dead in Matthew 9:18–26, and preached good news to the poor in Matthew 5:3. Some passages of the Old Testament (especially Is 26:19, 35:5–6 and 61:1) identify these works as things that God will do. The Lord doesn't answer a lot of our questions either. Sometimes we have to look around us and interpret the good works taking place as confirming signs of God's presence. To a person of faith, the witness of God's love and providence is abundantly clear. To a person who lacks faith, life is nothing but chance and coincidence. Either way, Jesus doesn't make a decision of faith for us. At best, He points our attention in the right way and asks us to make our own decision of faith for Him. When we do so, our eyes are opened to see the wonder of God's presence in ways we could never have previously imagined. The poet Gerard Manley Hopkins commented on this when he said, "The world is charged with the grandeur of God."[4] It should be noted that Jesus does not tell John's disciples to watch Him only in glorious moments when He preaches to the crowds or when He walks on water or when He feeds the five thousand with a few loaves and fish. Rather, He tells them that they will come to know Him best in ministry to the suffering and downtrodden. There are certain settings in which we can come to experience God's presence in a more immediate and intense way than others. These settings are called "privileged places of encounter". Jesus identified Himself with the poor and

---

4. G. M. Hopkins, "God's Grandeur" in *Poems and Prose* (London: Penguins Classics, 1985).

the suffering when He said, "Whatsoever you do to the least of these, you do unto me" (Mt 25:40). When we are close to those who suffer, we will be close to the Lord and we will see the presence of God more clearly. Disciples who have trouble recognizing the Lord present in those who suffer will have even greater difficulty recognizing God present in Jesus on the cross of Calvary.

> *When have you made a decision of faith for God in your life? What prompted it and how do you identify with John the Baptist's disciples who seek clarification?*
> *What are the signs of the times today that reveal to us the reality and presence of God?*
> *Jesus continues His works through the gift of the Holy Spirit in the Church. How are people today drawn to Jesus through these ministries?*
> *Which of the works of Jesus has touched your life in a personal way so as to awaken the gift of faith in you?*
> *When has your faith grown because you experienced the Lord's presence while serving Him in a privileged place of encounter?*

The final part of Jesus' discourse is a challenge to the crowds when He asks them, "What did you go out to see?" He uses the example of a reed shaken by the wind and someone clothed in soft garments. The reed shaken by the wind is probably a reference to someone who changes their opinions based on political convenience. The person dressed in soft clothes is probably an image of comfort, prestige, and high society. Herod actually did fit both of these images and even used a reed on coins minted during his reign when he founded the city of Tiberius in AD 19. Jesus challenged the crowds to be clear about why they went to the desert and to respond accordingly to the one they heard speak. If they went to hear the latest political or religious opinion, then that's a matter of interest, debate, and discussion; but if they went to hear a prophet, they should be heeding every word that John preached as coming from the mouth of God. If they went to see the latest and most beautiful fashion, then that's a matter of competitive consumerism, culture, or artistic interest; but if they went to hear a prophet, they should be prepared to embrace the difficult sacrifices needed so as to change their lives and return to right relationship with God and others. Jesus issues the same challenge to us every time we encounter the word of God in prayer, Scripture study, and other sources of divine revelation. We cannot remain neutral in the face of a religious encounter; we will either respond to God with acceptance or reject the Lord with indifference. This challenge is particularly relevant for us during this Advent time when we are encouraged to seek a deeper encounter with the Lord. We are cautioned to not only seek that encounter but to also respond appropriately to it.

Why do you come to Mass and receive Communion?
What do you look for in the homily or the reading of the Scriptures?
What do you do when you are presented with an opportunity to grow in faith through a particular ministry?
What are some of the religious opportunities (like the preaching of John the Baptist) that have changed your life?
What are some of the religious opportunities you wish you had participated in but didn't?
In what ways can we try to diminish the power of God's Word and so exempt ourselves from needing to be changed by it?

Fourth Sunday of Advent

Our Scripture passage for this Sunday comes from the Gospel of Matthew 1:18–24. In this passage, we read about Joseph the just man who allows his life plans to be changed by the will of God revealed to him in a dream. As we enter these final days of preparation for Christmas, this passage offers some particular points for our reflection.

Joseph was in a dilemma as to what he should do. We are told that he was a "just" man. That description means Joseph is someone who kept the law and obeyed it. However, the law (Dt 22:23–27) presented quite harsh consequences for women in such a situation as Mary; that is, with child, and the betrothed husband was not the father. At the very least, such a woman was to be publicly humiliated, and in a worst-case scenario she could even be stoned to death for disgracing her household. Although he was an observer of the law, Joseph chose not to subject another human being to such a cruel fate. He had to decide whether he would keep the letter of the law and expose Mary to shame or allow his actions to be guided by compassion and mercy. This is a situation Jesus will address in the Gospel of Matthew very clearly when He teaches us that the greatest law is that of loving God and our neighbor. Everything else is subject to that one great commandment. Christianity is not a matter of blind adherence to laws and rules. Rather, we are to consider the impact our actions have on other people's lives and be guided by the principles of authentically faithful mercy and compassion. After all, law was made for man and not man for the law (Mk 2:27). Jesus will teach us the primacy of love as the interpretative element for all laws when He says:

> You have heard that it was said, 'You shall love your neighbor and hate your enemy.' But I say to you, love your enemies, and pray for those who persecute you, that you may be children of your heavenly Father, for he makes his sun rise on the bad and the good, and causes rain to fall on the just and the unjust (Mt 5:43–45).

Joseph was ready to go beyond being just; he was ready to be merciful even if it meant not observing the law. Even in his feelings of hurt, anger, confusion, and betrayal, Joseph still cared about Mary and didn't want to inflict any injury upon her. In the words of Saint John Chrysostom, "Joseph determined to conduct himself now by a higher rule than the law, for now that grace was appearing; it would be fitting that many tokens of that exalted citizenship be expressed."[5]

> *How does the example of Joseph challenge you?*
> *How can the strict observance of laws today end up hurting people rather than helping people?*
> *When have you had to break a rule in order to be merciful to someone?*
> *Joseph risked the misunderstanding of others when he took Mary into his home. When have you risked being misunderstood for being merciful to someone else?*
> *What is the greatest law that governs and interprets your family life?*
> *What is the greatest law that governs and interprets your professional life?*

Although Joseph thought he was being quite heroic in choosing to be merciful to Mary, the reality is that God had something even better in mind. God wanted Joseph to be a part of His Divine Plan for the world and to provide a home for Jesus. That is a mission Joseph could have never imagined on his own. Rather, it was a revelation of God's will that became manifest to him. God's plan called Joseph to go beyond being merely heroic and to become a person who is heroically holy. That understanding of God's will unfolded for Joseph in the context of a dream. God continues to use our imagination as the place where we are inspired to know the Lord's will. We can choose to focus our imagination on images of revenge, or self-pity, or triumph, or any other way to resolve the challenges we face. We can also choose to focus our imagination on what Jesus would do in a similar situation as ours. A person

5.   St John Chrysostom, "The Gospel of Matthew: Homily 4.4" in *Ancient Christian Commentary on Scripture*, New Testament, Ia, Matthew 1–13 (Downers Grove: Inter Varsity Press, 2001), pp. 14–15.

doesn't have to be Christian to act in a heroic way, but Christians are called to act in a heroically holy way. As disciples, we are called to rise above the highest standards of the secular world around us and to bear witness in our lives to the very holiness and sacrificial love of God. That means being much more than just a nice person. When we choose to use our imagination as a method of prayer, the Lord will inspire us to see how we can live out God's will not just in a heroic way but even in a holy way. It is literally mindboggling to gain a glimpse of how God calls us to live each day. When we open ourselves and sincerely ask the Lord to inspire us so that we might be the instrument of His salvation and redemption in the world, then we are offering the Lord the gift of our lives to use according to His will. It is at this moment that Joseph reveals another great quality. Joseph was not only a dreamer, but he also acted on that moment of inspiration. The Gospel tells us that when he awoke, he took Mary into his home; he did as the angel had commanded. It's one thing to imagine what God's will wants to accomplish in and through our lives; it's quite another thing for us to let the Lord use our lives to do that will.

> *How have you used your imagination as a resource for prayer?*
> *What are some of the ways that we dismiss inspired moments so as to not respond to them?*
> *What are some of the daydreams with which God is inspiring you at this time?*
> *Have you ever been surprised to learn that someone else is being inspired with the same faith-filled dream as you, and have you found it meaningful?*
> *What is the holiest thing you can imagine doing today?*
> *Who are some of the faith-filled dreamers of our time who see and respond to the will of God?*

Throughout this Advent time, we have been focusing our attention on what it means to prepare for the coming of Jesus. One of the ways Jesus is present to us is through the lives of faithful Christians who manifest "God with us" (Emmanuel) by their actions of saving love for others. God can accomplish His will without us, so it is worth considering why the Lord wants our cooperation in His plan.

Perhaps it's because the Lord wants to give us the privilege and joy of bringing His presence to others. God delights in letting us be His co-workers! That cooperation can only happen, however, when we say "Yes" to the will of God and give the Lord permission to use our lives in an active response of generosity and enthusiasm. Part of our Advent journey is about leading us to that moment of faithful surrender so that we can become a selfless conduit of God's grace for others. That's what Mary did with her "Yes", that's what Joseph did with his "Yes", and that's what we can do with our "Yes". People who say "Yes" to eagerly accomplish the Lord's will can change the world. Saint Catherine of Siena challenged Christians in the four-teenth century to be such heroic witnesses of faith when she said, "If you were to become who God intends you to be, you would set the (world) on fire."[6] In the final verse of Matthew's Gospel, Jesus fulfills His earthly ministry by assuring His disciples that He will be "with them always" (Mt 28:20). Our Lord can give this assurance because His presence in the world will always be known through the lives of heroic people of faith who say "Yes" to God's will and offer themselves for the Lord's work.

> *Who exemplifies heroic spiritual surrender in their lives?*
> *How do you know that "God is with you" ("Emmanuel")*
> *each day?*
> *Who has inspired you to want to live a heroic life?*
> *Who has inspired you to want to live a holy life?*
> *What are some of the limits or qualifications (or even expi-*
> *ration dates) we can put on our "Yes" to God?*
> *This reading shows us what great things can happen when*
> *people say "Yes" to God. What are practical examples of*
> *things you think happen when people say "No" to God?*
> *When we pray about difficult situations in our world, we*
> *oftentimes ask God to do something; has it ever occurred to*
> *you that God did do something—He created you?*

Joseph is an interesting figure in the Gospel. We don't know much about him except what we read in the Gospel of Matthew. Most

---

6.   St Catherine of Siena, *Adaptation of Letter T368*. For a systematic
      edition of the letters, see S. Noffke, *Letters of Catherine of Siena*,
      vols. 1-3 (Arizona Center for Religious Studies, 2007).

Scripture scholars consider it probable that Joseph died sometime prior to Jesus' public ministry and that explains why Mary, Jesus, and the family are mentioned later in the Gospel accounts but never Joseph (Mt 12:46–50). In many ways, Joseph is a hidden yet essential part of the Gospel message. God needed Joseph to provide a nurturing home for Jesus and a caring husband for Mary. It takes a man of outstanding qualities to offer his life for such a mission and to do so humbly, quietly, respectfully, sacrificially, and so forth. Joseph worked day in and day out to provide for the family he accepted when he said "Yes" to God.

> *In what ways do you identify with Joseph?*
> *What do you think was Joseph's greatest virtue?*
> *What do you think was most difficult for Joseph in his role as the foster father of Jesus?*
> *What opportunities do you have to care for someone for whom you are not legally responsible?*
> *If you were to pray to St Joseph for inspiration today, what would be your prayer?*

Solemnity of Christmas
(Midnight & Dawn)

Although the Solemnity of Christmas does not necessarily occur on a Sunday, it is such an important and pivotal celebration in the life of the Church that it warrants inclusion in this series of Sunday Gospel reflections. This is true not only because of the prominent place Christmas holds in our society but also because of the profound nature of the infancy passages as recorded in the Gospel of Luke. Although there are optional Gospel passages which can be used at Christmas Masses (depending upon when those Masses are celebrated), the passage we will study for this reflection is taken from the Gospel of Luke 2:1–20.

The story of Jesus' birth in Bethlehem is a familiar one, and because of that we can easily miss the significance of the many important and meaningful details Luke mentions. These details tell us important information about who Jesus is, what our Lord's mission will entail, how we can encounter Him, and what the proper response is to that encounter. Let's study each of these aspects to see what insights we can gain and lessons we can learn to guide us in our discipleship.

The infancy narrative from Luke's Gospel contains particular details which help us better understand the identity of Jesus. First, Jesus was born in the midst of vulnerable homelessness and inhospitable poverty. Our Lord's identification with such circumstances at the moment of His birth prepares for His ministry later in the Gospel when He will demonstrate preferential compassion for those who suffer similar conditions. Francis of Assisi frequently meditated on the conditions of our Lord's birth because he saw in that moment Jesus' identification with the poor and the outcast.[7]

Second, at the moment of Jesus' birth the multitude of angels proclaimed Jesus as the source of peace (Lk 2:14) with the titles

---

7.   St Bonaventure, *Vita di S. Francesco d'Assisi* (Assisi: Edizioni Porziuncola, 2008), Chap. 9, 5, p. 111.

Savior, Christ, and Lord. All of these titles of implied majesty were direct challenges to the authority of the Roman Emperor Caesar Augustus (Lk 2:11). Augustus was hailed as the "Savior" of the people and was given credit for bringing "Peace". The famous Altar of Peace reconstructed on the banks of the Tiber River in Rome was originally built to celebrate the end of the civil war between Mark Anthony and Augustus following the death of Julius Caesar. This passage from Luke's Gospel tells us that the true source of peace is lying in a manger in Bethlehem and not on a throne in Rome. It also tells us that the one who can truly save us is found in a small town of Judea and not the capital of the Roman Empire. The title Lord was equally as revolutionary and subversive. While it was a statement of Jesus' divinity as God, it was also a title claimed by the Roman Emperor. For this reason, Luke goes out of his way in chapter 2, verse 1 to situate the birth of Jesus in the context of world events because what happens in the small town of Bethlehem will reach the farthest corners of the world. The title "Christ" is an identification of Jesus as the long-awaited Messiah of the Jewish people.

Third, the most important revelation of Jesus' identity occurs when we are told that He is the "Firstborn" who was "wrapped in swaddling clothes". The proper way to translate the verse of Luke 2:7 would be as follows, "And she gave birth to her son the Firstborn and wrapped Him in swaddling cloths…" The term "Firstborn" (Greek *prototokos*) was a significant title first used in the Old Testament in reference to the people of Israel (Ex 4:22 and Jer 31:9) and then in the New Testament as a description of Jesus in reference to His eternal relationship with the Father ("Firstborn among many brothers" in Rom 8:29, "Firstborn of all creation" in Col 1:15, 18, "Firstborn from the Dead" in Rev 1:4–5, "The Firstborn" in Heb 1:5–6).[8] To call Jesus the "Firstborn" is a statement of our Lord's divinity. We are then told that Jesus was "wrapped in swad-

---

8.   In the Septuagint, the text of Ex 4:22 is read, "σὺ δὲ ἐρεῖς τῷ Φαραώ· τάδε λέγει Κύριος· υἱὸς πρωτότοκός μου Ἰσραήλ"; Jer 31:9 [Jer 38:9]: ἐν κλαυθμῷ ἐξῆλθον, καὶ ἐν παρακλήσει ἀνάξω αὐτοὺς αὐλίζων ἐπὶ διώρυγας ὑδάτων ἐν ὁδῷ ὀρθῇ, καὶ οὐ μὴ πλανηθῶσιν ἐν αὐτῇ· ὅτι ἐγενόμην τῷ Ἰσραὴλ εἰς πατέρα, καὶ Ἐφραὶμ πρωτότοκός μού ἐστιν;" and Col 1:15, "ὅς ἐστιν εἰκὼν τοῦ Θεοῦ τοῦ ἀοράτου, πρωτότοκος πάσης κτίσεως."

dling clothes". The Old Testament references to swaddling clothes (Ez 16:4, Wis 7:1–6) all point to the ordinariness of an everyday human experience surrounding the birth of a baby. The point is that all people are wrapped in cloth at their birth; it is a statement of our common humanity. That's why these two descriptions are so important when they are put together, because it is Luke's way of describing the Incarnation of the Eternal Word who became Flesh. Or, as Luke would put it, the "Firstborn" was wrapped in "swaddling clothes". It is the statement that God has become man. As disciples, we need to be clear about who Jesus is and where we find Him. To Him alone belong the Kingdom, power, and glory. From Him alone comes peace and salvation. In Him alone are heaven and earth united as God and man are joined in one person. Jesus will continue to identify Himself with the poor and the outcast. Through us, His disciples, He will reach the far corners of the world including the deepest recesses of our own world. Our encounter with Him is nothing less than an encounter with the eternal God.

> *Which of these revelations of Jesus' identity most challenges you as a disciple, and why?*
> *Why do you think Luke took such great care to tell us so many things about Jesus when our Lord was just an infant in the small town of Bethlehem?*
> *If you were to tell someone who Jesus is, what descriptions would you use?*
> *Where do you go to find salvation and peace?*

Luke also includes a significant detail when he tells us in verse 7 that Mary, "...wrapped him in swaddling clothes and laid him in a manger, because there was no room for them in the inn". This identifying location of the manger is related again by the angels in Luke 2:12 when the multitude informs the shepherds where they will find the Savior. The word "manger" means a place of feeding, and it is where the food was offered so the flock could be nourished. Just as Jesus was "wrapped" and "laid" in a manger at His birth, so too the Lord will be "wrapped" and "laid" in a tomb at His death (Lk 23:53). Also, it should be noted that "inn" is not the best translation for the Greek term *kataluma*. Sometimes this term will be better translated by "the place where travelers lodged". Although that is a lengthy translation it is actually more accurate and describes the accommodations normally provided to travelers as an expression of hospitality. This term becomes more important because in Luke 22:11 we are told that it is in a *kataluma* that Jesus celebrates the Last Supper with His disciples and institutes the Eucharist. With this final interpretive connection, we can now understand the profound meaning of what happened in Bethlehem: Jesus, the eternal Son of God became Man—who will give His life for us on Calvary and in the Eucharist at the Last Supper—is now being placed in the manger to become food for the flock. This is a very powerful and beautiful understanding of the Eucharist in Luke's Gospel. When the shepherds receive the good news (Gospel) of Jesus' birth, they are told that they will find Him "in a manger". Luke wants all disciples to be able to recognize the Firstborn of God in the food of the Eucharistic banquet. It is for this reason that Luke later includes the important story of the journey to Emmaus and the two disciples who come to recognize the Risen Lord in "the breaking of the Bread" (Lk 24:30–35). If we want to meet the Lord this Christmas, then there really is no better place to find Him than in "Christ's Mass"! The same God who assumed our human condition in the Incarnation freely chooses to give Himself to us as "food for the flock" in the Real Presence of the Eucharist. The word Bethlehem is a Hebrew term that means "House of Bread". How appropriate it is that the Bread of Life is now born in the House of Bread! As disciples, this is good news for us. It challenges us to look beyond the physical elements of bread and wine and to see the Eucharistic presence of the Risen Lord. It also guides us in our search for Jesus so that we might know how and where the Lord offers Himself to us. Reflecting on this mystery Edith Stein said, "The child in the manger opens his arms and his smile already explains what he will later say, 'come to me those who are labored and burdened' (cf. Mt 11:28)."[9]

How does this image of Jesus being laid in the manger help deepen your appreciation of the Eucharist?

---

9.   E. Stein, "Le Mystère de Noël (Ger: *Das Weihnachtsgeheimnis*)" in *La Crèche et la Croix* (Paris: Ad Solem Editions S.A., 2007), p. 23.

*Jesus was placed in the manger in the midst of an inhospi-
table and even hostile situation of rejection. Who do you
think was most encouraged by our Lord's presence in that
setting, and who is most encouraged today by our Lord's
Eucharistic presence in similar circumstances?*

*What would your response have been to this event if you
had been present at Bethlehem, and how does it inspire
and challenge your response to similar situations today?*

The next section of the infancy narrative goes on to relate how
the shepherds received the good news of Jesus' birth and of their
response to that news. We are specifically told that the shepherds
said to one another, "Let us go, then, to Bethlehem to see this thing
that has taken place, which the Lord has made known to us" (Lk
2:15). Later we are told that the shepherds returned glorifying God
for all they had heard and seen (Lk 2:20). Both of these actions are
important and offer guidance for us as to how we should respond
to messages of faith in our lives. First, it is significant that the
shepherds were not content to only hear about Jesus, but they
were motivated to go and meet the Lord for themselves. This is
an important dynamic that should be taking place in our lives as
disciples as well. Every revelation of God, every truth of our faith,
is meant to draw us to the divine encounter, and if we settle with
mere knowledge, we have not fulfilled the intended purpose of the
good news we receive by faith. The difference between learning
about God and actually encountering God has been likened to the
difference between reading a recipe and actually tasting the meal.
Jesus wants to draw us to Himself, and anything we learn about
the Lord is meant to motivate and facilitate such an encounter. The
shepherds were told where to find Jesus, what He looked like, and
who He was. With that knowledge they then put forth the effort
to go and meet the Lord for themselves. Luke wants all of us as
disciples to be motivated in the same way.

Second, it is important to note what the shepherds did after
they met the Lord; they praised God and returned to their flocks.
The image of the shepherds is an interesting one and can function
on various levels. Some Scripture scholars see the shepherds as
symbols of the poor and outcasts who become the first to receive
the good news of Jesus' birth. Other Scripture scholars think the

shepherds more aptly represent the leaders of the Christian Church who care for the flock. This second interpretation would most certainly be in line with other New Testament writings that relate the ministry of Jesus, the apostles, and their successors to that of shepherding (1 Pt 5:2–4, Jn 21:15–17, Mk 6:34, Mt 9:36, Jn 10:11–18). This response of the shepherds should inspire us to act in the same way. They took the message of their encounter with Jesus back to their flocks. In a real sense, they had nothing to give their flocks until they themselves had experienced the Lord! It is because of their personal encounter with Jesus that they can now lead their flocks to the Lord as well. When we encounter the Lord, it is never meant to be an experience that we keep to ourselves. Rather, we are to praise God for that grace and share it with those entrusted to our care so that they too can experience the Lord and be transformed by God's love.

> For what experience of God in your life do you offer greatest praise and thanksgiving?
> How can you lead others to that experience in their lives?
> Why are people all too often content to just learn about God but not motivated to encounter God for themselves?
> Why do you think Luke put such emphasis on the importance of personal encounter with Jesus for disciples?

Finally, in Luke 2:19 we are told that Mary kept all these things, pondering them in her heart. The image of Mary is important because she embodies what it means to be a disciple. She was the first one to hear the Word of God and to do it (Lk 1:38 and Lk 11:28). In this moment, then, Mary is teaching us the importance of reflecting on the experience of God lest we fail to grasp the significance and meaning of the Lord's action in our lives. It is only when we take time to prayerfully reflect on the events of our lives that we can come to understand those things from God's perspective and see the presence of God with us. Such reflection requires periods of sacred silence in a person's life. Silence is the door through which God enters our heart and soul. Without silence, we can't have any meaningful awareness of God or bring into coherent meaningful focus the realities of our lives. That is why the English scholar, T. S. Eliot, claimed that a tragedy occurs when we have the experience but miss the meaning.[10] The philosopher, Socrates, is credited with articulating the importance of such reflective contemplation when he said, "The unexamined life is not worth living for a human being."[11] Mary reminds all disciples of the importance of faith-filled reflection on the events of God in our lives. Indeed, through the door of silence God can enter our hearts, minds, and souls and help us to understand deeply the meaning of the Lord's action in our world.

> *How do you incorporate silence into your life of faith?*
> *What are the challenges you face in fostering periods of reflective silence each day?*
> *What spiritual insights have you gained through reflective contemplation?*

---

10. T. S. Eliot, "The Dry Salvages" in *Four Quartets* (Orlando: Harcourt, Inc., 1943), p. 35.

11. D. Leibowitz, *The Ironic Defense of Socrates: Plato's Apology* (Cambridge: Cambridge University Press, 2010), 38a, p. 161.

Feast of the Holy Family

Our Scripture passage for this Sunday comes from the Gospel of Matthew 2:13–15 and 19–23. In this passage, we read about Joseph taking Jesus and Mary to Egypt in order to protect them from Herod's violent intent. This passage offers several points of reflection for us as we apply its message to our own families and especially to the Church as the Family of God.

One of the obvious messages in this Gospel passage is that of protecting the vulnerable in our midst. Joseph cared for Jesus and Mary by removing them from situations of danger. Children are still vulnerable to harm throughout the world today. The protection of children is a responsibility we all share because Jesus Himself identified with them when He said, "Whoever receives one of these little ones in my name, receives me." Some threats to children are obvious, such as abortion, physical harm, violence, abuse, and sub-standard health service; other threats are more subtle, such as consumerism, secularism, perfectionism, media, and sub-standard education, as examples. Parents have a particular responsibility to protect their children from the destructive influences of the world around us. Such protective efforts may include limiting media exposure, Internet usage, and social networking sites that can cause low self-esteem and even addiction. It is not easy to be a parent in our contemporary society, so it is important for parents to form healthy associations with people who share their faith-based values. This larger supportive community can reinforce efforts and provide extra vigilance so that destructive influences and behaviors are minimized.

> *What do you think are the most harmful influences affecting children in your family?*
> *What are the most harmful influences affecting children in our city, country, and world?*
> *What can you do to protect children from those influences?*

*What can your faith community do to better protect the chil-
dren in your midst and equip parents to identify destructive
influences and impede them from reaching their children?
Who else is vulnerable in our families, parish, or society
and needs our help to protect them?*

Herod wanted to destroy the child Jesus because he saw Jesus as
a threat to his Kingdom. Later in Jesus' life there will be another
Herod who will seek to harm the Lord as well and silence His
message. Herod represents all those forces that are opposed to
Christianity and threatened by the message of the Gospel. It's hard
to imagine Herod being threatened by a very young child in Bethlehem but that fear only demonstrates the shallowness and fragility
of Herod's sense of self. Today we experience similar situations in
which people can be threatened by the message of the Gospel and
seek to silence that message by destroying disciples who witness
it. The destruction may not be a physical attack but it may involve
damaging another's reputation or threatening other actions that
could make a person's life more difficult.

*Who are some of the people or groups today that are threat-
ened by the message of Christianity and the mission of the
Church?
What are the ways in which those forces try to undermine
our Lord's message of faith or to harm people of faith?
What is the Christian way to respond to such attacks?
What opportunities do you have to help defend the message
of the Gospel and the mission of the Church?
What can your faith community do to better prepare people
to identify and respond to the forces that oppose Christianity?*

Joseph took Mary and Jesus into Egypt for refuge. Egypt, after the
founding of Israel, had actually been a traditional place of refuge
for Jews (cf. 1 Kgs 11:40, Jer 26:21). Even the High Priest Onias IV
sought refuge there during the Maccabean era. Places of refuge are
important for all of us. This is especially true for immigrants, like
the Holy Family, who seek asylum. Imagine what would have happened if Joseph were not allowed to cross the borders into Egypt!
While the threats and stresses are different for each of us, the ability
to identify and utilize places of refuge are important to all of us.

Our personal refuge may be a place of prayerful quiet where we can go to renew our relationship with God and heal from the wounds of the day. Refuge may also exist in holy friendships where we can speak honestly and openly about the assaults taking place in our hearts and souls. Refuge can also be very practical for peoples of the world who face violence and even lethal threats to themselves and to their families. As a Church, we have a responsibility to help people find refuge when they need it. This is especially true for the vulnerable in our world. Oftentimes we see images on television of strife-stricken peoples fleeing in desperation from the violent attacks of others. We cannot remain neutral in the face of such situations. God hears the cry of the poor and suffering—especially when others have become deaf to their appeals.

> *Where were places of refuge for you and your family when you were a child?*
> *Where are your personal places of refuge now?*
> *Where do your children find refuge? Who comes to you for refuge?*
> *What is our responsibility as a nation to provide refuge for those seeking it?*
> *Who in our world is most in need of refuge today and how can you assist them?*
> *Who comes to our parish seeking refuge, and what can we do to better serve them?*
> *Where do you find spiritual refuge?*

One of the most important responsibilities of marriage and family life is that of caring for children. Joseph and Mary were willing to change countries, cultures, and cities to protect Jesus. That effort required great sacrifice and incurred inconvenience for them. It was worth it. They understood that caring for their child was the greatest responsibility and most important priority of their lives. Their professional life, personal interests, and other individual concerns were all secondary to that one great priority. Sometimes people have difficulty putting their children and family first. It is not unusual to hear of fathers or mothers who become tired of the sacrifices required, day in and day out, to put others first. Also, Mary and Joseph weren't primarily guided by what their child

(Jesus) wanted; they did what God, in a dream, asked of them. Disciples are called to fulfill the will of God for others and not to merely please others by our actions. Doing what God wants for someone else may be very different from what that person desires for themselves. Maybe Jesus didn't want to go to Egypt. Nonetheless, Mary and Joseph knew what was needed, and they did what was the best for Jesus according to the divine plan.

> *What are some of the personal and professional sacrifices your parents made for you?*
> *What are some sacrifices and inconveniences you are willing to accept for the sake of your children?*
> *What are some of the mistaken priorities people can have today that cause them to lose sight of their primary responsibility to God and family?*
> *What can your faith community do to assist families in keeping first things first?*
> *What happens when parents do what their children want rather than what God wants for their children?*

Lastly, this Sunday is a great time to think about what it means to foster a Christian family in general. In the time of the early Church, it was common for families to have "codes" which they lived by. Oftentimes these codes summarized the primary values that guided a particular family's life, decisions, and actions. Saint Paul lists numerous such "family codes" in his letters. The second reading for this Sunday comes from Colossians 3:12–21 and is an example of such a code for the family of the Church.

> *If you were to create a Family Code of values for your family, what would be the three primary values you would choose (values that would be used to guide your life, decisions, and actions)?*
> *How would your family life change if you were then to live by those three primary values?*
> *As we approach a new year, what do you think would be the effect on your family relationships if you discussed this topic together?*

SOLEMNITY OF THE EPIPHANY

Our Scripture passage for this Sunday comes from the Gospel of Matthew 2:1–12. In this passage, we read the well-known story of the Magi who visit the child Jesus in Bethlehem and bring gifts of gold, frankincense, and myrrh. This passage offers some good points for our reflection and prayer.

One of the first things to note is that this passage contains the first words actually spoken by any person in Matthew's Gospel. The Gospel writers were careful to use the first words to establish a theme for their writing. Thus, the first spoken question, "Where is the newborn King of the Jews?" is a theme that will resonate throughout Matthew's Gospel. To be a king in the Jewish world was not just a political position of power. The Jewish people believed that God alone was their king and that any human regent had the responsibility to represent God. Some kings did a better job of being a representative of the Divine Image than others! The people looked to the king to manifest God's justice, mercy, wisdom, and protection. The Magi were seeking to see the face of God in human representation, and they didn't find it in Herod. Herod represented ruthless power and political cunning (he even executed three of his own sons). Throughout the Gospel of Matthew, Jesus will show us the face of the Father and in doing so He will authentically serve as God's perfect representative to the people. In witness to that authentic and complete representation, Jesus will properly be hailed as "King of the Jews" when He dies on Calvary. Herod caused others to suffer through his self-centered and untamed ambitious pursuit of power. Jesus suffered for others and opened the doors of God's mercy and forgiveness through His death and resurrection. Each of us in our baptism has received the commission to carry on the kingly ministry of Jesus. That means we are to be God's authentic representatives to the people with whom we interact.

Do people see Herod or Jesus in us?
Who represents the face of God, the heart of God, to you?

Who looks to you to be a minister of God's justice, mercy,
truth, wisdom, or protection?
In what settings are you a good representative of God?
In what settings do you find it most difficult to live out the
Kingly mission of your baptism?
If someone approached you and asked, "Where can I find
the King of the Jews?" what would you say to them?

Another interesting thing to note is that the wise men do not come to visit the babe in the manger. Rather, we are specifically told that they come to visit the child Jesus. There is a very significant difference between searching for a babe and searching for a child. The Greek word used for "child" (Greek *paidon*) refers to someone three to seven years old, not an "infant" (Greek *brephos*). That means that the wise men were journeying for years! That took perseverance. They did not go on a weekend pilgrimage or visit for just an hour on Sunday morning. What they did was a journey of life and faith that required commitment and resolve. For years they wandered looking for Jesus until they found Him. They were seekers who were not deterred by the lack of immediate results for their efforts. That is an important message for us because sometimes we can become frustrated in our faith life if we do not sense immediate results to our prayer or at least the effects of God's presence. We live in a culture of immediate gratification and can easily lose patience or interest when our efforts are not immediately successful. The example of the Magi should inspire and edify us to examine our own lives as disciples and identify ways in which we have allowed our expectation for immediate results to deter us from our commitment to Christ. If the Magi could search for years, certainly we can persevere during difficult and dry times of prayer as well. The Gospels are full of stories of people who persevered in their desire to encounter Jesus. Many of these people had to overcome the objection of the crowds, the cultural expectations of others, and even their own shame in order to finally meet the Lord. Certainly the example of these Magi and the people of perseverant faith are presented for good reason, so we will not give up or lose hope in our discipleship.

When has the expectation for immediate results affected your resolve in prayer or discipleship?
What is a grace or gift from God that you have been seeking for years?
Who is an example of faithful perseverance for you?
How can a faith community help people who struggle to find Jesus?
Why do you think it took the Magi years to find the Lord?

The gifts the Magi brought are all symbolic statements of who Jesus is. Gold is the gift proper for a King. Frankincense was offered by the High Priest to God in the Temple of Jerusalem. Myrrh was used as a perfume in the burial preparation of a body. Thus, the identity of Jesus is manifested in these three gifts: He is King, God (and/or High Priest) and Man (someone who will die). In one way or another, each of us makes the statement of who Jesus is to us based on the gifts we offer from our lives. For some, Jesus is a small part of their lives whose reign extends only to an hour on Sunday morning. Such a limited understanding of Jesus will be reflected in an equally limited gift of one's life to the Lord. For others, Jesus is the Lord of their lives twenty-four hours a day and seven days a week. Such a comprehensive understanding of Jesus will likewise be reflected in an all-encompassing gift of one's life to the Lord. We tend to give a person the gift that is appropriate because we believe they deserve it and that they can use it.

When it comes to Jesus, what does the Lord deserve from your life?
Who is Jesus to you?
How do you manifest your faith in Jesus through the gifts you offer Him?
What are the gifts you offer to the Lord for Him to use?

The star has historically been interpreted as a symbol for the light of faith leading people to Christ. For each person the path to Christ is unique and personal yet there are some common elements. For example, some people are led to seek God through the wonder of nature (the natural sciences). Others are led to seek God through events of salvation in their lives. Still others are led to seek God because of the influence of another person of faith. God reveals

Himself to us in a variety of ways, but there comes a point where we need to consult the Scriptures to really learn who God is through the person of Jesus. A story is told about St Francis of Assisi who took Lady Poverty to a hill and said to her, "This, Lady, is our cloister."[12] By this he meant, "The world is the place where we encounter God." Regardless of what events may have initiated our journey of faith, Scripture is a necessary step in the process of completing that journey and fully grasping the truth of who God is. That is why the Magi could not complete their journey until the Scriptures were consulted. The Word of God in Scripture sheds light on our experiences of faith and more clearly reveals to us the reality of God working in our lives. When we read the Scriptures, we grow in understanding and our eyes are opened to see clearly the character of God. We also unleash the power of God's Word in our hearts when we read the Scriptures. The Letter to the Hebrews attests that the Word of God is alive and powerful and that it can accomplish great things in our lives once we encounter it (Heb 4:12).

> *How has the study of Scripture opened your heart and mind in new ways?*
> *What have you learned about God through your reflection on the Word that you did not previously understand just based on your personal experience or the experience of others?*
> *What was the "light" that led you to desire to meet Jesus in a deeper and more personal way?*
> *Who is someone you know that is searching in the darkness, and how can you be a light to them?*
> *What can you do to foster your love for the Word of God in Scripture and share that love with your family and friends?*

Lastly, one cannot help but think about the contrast between the Magi and Herod. Herod had all the knowledge of Scripture but did not seek Jesus. The Magi were gentiles who searched in the darkness without the knowledge of Scripture but were willing to travel far distances to meet this newborn king of whom they only

---

12. *Sacrum Commercium sancti Francisci cum domina Paupertate,* Ed. Stefano Brufani (Assisi: Edizioni Porziuncola, 1990), chap. 30, ed. 173.

had vague knowledge. Herod saw Jesus as a threat to his way of life. The Magi saw Jesus as the source of new and deeper life. Herod lived comfortably in his palace in Jerusalem. The Magi wandered through cold nights and long days to fulfill their journey of faith. Herod had so much but gave nothing. The Magi had only what they could carry, but they gave everything they had. When it comes to our life of faith, Herod represents that attitude that tries to put God in the passenger seat while we control our own destinies. As the saying goes, "If God is your co-pilot, then it's time to trade places." Herod had no interest in trading places. The Magi, on the other hand, were eager to pay homage to the true Lord and King of their lives. Herod was un-changed by the birth of Jesus. The Magi were transformed by their encounter with Jesus and even returned home "different" from the way they came.

When does the message of the Gospel become uncomfortable or challenging for you?

When have you gone outside of your comfort zone to serve the Lord?

What do you admire most about the Magi and their journey of faith?

What aspect of Herod do you find most troubling?

What experience of God in your life has most changed you such that you became a different person because of that experience?

Jesus offers Himself to us in every Eucharist we celebrate. How can the attitude of Herod creep into our thoughts and prayers at Mass?

It's interesting that one of the most common images of early Christian art in the catacombs of Rome is that of the three Magi worshiping Jesus. Why do you think the early Christians of Rome identified with the Magi so strongly during the times of persecution?

FEAST OF THE BAPTISM OF THE LORD

Our Scripture passage for this Sunday comes from the Gospel of Matthew 3:13–17. Each year we read a different version of this moment in the life of Jesus and gain distinctive insights from the Gospel. This is a passage with which we are all familiar that tells us of the baptism of Jesus by John in the Jordan River. There are some significant elements to this passage that are worthy of our reflection.

The first thing to note is that Jesus chooses to be baptized by John. Our Lord's action is troubling to John because he clearly acknowledges that Jesus is the greater one and that Jesus has no need of repentance. Nonetheless, Jesus desires John's baptism, and our Lord speaks His first words in the Gospel of Matthew when He says, "It is fitting for us to fulfill all righteousness." These are important words. Jesus did not need John's baptism because Jesus had no sin. Even so, Jesus understood that some things are done out of righteousness rather than out of our personal need. Jesus was baptized not because He needed to be cleansed in the waters but because He wanted to give to the waters of baptism the power to cleanse us all! He joined with sinful humanity in a moment of solidarity not because He Himself was sinful but because He wanted to identify with us so as to lead us in the way of salvation. Sometimes we do things not because we need to do them for ourselves but because it is our duty to "fulfill all righteousness" so that others can benefit.

For whom do you need to be a leader in the ways of faith? What do you do in your faith life to set a good example for others to follow?
Who in your family, friends, or professional life seems to be waiting for someone to give them a good example to follow, and what can you do to provide that example?

Matthew tells us that at the moment of Jesus' baptism the "heavens opened." That is a significant statement. It means that in the baptism of Jesus there is a new possibility of communication between God and mankind. Indeed, Jesus has opened a new possibility of communication by bringing the compassion and forgiveness of the Father to the world. We now have an access to God that was not possible before Jesus' life and ministry. The door that was opened in the baptism of Jesus was immediately utilized when the Father spoke. God is constantly seeking to be an intimate part of our lives, and the Lord readily responds when doors are opened. Like Jesus, we can encounter the Lord with greater immediacy and clarity when we place ourselves in a state of openness, vulnerability, and solidarity with those in need. The Father was well pleased, both in who Jesus is as His son and in what Jesus did by being baptized. God wants us to foster that same vulnerability and openness in our own lives. Creating this openness requires humility because we cannot cause God's self-communication and revelation to us. If we could cause it, it wouldn't be God. This openness also requires an acknowledgement of our need for God and of our desire to conform our lives to God's will. Ultimately, the openness that God desires of us is that we trust Him no matter where He leads us or what He asks of us. In our baptism we promise to live such openness as members of the Mystical Body of Christ. This passage reminds us that God wants nothing less than intimate communion with us, and the Lord waits for us to take down the obstacles and barriers of our own construct that prevent such an open relationship of trust and confidence.

> *When do the heavens open for you in such a way that you experience a privileged communication/communion with God?*
> *What is the connection Jesus makes in your prayer life with God?*
> *For whom do you pray the heavens will open so they can be in deeper communion with God?*

Matthew also tells us that the Spirit of God descended like a dove on Jesus at His baptism. That is a direct allusion to Genesis 1:2 where the Spirit of God hovered over the waters at the beginning of creation. In making this connection, Matthew is telling us that there is a "new creation" happening in Jesus (cf. Mt 1:1, 1:18). The waters of Baptism bring about a new creation for all of us. The old order of sin passes away, and we are regenerated to become a new person born in innocence of water and the Spirit.

> *What do you think is the newness that Jesus brought to the world of His time?*
> *What is the newness Jesus wants to bring to the world of our time?*
> *Who are the people who most need a "new beginning" or "new genesis" for their lives?*
> *When have you needed a "new beginning" in your life?*
> *How can we be people who help others realize God's mercy and choose to start again a new life in Christ?*

Baptism gives us all a new beginning as we are "re-born" of water and the Spirit; the Sacrament of Confession is called the "Second Washing" because it, too, allows us to have a new beginning through the forgiveness of sins.

> *How has your experience of Confession been a new beginning for you?*
> *Oftentimes we need to find a way to establish a new beginning within our relationships (especially marriage) but rather than hitting the "re-set" button, we sometimes find it more tempting to hit the "re-play" button! How does this Scripture passage inspire you to desire a new beginning in Christ rather than "re-play" in anger?*

When the Father speaks from heaven, He proclaims Jesus to be "My Son, My Beloved, In Whom I am Well Pleased." Each of these phrases is a great title that has deep roots in the Old Testament (My Son in Ps 2:7 [David], My Beloved in Gn 22:2 [Isaac], In Whom I am Well Pleased in Is 42:1, 44:2 [the Suffering Servant]). Thus, the Father is establishing the pedigree of Jesus by showing how figures in the Old Testament demonstrated the characteristics that will mark Jesus' life and ministry. Jesus was 'pre-figured' in the Old Testament by these images. In a real sense, we all inherit a certain pedigree and have been formed according to the character of others. Likewise, most of us are responsible for influencing the life of someone else just as we have been influenced.

As you look at your life, from whom do you get your traits (good and bad)?

What are the good qualities you are passing on to others?

What are the weaknesses you pray others do not inherit?

If the Father spoke to you as He spoke to Jesus, what three people would He identify as the "pedigree" for who you are in His eyes?

How did your father or mother express their pride and love for you?

Who in your life needs to hear you express your pride and love for them by your statement, "You are my beloved son/daughter; in you I am well pleased"?

First Sunday of Lent

Our Scripture passage for this Sunday comes from the Gospel of Matthew 4:1–11. In this reading, we hear of Jesus being led into the desert for forty days where He is tested in a variety of ways. His experience offers several points for our reflection and prayer.

The first thing to notice is that each of the temptations begins with the phrase, "If you are the Son of God..." (Some translations read, "Since you are the Son of God..."). Satan is not tempting Jesus to deny His identity but rather to prove Himself in a way that goes against obedience to the Father's will. Satan is testing Jesus to see what sort of Son of God He will be! In Jesus' responses, we see the Lord humbly, faithfully, and obediently accepting His human condition rather than asserting His own will and exercising His divine power. That is a challenge to us because Satan uses the same tactic to tempt us. We may know that we are "Christians", but the challenge is to ask, "What kind of a Christian am I?" There are lots of ways to answer that question. Perhaps we are Christians who think it's enough to go to Mass each week but that's it. Perhaps we are Christians who recite daily prayers but have no other connection with the Lord in between those prayers. We need to remember that in our baptism we were claimed completely and eternally by Christ. We belong to Him not just one hour a week or even one hour a day. We belong to the Lord at all times and at all places. Sometimes we can be tempted to define our discipleship based on what we find convenient or expedient. This temptation of Jesus is addressed to us every time we face the similar temptation to settle for a lesser definition of discipleship than what Jesus has given us. When we strive for anything other than the fulfillment of God's complete will in our lives then we are succumbing to the temptation to justify our actions based on our own wants rather than basing our actions on God's will.

What is your identity (husband/wife, father/mother, Christian, career, and so forth)?
When are you tempted to act contrary to your identity?
We form our sense of self in relationship to others; Jesus knew Himself first and foremost in relationship to the Father.How do people today seek a sense of "self" in relationship to things other than God (possessions, power, position, human relationships, work, pleasure, and so forth)?
What helps us to find and keep our primary identity rooted in relationship to God?

Second, it is significant that Jesus was tempted to turn stones into breads. It is important to notice the plural in this temptation (breads). Matthew is giving us an insight into the real meaning of this temptation. You see, only one loaf would have been needed to satisfy Jesus' own personal hunger. The use of the plural indicates that Jesus was tempted to make bread not just for Himself but for others as well. This temptation becomes more meaningful when we realize that one of the common first century expectations of the Messiah was that He would re-produce the miracle of manna and there would be a lavish supply of food for humanity. By turning the stones into breads, Jesus would be giving in to others' expectations of how He should act as the Messiah. Anyone who can feed the multitudes gains enormous political power (even current-day regimes understand this dynamic). Jesus will not allow himself to be controlled or dominated by popular expectations of how He should act or what He should do. Rather, His life and His actions will be guided by every word that comes from the Father.

Whose expectations influence your life?
When have you been tempted to appease others' expectations even though it is not what you knew to be "right"?
Jesus relied on Scripture to counter the false expectations of others. What do you rely on to give you strength in such moments?
When can others' expectations be a good and healthy thing?
What are God's expectations of you today as His disciple?

Third, Jesus is tempted to throw Himself off the pinnacle of the Temple in Jerusalem so as to test the promise of Psalm 91:11–12 that,

"... he commands his angels... to guard you wherever you go. With their hands they shall support you. He will give his angels charge of you... and on their hands they will bear you up." This temptation shows us that even Satan can use Scripture to confuse us for his own benefit! Jesus is able to preserve Himself from being misled or confused by knowing which Scripture verse was applicable in which moment. All texts of Scripture have a context; when we remove texts from their context, then those texts become a pretext and we are in danger of misreading them. The context for Jesus' life and ministry is obedience to the Father's will as someone who will not test the Father's promises or make the Father prove Himself.

> *When do you find yourself wanting to make God "prove Himself"?*
> *When do you doubt God's presence with you?*
> *Sometimes people put themselves in harm's way and then expect God to save them from the consequences of their own irresponsible decisions. What does that statement mean to you?*
> *What are the primary temptations to reckless living people experience today?*
> *Who taught you to be responsible and accountable for your actions? How are you teaching others that same lesson?*
> *How can Scripture verses be used today in deceptive ways?*
> *What helps you discern the difference between Scripture that is correctly used and Scripture that is incorrectly used?*

Fourth, Jesus is taken to a high mountain and shown all the kingdoms of the world. Satan promises Jesus authority over all these kingdoms with the condition that Jesus pay homage to Satan. This is a very subtle but real temptation. You see, Jesus is being tempted to allow the worldly values of power, force, intimidation, and so forth to guide His life. By doing so and accepting the ways of the world, Jesus would be de-facto paying homage to Satan! None of us has idols in our homes, and yet we end up paying homage to forces that oppose God every time we agree to settle for the world as it is and allow worldly values to guide our lives. Jesus was tempted to rule the kingdoms of the world by capitulating to the Devil's kingship over that world. Instead, as St Chromatius said in the fifth century, "The Lord withstood temptations from the enemy that He might restore victory to humankind and He thereby made sport of the devil."[13]

> *When are we tempted to accept the status quo of the world as our guiding principle?*
>
> *How can selfishness and practical disregard for God's existence (that is, living life in a personal or professional way as though God does not exist) affect our actions?*
>
> *Jesus could have it all if He would just cut a few corners of fidelity. When are you tempted to act contrary to God's will for the sake of "getting ahead" by cutting corners on ethics, morals, or faith principles?*
>
> *At the end of Matthew's Gospel, Jesus will be given all power and authority on earth, but it is only after He obediently fulfills the Father's will to die on the cross. When have you been rewarded for your fidelity after first being crucified for it?*
>
> *What are "short cuts" people use today for the sake of success but at the expense of Christian ethics?*

Lastly, this Sunday is a good opportunity to reflect on the three primary spiritual practices associated with the Time of Lent: prayer, self-denial, and works of charity. While these practices are to always be essential components of a disciple's life, the forty days of Lent are a time when we are asked to intensify them so as to become more faithful to God's Word as did Jesus in the desert. Deepened prayer helps us to hear the Word of God more clearly and to become more responsive in following the Lord's will in our lives. Prayer also increases our love of God by deepening our relationship with the Lord. Self-denial frees us from being enslaved by our appetites or dominated by wasteful practices. Self-denial, especially fasting, also awakens us to the needs and sufferings of others and allows us to experience the frailty of the human condition so as to grow in compassion for those who live in constant need. In performing charitable works (almsgiving), we express our love of God in our

---

13.   St Chromatius, "Tractate on Matthew, 14.5" in *Ancient Christian Commentary on Scripture*, New Testament, Ia, Matthew 1–13 (Downers Grove: Inter Varsity Press, 2001), p. 64.

love of neighbor and begin to make a practical difference in the lives of others as a witness of our discipleship. Charitable works (almsgiving) also challenge us to let go of the false security of our possessions and the illusion of self-sufficiency by our responsible care for others. Thus, these three practices are interconnected. Prayer, self-denial, and good works all lead us into a practical and more profound love of God and neighbor. Lent is not so much about what we "give up" but rather what we "give to" God and others.

> *How can you deepen your prayer life during these forty days of Lent so you can hear more clearly the Word of God being spoken to you?*
>
> *What are some of the enslavements you experience, and how can the practice of self-denial help free you from being governed by those enslavements ("Do you control your desires, or do your desires control you")?*
>
> *Who needs to experience your mercy and charitable works, and how can you express your love of neighbor in a new way during this Lenten time?*

SECOND SUNDAY OF LENT

Our Scripture passage for this Sunday comes from the Gospel of Matthew 17:1–9. This is the account of the Transfiguration of Jesus and the revelation of His glory to the disciples. Note that the account of the Transfiguration is also related in the Gospels of Mark and Luke, and those passages are read on Liturgical Years B and C respectively. For more insights into this moment in the life and ministry of Jesus as related in the Gospels of Mark and Luke, the reader is encouraged to consult the *Come Follow Me* reflections for the Second Sunday of Lent for those Liturgical Years. As we continue our journey through the season of Lent, this passage offers some good points for reflection and prayer.

When you think about the experience of Jesus' transfiguration, it is interesting to consider the question, "Who really changed in that moment?" On the surface it seems that Jesus is the one who was changed, but that's not really the case. Jesus simply allowed others to see His glory as the Son of God, but Jesus remained the same both before and after the experience of the Transfiguration. The people who were most changed by that moment were the disciples. They were given an experience of insight into the presence of God with them (Emmanuel), and that insight was meant to change the way they saw and experienced life from then on. Moments of revelation are meant to change us as well. Like Peter, James, and John, we are all given experiences of God's grace when we recognize "God moments" in our lives. These are our mountaintop experiences, and they are usually wonderful moments of blessing. They also have a purpose, which is to change us in a permanent way so that we can face with deepened faith the situations of our lives from then on. Mountaintop experiences of God's revelation are real, but they don't last forever. Jesus always leads us down the mountain, and He continues to accompany us (Emmanuel) as we walk through the daily challenges of discipleship. Mountaintop experiences of faith give us a glimpse of what life in Christ is like to sustain us when we encounter a world devoid of God's love and hostile to the Gospel.

> *What have been some of the "mountaintop" experiences of*
> *God in your life that have changed the way you live?*
> *How do you keep alive the memory of those experiences as*
> *you face the challenges of daily life?*
> *How can a faith community help others recognize and*
> *respond to mountaintop experiences in their lives?*

Peter was happy to be in this moment. In Matthew 16:15 Jesus posed this question to His disciples: "Who do you say that I am?" Although Peter responded to that question, his answer failed to capture the full reality of Jesus' identity. Then, just a few verses later, Jesus taught His disciples that He must suffer and die before rising from the dead (Mt 16:21). Of course, Peter knows that where Jesus leads the disciples must follow (cf. Mt 16:24). The disciples didn't like the message that Jesus would lead them to suffering and death. They wanted to follow a messiah who would lead them to victory and glory instead. That's why Peter is so overjoyed to now see this moment of the transfiguration. Peter is able to experience the reason for which he himself was following the Lord: glory, honor, and exaltation. Peter wants to freeze the moment and capture the presence of Jesus where discipleship is comfortable, rewarding, and glorious for him. Peter does not want to leave that mountain and follow Jesus to Jerusalem because he knows what awaits them. It's as if Peter is saying, "Let's stop here, Lord, we've gone far enough." Peter thought he had reached the satisfactory destination of his discipleship when he found a place of comfort and glory. However, the faith to which Jesus calls Peter and us is lived out in daily discipleship as we progress step by step on our journey to Jerusalem with the Lord. It is a discipleship that does not stop at a place that is comfortable but one that faithfully follows where ever Jesus leads. Sometimes we can be like Peter and not want to take the next step of faith because of the discomforting challenge it will present. This passage is a correction to our complacent discipleship that reminds us of the ongoing need to follow Jesus and never settle for "far enough" or "good enough" when it comes to our faith lives.

What tempts you to stop short and settle for "good enough" when it comes to your life of discipleship?
How can we become complacent in our faith and want to stop deepening our discipleship?
How can people today be tempted to seek only glorious moments rather than the strength to endure sacrificial moments in their faith?
What is a step of faith that you are hesitant to take because you find it appealing, comfortable, and predictable to stay right where you are?

Another aspect of Peter's response is worth considering. In Matthew 16:22, Peter previously tried to correct Jesus' teaching concerning the necessity of His own suffering and death. Peter wanted to follow a glorious Messiah, not a crucified one. Sometimes people today can have the same mistaken faith of Peter and believe the gospel of health and wealth—namely, that following Jesus brings us a blessed, easy, and glorious life. When we believe that, we misunderstand the purpose of discipleship and are unable to accept the challenges and difficulties (crosses) that are a part of following the Lord faithfully as He leads us through His death and resurrection. We have mistaken faith when we want Easter Sunday without Good Friday. Such is the desire of Peter in this Gospel passage. Following Jesus Christ doesn't necessarily make our lives easier, but it always brings blessings. Saint Teresa once said, "God makes our ills count as gain."[14] Discipleship often requires us to accept greater challenges.

What are some of the difficulties you have had to accept because of your discipleship?
How does the false gospel of "health and wealth" affect people today in their prayer and expectations of Jesus?
What examples can you think of in which people have actually stopped being disciples because they were called to leave the mountaintop and embrace the cross?
Peter initially followed Jesus because he perceived Him to be the Messiah in a worldly sense. Why do you follow Jesus?

14. St Teresa of Avila, "Oh Hermosura" in *Complete Works,* Vol. III, Trans. By A. Peers (London: Burns and Oates, 1946 (rpt. 2002), p. 284.

Peter didn't quite know how to respond to this moment of revelation, and so he immediately starts to talk. Peter mistakenly thinks that this moment of glory is the goal of Jesus' ministry, so he seeks to enshrine this moment and make it last by building tents. It is in the midst of Peter's talking that the voice of the Father interrupts and announces, "This is my beloved Son... Listen to Him!" That statement has two meanings. First, it is a statement to Peter that he needs to stop talking and forcing his interpretation on the moment. Rather, Peter needs to listen to Jesus explain and interpret the moment for him. We can do a lot of talking in our prayer as well. Sometimes God wants to remind us that we need to listen more than speak. God knows what we need before we ask; our prayer is meant to open us to do God's will, not talk God into doing our will!

The second part of the Father's statement is intended to direct our listening to Jesus as the only one who authentically communicates God's will for our lives. The Father announced Jesus as His own divine son, and listening is the proper response. This command means that disciples should not only hear Jesus but actually listen to Him. To "listen" to the Son of God means paying attention to the teachings of Jesus with openness, receptivity, and a desire to respond. It means being attentive to the message of the Gospel and seeking ways to apply it to our daily lives. It also means that when we have lots of other influences attempting to tell us what to do (culture, friends, business world, media, temptations, and so forth) that we choose not to listen to those influences but instead listen to the voice of Jesus. It means that when we make any decision, we choose to seek out and listen to the guidance of Jesus and not the other forces at work in our lives. This is a rather powerful teaching for us as disciples. Both elements of the Father's correction and instruction speak to us as we live our lives each day. We are surrounded by so many influences that are not the Son of God. When we realize that Jesus is given to us to lead us and guide us to the Father, then we can better understand the great responsibility we have to accept His leadership and guidance as authoritative and authentic and not just one more opinion of how we should live our lives. During this second week of Lent, we are invited to examine the many influences that try to give us guidance and direction and to remove those things that do not come from Jesus. He alone is the Son. Anytime there is a competing or conflicting influence, the voice of the Father serves as an admonition reminding us to listen only to His Son.

> *To whom do you listen in those moments when you must decide between competing perspectives? How do you "listen" in your prayer?*
>
> *What are the competing voices that try to influence your decisions and actions?*
>
> *What is a decision that you must make now, and how will you take it to prayer so you can listen to Jesus?*
>
> *God is the one who can best interpret for us the meaning of significant experiences in our lives. What is an experience or situation in your life for which you need to seek God's interpretation?*

THIRD SUNDAY OF LENT

Our Scripture passage for this Sunday comes from the Gospel of John 4:5–42. In this passage, we read about Jesus encountering the Samaritan woman at the well and the impact our Lord has on her life. This story offers several points worthy of our reflection and prayer during this sacred time of Lent.

The passage begins by telling us that Jesus had to go to Samaria. That's not a geographical necessity. Rather, it is a statement of God's will that the message of the Gospel should move outside the Jewish world and be presented to the rest of humanity including women and Samaritans. The Gospel isn't just for those who are like us, whomever that may be. It is also for those whom social conventions deem marginalized. By bringing the Gospel to the Samaritan woman, Jesus is inviting her to be a disciple who can become a missionary capable of bringing other marginalized people to Him. In a similar way, God asks us to go outside our world of comfort and familiarity so as to encounter others and in doing so to encounter the Lord. We will meet Him in Samaria! When we choose to only associate with people who are like us, we cannot be effective witnesses of Jesus to those who most need Him. We like to meet God on terms that are comfortable and when we are in control, but God reveals Himself to us on His terms, which require us to surrender and experience vulnerability. There are privileged places of encounter where we can experience Jesus more readily and intensely. These are the settings and people with whom Jesus freely chose to identify Himself: the poor, the suffering, the imprisoned, the sick, the oppressed, and the outcast.

> *What opportunities do you have to show God's love to the marginalized in your world (professional, personal, family, friends, and so forth)?*
> *When have you encountered the presence of God through your contact with the outcasts?*

When has your personal experience of vulnerability or weakness become the setting in which you experienced God's presence in a privileged way?

When have you experienced God's love reaching out to you when you felt marginalized?

There is a point when disciples are called to become apostles who freely share with others the gift of faith they have received; that's the moment when the woman goes to tell others about Jesus. For whom have you been an apostle of Jesus in order to help them recognize and encounter the Lord in their lives even as you have encountered Him in yours?

It is interesting that Jesus comes to the well at the hottest hour of the day and asks the woman to do Him a favor. Namely, He requests a cup of water. In response, she opens herself to dialogue rather than simply dismissing our Lord's request. She thinks that in giving Him a cup of water she would be doing Jesus a favor. In reality, she was allowing the Lord to do her a favor. Inconveniences are the vehicle through which God sometimes invites us to open ourselves to receive His grace as well. If we only knew the gifts God wants to give us when we open ourselves to Him with greater generosity and availability. Think of how many times in your day you experience brief moments of inspiration inviting you to stop and consider doing good for others. These moments can be inconvenient, yet they can also be opportunities to allow the Lord to use our lives just as He used the life of the woman of Samaria. God is never outdone in generosity, and we are always blessed with more than we give when we offer to the Lord the gift of our time and talent to do His will. We would all be willing to invest our time and energy in an opportunity if we were guaranteed a greater gift in return. We are called to be generous disciples of Jesus who willingly respond to such moments of inspiration.

What are some of the inconveniences you experience that could be invitations from God to open your life to others and so be blessed by the Lord?

When has responding to someone else's need been a moment of grace and deepened your faith?

*When has a brief gesture of kindness for someone else ini-
tiated for you a deeper relationship with God or others?
What can you do to make yourself more receptive and responsive to inconvenient moments of inspiration in your day?*

Faith is a process because God always wants to lead us more deeply
into relationship with Him. We see that desire and process taking
place in the conversation between Jesus and the Samaritan woman.
At the beginning of her interaction with Jesus, she refers to our
Lord simply as a "Jew". Then she calls Him "Sir". Eventually she
acknowledges that He is a "Prophet". Finally she wonders if Jesus
could be the "Messiah". Her faith remained incomplete throughout this process of encounter, and for that reason Jesus calls her
to even deeper faith and reveals Himself to her as "I AM". That is
a very important statement because "I AM" is the divine name of
God given to Moses in Exodus 3:14. Jesus is revealing to her that
He is God. Although she does not grasp this revelation, Jesus continues calling her to deeper faith. So, too, our Lord calls each of
us to ever-deeper knowledge of Him and ever-greater relationship
with Him. This call to deeper faith occurs through the events of
our lives and the conversations of our prayer. God calls us to trust
Him evermore, and when we accept that invitation, then the Lord
reveals Himself to us with greater clarity. Deepened knowledge of
God leads to deepened trust in God. We, like the woman, can find
ourselves being called to leave behind our former preoccupations
(the water jar) and become messengers of faith to others like she
did for her village. How we understand Jesus determines how well
we will serve Him. The woman in the story was not motivated to
bring the message of her encounter with Jesus to the town until she
realized He was the fulfillment of God's plan for her life.

*What have been some of the significant milestones in the
development of your faith life by which you came to know
the Lord more clearly?*
*How has deepened faith practically expressed itself in more
committed discipleship in your life?*
*What adult faith enrichment opportunities or experiences
have opened your eyes to see the Lord more clearly and
respond with more committed discipleship?*

> *What can you do this next year to take the next step in*
> *deepening your faith or becoming more active in the mission*
> *of the Gospel as a disciple?*

Next, Jesus leads the woman to a personal encounter with Him so that she can worship in "spirit" and "truth". Jesus Himself will later state in John's Gospel that He is "the Way, the Truth, and the Life" (14:6). Truth is not a concept but a person: Jesus. The same topic came up in the conversation with Pilate in which the Lord remained silent and presented Himself as the visible truth (18:37–38). To worship in "truth" is to worship Jesus. We read in the opening lines of John's Gospel that "The Word of God became flesh and made His dwelling among us. We have seen His glory, the glory of the one and only Son, who came from the Father, full of grace and truth" (Jn 1:14).

When Jesus conversed with Nicodemus in John 3:1–36, Jesus spoke of how the Spirit is the gift of God that allows us to be caught up in the very life and mystery of God. The Spirit, then, brings us into the life of the Trinity. We become a temple of the Holy Spirit when we are born again in baptism. To worship in Spirit is to live each day immersed in the life of God whereby we are unconditionally and totally directed to God. God is not limited to a mountain or a place or a sanctuary; God offers Himself in an all-pervading personal presence to the believer requiring our complete response and surrender.

> *What are ways in which we try to limit God's presence to*
> *certain places today?*
> *What part of people's lives can they find most difficult to*
> *surrender to the Lord?*
> *What does it mean to you when we say, "Truth is a person"?*
> *You are a temple of the Holy Spirit. When do you most*
> *sense God's movement in your life drawing you to Himself?*
> *Who is someone you know who demonstrates what it means*
> *to worship God in Spirit and Truth?*
> *In which of these two aspects of authentic worship do you*
> *most want to grow?*
> *How will you pursue that growth?*

One other dynamic in this passage that should be noted is when Jesus points out the previous five husbands of the Samaritan woman. Our Lord's discussion with the woman had yielded initial results, but she was still thinking on the earthly level of physical things (water). Jesus wanted to open her heart and mind to go to a deeper level but something was preventing that conversation from progressing. It is at this moment, in verse 16, that Jesus asks her to go and call her husband. Although this request is presented as something extraneous to their conversation it actually demonstrates that Jesus is trying to find another venue to lead her deeper faith. She responds by stating that she has no husband, which is the opening the Lord needs to point out her five previous marriages and the implied illicit relationship she is currently in. Scripture scholars debate whether or not this is an indication of the woman's sinful life and, if so, what such an indication means. Perhaps the woman was trying to hide a part of her life from the Lord because she was embarrassed for Jesus to see her as she really was. Perhaps the acknowledgement of her past and current illicit relationship was a sign of reconciliation and forgiveness. The significance of her personal background as an essential part of this conversation should not be underestimated since it was part of the good news she announced to her village. What is certain is that this revelation opened the door for the woman to take the next step in her faith and to proclaim Jesus as a Prophet. Most likely, Jesus reached a point in the conversation of faith where the dialogue could not continue until some particular obstacles were acknowledged and at least addressed, if not resolved. Honesty and complete disclosure was a necessary part of their communication at this point.

Sometimes our prayer becomes stagnant when we try to keep a part of our lives from the Lord as well. God knows us and loves us for who we are as part of His creation. Sin always mars the beauty of God's creation. Prayer is the place above all where we need to be honest and open with the Lord so that God can love us and heal us of our sinful past and lead us to fullness of life. When we try to offer a selective presentation of ourselves to the Lord, we are deceiving ourselves—not God. It is that falseness of self that often prevents our encounter with God from going deeper. There are times in our lives of faith when the same thing happens to us. The Lord wants to lead us deeply into communion with Him, but practices of sin in our lives can cause us to remain in a superficial relationship instead. It is out of mercy and love that the Lord helps us recognize these impediments to profound relationship. The awareness of the presence of sin in our lives allows us to identify the obstacles that are holding us back from deeply committing ourselves to God. Once we know the presence of sin, we can seek God's forgiveness and reconciliation in the Sacrament of Confession. The newfound freedom of forgiveness allows us to continue our journey of faith to deeper levels just as it did for the Samaritan woman.

> *When do you identify with the Samaritan woman who was stuck on a superficial level in her spiritual life?*
> *How has the Sacrament of Reconciliation given you the freedom, strength, and grace to deepen your spiritual life?*
> *If Jesus invited you to profound relationship with Him now, what current sinful practices would practically hold you back from accepting that invitation?*
> *Our Lord spoke to the Samaritan woman with honesty, love, and mercy. Who has loved you in such a way that they have actually helped you overcome obstacles to your spiritual growth?*
> *Who are you called to love with honesty and mercy so as to help them identify obstacles in their spiritual life in order to grow closer in communion with the Lord?*
> *Why do you think Jesus asked the woman to bring her husband?*
> *When has your relationship with the Lord been able to move forward because you choose to acknowledge and seek forgiveness for particular situations of sin in your life?*

Lastly, it is worth reflecting on the sequential development of themes in this gospel passage. Specifically, Jesus and the woman first speak about the gifts of God (that is, the well, living water, and so forth) but then Jesus moves the conversation from the gifts of God to the ultimate Gift of God, the very presence of God Himself in Jesus. Maybe the Lord wants to change our focus in the same away so that we pray not so much for the gifts but for union with the Giver. Basically, Christian faith is about relationship and not getting what we want. Sometimes we can so focus our prayer on what we want that we are more interested in the gifts God gives us than the gift of God Himself. This subtle movement in the gospel passage invites us during this third week of Lent to examine our prayer and purity of our intentions and petitions. God desires to be in relationship with us, and every blessing we receive from the Lord is a sign of His goodness and love. The Lord's blessings are meant to incline our hearts and minds to love God in return rather than walk away, only to come back when we need something else.

> *How do you feel when someone only comes to you because of what you give them rather than for who you are?*
> *What do you seek in your prayer—the gifts of God or communion with God Himself?*
> *When has a gift of God led you to a deeper relationship with Him?*
> *What can you do to more effectively seek communion with God?*

Fourth Sunday of Lent

Our Scripture passage for this Sunday comes from the Gospel of John 9:1–41. It is a rich scene in which Jesus gives both sight and insight to the man born blind. This reading tells us who Jesus is and what He means for our lives. At the same time, this particular reading is a teaching on the nature of sin and the challenge of discipleship. Here are several points for our reflection and prayer.

The passage begins with some interesting details that give us a key with which to understand the whole scene. For example, it tells us that the man was blind from birth. Actually the Greek text says that he was blind from his "genesis". That has a double meaning of both birth and creation. By using this term, John is telling us that Jesus is not someone who comes to simply restore things to the way they once were (that is, to return the world as it was before the Fall). Rather, Jesus comes to establish a new creation, a new Genesis, and He does it through touching the man's eyes with mud and having him wash in the waters of Siloam, which means the "Sent One". These are all images of the Sacrament of Baptism. You see, in baptism we become a new creation in Christ Jesus. Just as Adam was formed from the dust of the earth and infused with the Spirit of God (Gn 2:7), so now Jesus takes the dust of the earth and infuses it with Himself (symbolized by spittle). He then applies this remedy for blindness to the man's eyes for his healing. The word for healing in Greek is the same word for "salvation". What the Lord is offering this man is not only the healing of his blindness but also the gift of salvation by uniting him with God in Jesus. However, the man must cooperate with God's grace and follow Jesus' invitation by going and washing in the pool of Siloam. John tells us that Siloam means "Sent", and throughout John's Gospel Jesus states that He is the "Sent One" of God. Thus, to wash in the pool of the "Sent One" is to wash in the water that is Jesus Christ Himself. Wow! The man born blind represents all of us who are naturally born unable to see God and the world clearly, and who need to be re-created in the waters of Jesus (baptism) so as to receive the healing, saving gift of Himself. That new creation is not the goal of a Christian life; it is really just the beginning. What a beginning it is!

> *How does this passage change the way you understand baptism?*
>
> *How can a faith community help people to better appreciate the significance of their baptism, especially if they were baptized as children?*
>
> *When a person is baptized, they are given a lit candle with the words, "Receive the Light of Christ." When have you experienced Jesus opening your eyes in a moment of faith?*
>
> *To be immersed in the "Sent One" means that we share in the life of God and that the life of God permeates and defines us in every way. When are you most aware of the life of God in you?*
>
> *How can you foster greater awareness of, and responsiveness to, the life of God in you?*
>
> *How is it possible for us to allow the life of God to become diminished within us?*

In this passage, Jesus offers an important self-revelation when He says, "I AM the Light of the World." This is not only a statement of who Jesus is but also of what Jesus does for disciples. The image of light is important, especially for one who is born blind. With sight and light, a person can begin to see clearly. Jesus gives us the ability to spiritually "see" in the waters of baptism, but we still need to be illumined (light) in order to correctly use the gift of sight and see clearly. By identifying Himself as the Light of the World, Jesus is stating that He is the one who illumines our lives and helps us see the world from God's perspective. Through His life, death, and resurrection, as well as His teachings and ministry, Jesus is shedding light on our human experience and helping us see the world as God sees it. The gift of our baptism, then, may open our eyes and give us the capacity for faith, but we still need to become informed and mature by following the Light of the World and allowing the Lord's teachings to both help us interpret the events of our times and guide our response to those events. This illumination does not happen in a vacuum or just in the privacy of our individual prayer. Rather, the ongoing mission of the Church is twofold. First, it involves teaching disciples how to see the world from a Christian perspective. Second, it calls the Church to be the instrument by which Jesus sheds His light on our human situation. This mission is not only entrusted to those in official positions of ministry responsibility. All Christians, by virtue of their baptism, are to be active members of the Body of Christ by illuminating the human situation with the Light of Christ. This transition from darkness to light was described by Saint Gregory of Nyssa as the intelligence's yearning for understanding by which it gains access to the invisible and the incomprehensible, leaving behind what has been observed, in order to see God in His simplicity.[15]

> *How do you seek the Light of Christ in your life?*
>
> *What situation do you need to see from God's perspective now?*
>
> *What situations in our society or larger world need to be illumined with the Light of Christ?*
>
> *What ministries have most helped you mature in your faith?*
>
> *Who do you know whose eyes have been opened in baptism but still need to experience the light of Christ so that their situation can be illumined through your word and example?*
>
> *What are the obstacles that can obstruct the Church from becoming fully the effective instrument of God as the Light of the World?*
>
> *When was the light of Christ turned on for you?*

Jesus also tells us that He must do the work of God while it is day (Jn 9:4). There are two meanings to that statement. On the one hand, the work of God is first and foremost to bring people the gift of faith ("so that the world may believe" Jn 17:21). However, faith requires that we recognize and acknowledge God present and acting in the person of Jesus. Thus, the works of Jesus, such as miracles, are ultimately meant to accomplish the one great work for which Jesus was sent (so that the world might believe). When

---

15. Gregory of Nyssa, *The Life of Moses* (New York: Paulist Press, 1978), Book II, N. 163, p. 95.

we make the connection between an action of God in our lives and the presence of God in Jesus, then we have "seen the light" and can profess our faith in Jesus not just as a great man, or miracle worker, or prophet, or Messiah, or Son of Man, but as the very presence of God in our midst. That process of deepened faith confession is seen in the blind man's growing awareness in this passage. He slowly comes to believe in who Jesus really is because of the miracle Jesus performed. Jesus wants us to see the light of God's presence in our lives as well. Sometimes we are happy to experience the works of God, such as blessings, miracles, healings, but fail to follow through on the true work God wants to accomplish in us through those individual works: deepened faith in and commitment to Jesus as the one in whom God is present and through whom God acts.

> *What have been some of the works of God in your life?*
> *When has a work of God led you to deeper faith, and how did you express that deeper faith?*
> *How can a faith community help people correctly recognize the works of God in their lives and translate that awareness into deepened faith?*

The man born blind had to grow in his faith and understanding of who healed him. This growth did not happen in a pleasant and peaceful way. Rather, his growth in faith occurred because of the questions and challenges he faced. He grew in faith because he had the courage to stand up and face those challenges. He acknowledged what he did not know while at the same time standing firm with what he did know. Through this process of being challenged and questioned by others, he actually learned about Jesus and became a strong disciple. That can be an important lesson for us as well. You see, being a disciple doesn't necessarily make our lives easier. It oftentimes means that we are called to take a stand of faith and defend Jesus in our conversations as well—especially when we are challenged or questioned. Rather than seeing those moments as awkward situations from which we should shy away, we should see them as opportunities to witness to the Lord's presence and action in our lives and through that witness to grow in our discipleship. God's action in our lives doesn't necessarily make life easier; being a disciple can actually make life more difficult. Some people are angry, outraged, disappointed, shocked, or dismayed when we respond to the Lord as a committed disciple. Certainly that was true of the man born blind. Still, he remained firm in his faith.

> *When have you been questioned about your faith? What did you do?*
>
> *St Paul said, "I can do all things through Christ who strengthens me" (Phil 4:13). Who are people you know who have actually become stronger in faith because of the challenges and questions they have faced?*
>
> *Who are people who have actually become weaker in faith because of challenges and questions they have faced?*
>
> *What makes the difference between someone who is strengthened or someone who is weakened by challenges and questions?*
>
> *What can a faith community do to help its members grow in their faith when they face questions or challenges?*

Lastly, this passage is permeated with statements, questions, and presumptions about the nature of sin. At first, the disciples question whose sin caused the man to be born blind. That question reveals an understanding of sin that is primarily based on moral actions (either those of the man born blind or his parents). For the Jewish leaders, they based their understanding of sin on observance of the Mosaic Law. For this reason, they called Jesus a sinner because He healed on the Sabbath in violation of the Law of Moses. The Lord uses this scene as an opportunity to teach us a far more profound understanding of sin: one that is not based just on actions or observance of Law, but one that is based on our acceptance of the gift of God in Jesus. Sin, in John's Gospel, is when a person rejects relationship (faith) with God in Jesus. In John's Gospel, Jesus did not come to condemn the world but rather so that the world might have life (Jn 3:17, 12:47). Since our Lord did not come to bring judgment, that means we judge (and condemn) ourselves based on our decision to accept the Light of the World in Jesus or to reject Him and choose to remain in darkness and sin. Sin, then, is fundamentally our turning away from the life of God offered to us in Jesus.

*How does this radical understanding of sin in John's Gospel
challenge you?*

*How is it that good people can find themselves turning away
from deeper relationship with Jesus without realizing it?*

*In the Gospel of John, Jesus is offering us an opportunity to
live in relationship with him in each moment. When we say
"Yes" to that invitation, we are accepting His Light; when
we say "No" to that invitation, we are choosing darkness
and sin. How can you prepare yourself to live your day as
a "Yes" to God?*

Fifth Sunday of Lent

Our Scripture passage for this Sunday comes from the Gospel of John 11:1–45. This is the famous account of the raising of Lazarus from the dead. Jesus ends His public ministry on a high note with this greatest of all miracles. Jesus previously identified Himself with various "I AM" statements (I AM the living water, I AM the light of the world, and so forth), but in this passage He makes His greatest I AM claim yet: I AM the resurrection and the life. Each of these I AM statements tells us not just who Jesus is but also what He means for our lives. As with the other passages in John's Gospel, this reading has rich and profound meaning for us.

The passage begins by telling us about Lazarus' illness. Jesus does not want us to focus on the illness itself, however, so He explains that this tragedy is meant to be an occasion for God's revelation and glory. The passage then says that, "because Jesus loved Lazarus ... He delayed". That may strike us as odd. We would expect that our Lord's love for Lazarus would motivate Him to visit the sick man. Jesus explains that His love for the family will be manifested in works that demonstrate the glory of God and become the method by which the disciples come to faith. All of these statements give us an insight into the mind of God and how to read situations in our own world and personal lives as well. When we encounter situations of dire need, distress, or tragedy, we oftentimes find ourselves focusing on what's wrong, what's broken, and what needs help. By doing so, we can also begin to expect God to do something. However, Jesus wants us to approach situations of tragedy and ask the question, "How can I be an instrument who manifests the Glory of God in this moment?" That is a powerful re-orientation of our prayer and motivation for action. Additionally, we sometimes experience what appears to be God's delay when we are in a moment of need. Sometimes we expect the Lord to act immediately out of love for us, and we can become frustrated when Jesus doesn't do what we want and when we want it. This passage reminds us that Jesus is governed by something greater than human affections and expectations; He is governed by the will of the Father. Just because God doesn't act immediately is not a reason for us to doubt the Lord's love for us. Lastly, Jesus' love for His friends and the family of Lazarus is manifested above all by His giving glory to God and helping them come to faith. Perhaps the greatest gift we can give our family and friends is the same thing: deepened faith through a life that points to God and not us.

> _How do you manifest your love for your family and friends?_
> _What could you do to manifest your love for family and friends by showing them the glory of God and helping them become better disciples?_
> _When have you become frustrated or doubted God's love because the Lord has delayed His action in your life or the lives of your loved ones?_
> _How can we best teach people the virtue of patient endurance of faith?_
> _We all experience and encounter tragic situations, and Jesus doesn't want us to remain focused on what's wrong, what's broken, or what's injured; rather, the Lord wants us to be an instrument of God's glory in those situations. What are some of the tragic situations that have affected your life or the lives of others, and how can you be an instrument of God's glory in the midst of those situations?_
> _When have you been motivated to go with Jesus to bring God's glory to a desperate situation, even when it involved personal risk?_
> _Mother Teresa faced tragic situations every day, and when she needed someone to help her she would say to them, "Would you do something beautiful for God?" That was her way of showing that every tragedy is an opportunity to manifest the Glory of God. How can you do something beautiful for God today?_

Martha thinks she understands what Jesus is saying, and so we see her constantly interrupting Jesus and insisting on her own knowledge and interpretation of our Lord's statements. Because she presumes she knows all the answers, she fails to actually listen to Jesus. She remains locked in her false understanding of resurrection, her false understanding of Jesus' power (and lack of power), and her false understanding of the power of death. The tragedy of Lazarus' death has led her to cling more tightly to her own notions of reality than to accept Jesus' revelation of a new reality. In doing so, she cannot recognize the full power and authority of Jesus as the eternal Word of God in her midst. She has all the right language but not the right understanding. Her statements reveal that she considered Jesus just a miracle worker who could have intervened before things got too bad; or maybe a saint to whom God listens; or a teacher who gives us understanding and insight. She even considered Jesus as someone who had a special relationship with God and certain heavenly knowledge as the "Son of God", but she did not grasp that Jesus is in Himself the very presence of God. Had she grasped that truth, she would have trusted in what He had to say rather than her own presumptions. The way in which we understand Jesus affects how we approach Him as well and how we listen to what He has to say to us. Jesus is the presence of the Living God in our midst. The purpose of our prayer is to come before the Lord so as to receive what He wants to give and to trust that our connection with Him is stronger than even death itself. Thus, the ultimate prayer of a disciple, in the midst of any situation, is to be joined to the divine life of God in Jesus. When we fail to grasp who Jesus really is, we trust more in ourselves, or other people, or our knowledge and experience of the world, or our anger and frustration in the midst of tragedy.

> *How has your understanding of who Jesus is grown over the course of time?*
> *What are some of the images of Jesus that you have grown through as you have matured in faith?*
> *How have those different images expressed themselves in changed prayer?*
> *How do you most express your faith in Jesus as the eternal Word of God present among us?*
> *How might Martha's interaction have been different if she had grasped the true identity of Jesus?*

In this passage, Jesus makes His greatest claim, "I AM the resurrection and the life; the one who believes in me, even if he dies, will live and whoever lives and believes in me will never die." This statement manifests Jesus' present and future sovereignty over believers. Eternal life starts in this life and is stronger than death. Our connection to Jesus means that physical death has no power over us as believers. As such, our future must be determined by faith in Jesus and not governed by the certainty of death. It also means that our present is determined by Jesus' power of life and His gift of eternal life. Death doesn't change our relationship with God. Our relationship with God changes death! However, much of our lives can actually be spent chasing after things that pass away and don't last. Those are the temporal concerns of this world and they take up a lot of our time and energy. When we allow those concerns to dominate us, then we have actually allowed our lives to be defined by death rather than eternity with God. Although this Gospel message is oftentimes used for funeral homilies, it is really meant to change the way we live always and not just comfort us in times of loss. Every day of our lives is to be a manifestation of Jesus as the Resurrection and the Life within us. One of the Prefaces for the Funeral Mass highlights our transcendental vocation as sons and daughters of God with these words, "Indeed for your faithful, Lord, life is changed not ended, and when this earthly dwelling turns to dust, an eternal dwelling is made ready for them in heaven."[16]

> *What does it look like when someone lives their life determined by death as opposed to living their life determined by eternity with God?*
>
> *Who do you identify as someone that lives life with a constant focus on what is eternal rather than what is temporal?*
>
> *What does the statement, "Death does not change our relationship with God; our relationship with God changes death", mean to you?*
>
> *Jesus wept when He saw people believing more in their experience of death than in His word of life-giving power. When do you find yourself trusting more in the world as*

---

16.   See Preface I for the Dead in the Roman Missal, 2010.

it appears rather than in the world Jesus proclaims and reveals?

Which of the three "I AM" statements of Jesus, has meant most to you during these three weeks of Lent: "I AM the Living Water", "I AM the Light of the World", or "I AM the Resurrection and the Life" and why?

PALM SUNDAY

Our Scripture passage for this Sunday is extensive and covers nearly two entire chapters of Matthew's Gospel from 26:14 to 27:66. This weekend we celebrate the beginning of Holy Week with what is commonly known as Palm Sunday. In this reading, we hear of Jesus' Last Supper, betrayal by Judas, trial both before the Sanhedrin and Pilate, suffering, crucifixion, death, and burial. Various details are immersed in this account of our Lord's final hours of earthly ministry. Our reflection this week will focus on only a few of these details and how they affect our lives as disciples.

As you hear this Gospel being proclaimed, you will notice one disappointing manifestation of sin after another. It is like a cascade of humanity's sin, weakness, and failure all rising up at once against Jesus. Such an intentional concentration of malice is Matthew's way of telling us something about the effect of Jesus' death and resurrection. Jesus came to save us from our sins, and through His suffering, death, and resurrection He destroyed the power of sin and opened the way to eternal life. Thus, we should not be surprised to see the sinful actions of so many surrounding Jesus at this moment. Our Lord will take the worst the world has to offer and bury the power of sin forever. In the face of such malice, evil and hatred, Jesus responds with mercy and love on the cross. As a result of Jesus' death, we see virtue and faith begin to flow into the world as the veil of the temple is torn in two, the Kingdom of God initiated (for example, the earthquake and the saints rising from the dead), the centurion professes his faith, and Joseph of Arimathea care for the body of Jesus with respect and dignity. Indeed, darkness has not prevailed. The world has hope after all, thanks to the death and resurrection of Jesus. Here's a quick summary of the malice that surrounds Jesus and what it means for us on this Palm Sunday.

Betrayal

The passage begins with the betrayal of Judas as someone who would sell out a friend for self-gain. Perhaps Judas thought, "it's just business". Who knows? Why do we betray others by what we say and do? There are lots of reasons. Maybe we are angry or hurt and want to get even, perhaps we have a chance to get ahead at the expense of our friendship, or maybe we've out-grown the group we've been with for so long. Perhaps we want to ingratiate ourselves with someone at another person's expense. Whatever it is, Judas, the "Companion" of Jesus ("Companion" means "one with whom we break bread"), becomes the betrayer. He shares the meal ... and then shuns the friendship.

> *When have you experienced betrayal? What was the situation and motivation for that action?*
> *When has someone felt that you betrayed them?*
> *How do we betray Jesus when we "share in the meal" of the Eucharist but then sell out our loyalty at the first challenge to our faith when we leave the doors of the church?*
> *Do you think that Judas felt betrayed by Jesus?*

Spiritual Indifference

Notice how Peter, James and John fall asleep at a critical moment in Jesus' life? They had the opportunity to spend these important hours with a friend in need, but they fell asleep. They could have been part of a great moment, but they couldn't be bothered. Is it laziness or indifference? Whatever it was, they were given a great opportunity and they weren't interested enough to participate in it. Instead, they slept.

> *How many times have we been invited by God to be part of a great moment, and we chose to sleep through it instead?*
> *When have we had the opportunity to help carry out a work of the Gospel, but we couldn't be bothered?*
> *When have you seen spiritual indifference?*
> *What are the excuses people use to justify their lack of response to such moments?*

How can people keep themselves from falling asleep in their faith?

Violence

Jesus was peaceful throughout His ministry, so why did the crowd feel the need to come in violence? We see in this passage the presence of clubs, mobs, and swords. It is always a sign of failure when we resort to violence, intimidation, or force as a solution to problems. Our violence may not involve swords or clubs, but oftentimes it involves slander, gossip, and other personal attacks. It happens every time we attack or destroy the dignity of another person. Violence is our rejection of communion, reconciliation, respect, and solidarity; it is our endorsement of dominance, destruction, and corruption.

When have you seen people resorting to violence (speech or action) to solve their problems?
On whom do you impose your will, and how could you do so in a non-violent way?
Who has been "violent" towards you?
Who is violent towards the Church today?
How are people violent towards Jesus today?

Cowardice

The disciples fled when it became difficult to follow Jesus. They chose to save themselves rather than embrace sacrifice for the sake of their faith and loyalty to Jesus. Sometimes we can experience cowardice when we are called to stand with Jesus in a moment of challenge as well. This happens when we are confronted with situations or opinions that go against our faith. It makes it all the easier to fall asleep when others around us are sleeping as well; one of the principles of survival is that there is "safety in numbers". Sometimes we find safety in numbers as well when we choose not to respond to faith challenges because others around us are not responding.

*What do you do in moments when you are confronted with
situations or opinions that go against your faith?*

*Oftentimes we remain quiet or prefer to shy away from a
direct response. What are situations you have faced when
your faith has been challenged, and how did you respond?*

*What are typical challenges to faith from which people
shy away?*

*How can a faith community better prepare people to be
courageous disciples?*

Deceit

As Jesus is on trial, we see a host of false witnesses coming forward.
These are people who are using this opportunity in order to appease
those who have power and influence. Basically, they are lying for
the sake of getting ahead and promoting themselves in the eyes
of others ... all at the expense of Jesus. Sometimes we lie for the
same reasons—to get ahead, to make ourselves look better, and so
forth. In doing so we always sin against Jesus who tells us that He
is "Truth" and that the truth will set us free (Jn 8:32).

What are typical situations that motivate people to lie today?

When has someone lied to you?

*When has telling the truth been difficult for you to do because it
isn't what others wanted to hear or what others wanted you to say?*

Blaming

As Peter is standing around the courtyard, the crowds begin to
question him about his friendship with Jesus. Peter not only denies
Jesus, but he also rejects Him and "blames" Jesus by swearing he
does not know Him. Peter wants Jesus to take on all the suffering
and punishment so that Peter doesn't have to do so himself. Peter
doesn't want the truth to be known; he wants no part of Jesus'
suffering. When we blame others while pretending to be faultless
ourselves, we are denying our responsibility as well. We become
content to make others pay the price so we don't have to. We also
see this action occurring through the crowds and others who mock

Jesus on the cross. They ridicule Him in such a way that they are blaming Jesus for this situation and laughing at the tragedy of His crucifixion. In doing so, they are attempting to absolve themselves of responsibility for the role they have played in His suffering.

> *In your family and professional life, who are the people who are typically "blamed" when things go wrong?*
> *Who do we blame when things go wrong in the Church?*
> *When do people find it easy to blame God?*
> *When have you stood up to stop the blame game and assumed responsibility?*

Political machinations

The trial of Jesus shows how easy it is for people to be used as expedient pawns in games of power and deceit. In the process of such inhumane pursuits, the innocent always suffer. Even today people can be treated harshly in an effort to set an example for others to heed. It is common for the media to sensationalize current events for the sake of promoting certain agendas and sacrificing people in the process through ridicule or defamation. The trial of Jesus shows us how political decisions on all levels can end up hurting innocent persons in the process. We should be careful to never put ideology or any cause before love of God and neighbor. If we are hurting people in order to help people, then something is wrong.

> *What social agendas or policies are hurting people today?*
> *Who are the innocent who are suffering because of ideology or political causes?*
> *Who is de-humanized in your work environment and how does it occur?*
> *How can you restore human dignity to someone who has suffered unreasonably or unjustly?*
> *How do you know when someone's suffering has become disproportionate to the wrong they have done?*

Despair

Finally, we see Judas giving in to despair. He trusted more in his own sin than he did in God's mercy. That is the ultimate sin against the Holy Spirit because Judas did not believe that God could or would forgive him. In his despair, he turns away from Jesus in an irrevocable way.

> *What leads people to despair today?*
> *Who do you know of that trusts more in their own failure, weakness, and sin than in God's power of transformation and forgiveness?*
> *Oftentimes we show our despair by our unwillingness to even ask forgiveness. What sins do people find most difficult to confess in the Sacrament of Reconciliation?*
> *How can a faith community help people to never despair and to always have confidence that God's mercy is greater than their sin?*

In response to all this malice, Jesus does not condemn those around Him but continues to fulfill God's will by dying on the cross for them and for us. In doing so, He takes the sin of humanity to the grave with Him and leaves it there while He Himself rises to bring us good news. Love is stronger than hate, life is stronger than death, and forgiveness is greater than sin. We may be weak and sinful, but we remain His disciples—if we are willing to accept the triumph of the cross and allow Jesus to be the Lord of our lives once again. That's good news for all of us during this Holy Week and every week. Sin never has the last word in our lives unless we want it to.

> *Which of the above sins do you encounter most often?*
> *How can you bring the good news of Jesus to those who manifest these sins?*

Take time this week to prayerfully accompany Jesus through the final days of His life and ministry so you can more deeply appreciate the depth of God's love and mercy in your life. [17]

---

17. The insights used in this reflection were largely gained from the Word on Fire website and represent the work of Most Rev. Robert Barron.

Lord Jesus Christ
may your death be my life,
and in your dying may I know how to live.
May your struggles be my rest,
your human weakness my courage,
your embarrassment my honor,
your passion my delight
your sadness my joy,
and in your humiliation may I be exalted.
May I find all my blessings in your trials.
Amen.

—Prayer of St Peter Faber, SJ

SOLEMNITY OF EASTER (VIGIL)

Our Scripture reading for the Easter Vigil comes from the Gospel of Matthew 28:1–10. This passage tells of the women who come to the tomb and find the angel sitting on the stone. The angel then sends them to be the first witnesses of the resurrection to Jesus' Disciples whom Jesus later calls His "brothers". Finally, the women meet Jesus on their way and pay Him homage while He instructs them to "Be not afraid". Each of these elements has important meaning for our reflection on this Easter Sunday.

It is significant that the angel rolled away the stone and then sat on it. There is a important reason why Matthew has told us this curious detail about the angel sitting on the stone. The stone was the obstacle that would block the women from entering the tomb so as to experience the Resurrection. The stone is what would separate them from their encounter with Jesus. The stone is the barrier that stands in the way of their next step of discipleship. To enter the tomb and experience the risen life of the Lord is a symbol of our baptism when we are immersed into the death and resurrection of Jesus. The stone stands as an obstacle to that experience of sacramental encounter with the Lord. It would not take any real effort for an angel to roll the stone away, so we should wonder why the angel chose to sit on the stone once it was rolled away. It wasn't because the angel was tired; rather, the angel was making a statement and Matthew wants us to pay attention to this truth—the stone has become a throne! Matthew is telling us that the power of Jesus' resurrection is able to turn the obstacles of our lives into the thrones of God's glory. That's a powerful message. The stone that Pilate had sealed in an effort to suppress the Gospel message has become the throne of God's glory. Every stumbling block for us can be turned into a stepping stone of discipleship through the power of the resurrection. What was meant to be an instrument of defeat can become the symbol of triumph. Certainly that was true with the cross of Calvary, and it is meant to be true for every cross we face as well. This reflection invites us to consider the many obstacles we face in our desire to encounter the Lord deeply in our lives. Perhaps it is a personal weakness, addiction, painful situation, or some other seeming impediment that is beyond our ability to overcome. The power of God can do for us what we cannot do for ourselves. That is part of the good news of the resurrection of Jesus. Our hope is not in our own strength but in God's all-powerful ability to transform us through grace. The women were so concerned about the stone because they knew it was beyond their power to move it. When we know the power of God, then we can submit our lives to the Lord with confident trust.

> *What are the stones that are current obstacles to greater faith (love of God and neighbor) in your life?*
> *When has an apparent moment of failure in your life turned into an incredible experience of God's triumph?*
> *When has God used a situation of tragedy to bring about a great growth and grace in your life?*
> *What do you think of when you hear the statement that God can turn the "Stone of defeat" into the "Throne of triumph"?*

It is interesting that the angel specifically sends the women to bring the message of the resurrection to the disciples. It is also significant that, when Jesus meets the women on the way, He sends them to His "brothers". This term implies that the previous relationship of faith and affection that was established during the Gospel story remains even after the cross. This is an important statement. We need to remember that the disciples suffered major moments of failure during our Lord's passion. Indeed, we can easily recall their sins of denial, cowardice, spiritual indifference, blaming, and so forth. However, despite these sins and failure, their relationship with the Lord was not destroyed. Rather, Jesus clearly affirms that they remain His "brothers" despite their sin, and the angel affirms that they are still His "disciples" regardless of their failure. This is a very important teaching for us, and we are meant to receive encouragement and consolation through it. As St Paul teaches, "What will separate us from the love of Christ?" (Rom 8:35). Indeed, not even our failures or sin will cause God to reject us as His disciples and brothers (or sisters). God loves us and calls us His own despite our shortcomings and weaknesses. That is really good news, isn't it? In the face of such incredible mercy and love, we need to reflect on what should be our proper response. We may see ourselves as sinners who deny, betray, and run away from the Lord, but in the eyes of Jesus we are still His brothers and sisters. This knowledge should give us the assurance we need to always seek out the Lord's mercy and to never give in to the temptation of believing that our sin is ever greater than God's love. With this confidence and trust, we can approach the throne of grace and experience the joy of renewed companionship with the Lord.

> *When has someone loved you when you didn't deserve the relationship?*
> *Who do you love despite their weakness or failure?*
> *What failures cause people to doubt God's enduring love for them?*
> *Jesus welcomes us back into relationship with Him if we are willing to accept that relationship and be reconciled. What keeps people today from reaching out and experiencing God's forgiveness and mercy so as to enter into relationship once again with the Lord?*
> *When is it easier for someone to see himself as a failure or sinner rather than as someone in whom God is confident and whom God calls a brother (or sister) and disciple?*

When the women meet Jesus on the way, Matthew states that they did Him homage. This means that they worshipped Him. At significant times in Matthew's Gospel, we are told about people who paid homage to Jesus (especially the visit of the three Magi in Mt 2:2, 8, 11 and the disciples in Mt 28:17 but also in Mt 8:2, 9:18, 14:33, and 15:25). Homage and Worship are the proper responses to Jesus as God. Throughout Matthew's Gospel, Jesus has been stressing the necessity of recognizing that God is present, speaking, and acting in His very person. To reject Jesus is to reject God; to accept Jesus must mean nothing less than to worship Him. When a person worships God, they are placing their entire life at God's service to be used by the Lord for His work in the world. Worshipping is not so much a matter of saying words, reciting prayers and singing songs; rather, it requires the surrendering of every part of our life to be guided by the Lord in all our decisions and actions. That's not easy to do. To use a metaphor, sometimes we like to draw close enough to the divine fire that we are warmed by it, but not so close that we are burned by it. Following this image, to worship Jesus means that we draw so close to the divine fire that we allow our lives to be completely consumed by it. Jesus revealed the Father to us, and in doing so He has made God's will known to us.

> *When are you most in tune with God's will in your life?*
> *In what ways can we fall short in our response to Jesus and end up not giving Him the true homage and worship He deserves?*
> *Who do you allow to direct your decisions and actions?*
> *To express their devotion to Jesus, the women embraced His feet. What posture of prayer do you find most expressive in your acts of homage and worship?*
> *Worship and homage have become casual terms in our current parlance; whereas Matthew used them sparingly and specifically. How has our casual usage of these terms caused us to lose sight of their significance and actually led us to misunderstand them?*

When Jesus greets the women, His first words to them are, "Do not be afraid!" These are probably the most common words of Jesus in the Gospels. Fear governs so much of people's lives and can paralyze them into passivity and silence in their faith. When we are afraid, we enter into a world of self-preservation and control. That is not the atmosphere in which the Gospel can take root and grow. Disciples are called to be courageous, trusting, and generous in their practice of faith. Such a witness requires that we be motivated by confidence in God's protection, presence, and care so as to be free in our response. Our Lord knew that disciples could be easily paralyzed by fear, and so His command to "be not afraid" speaks to us whenever we find ourselves becoming passive or silent as His witnesses. The fear of failure, fear of sacrifice, fear of rejection, fear of insufficiency and so forth are essentially incompatible with the life of committed discipleship. It takes a lot to overcome these very human fears. There are times when we become aware of God's presence with us in a way that cares for our needs or protects us from harm. These experiences remind us that we are not in control of our world after all and that we are loved by the All-Powerful Lord of Heaven and Earth. When we know and experience that loving presence, we can let go of our fears and become courageous witnesses. We can also be inspired by the courageous witness of others in such a way that their faith strengthens our faith. St John Chrysostom said in a homily, "To be afraid is not for you but for those who crucified Jesus."[18]

> *What are some of the fears that surface in the course of your day?*
>
> *What are some of the fears that prevent people from being good disciples and witnesses of the Gospel?*
>
> *What fears prevent us from approaching Jesus with confidence and openness?*
>
> *What do you think the women were afraid of?*
>
> *What are some of the important fears that you have had to overcome in your life and how has God helped you do that?*

---

18. St John Chrysostom, "The Gospel of Matthew, Homily 89.2." in *Ancient Christian Commentary on Scripture*, NT 1b, Matthew 14-28 (Downers Grove: Varsity Press, 2002), p. 307.

SECOND SUNDAY OF EASTER

O
ur Scripture passage for this Sunday comes from the Gospel of John 20:19–31. In this passage, we read about Jesus appearing to the disciples in the locked room on the first day of the week, breathing on them with the gift of the Holy Spirit, and sending them out to be ministers of forgiveness, peace, and joy for others. The passage ends with the Gospel writer's interesting statement about Jesus doing and saying many other things that are not contained in his writing. For additional insights into this Gospel account that are not discussed in this reflection, please refer to the volumes of *Come Follow Me* for Liturgical Year B or Liturgical Year C.

The first thing to notice in this passage is that all these events occurred on the first day of the week. That day is Sunday. It is no accident that so many experiences of God's presence, peace, reconciliation, and mission are all experienced on the Lord's Day. John is trying to tell us what should be happening when we celebrate the Lord's Day as well. The Lord's Day offers us opportunities to give God the gift of time by coming to Mass and praying. In the words of St John Paul II, "It is the day that shapes the rhythm of life for Christ's disciples."[19] It also offers us the opportunity to spend quality time with our family and friends, thus strengthening the bonds of community. God wants that! Family time should never be a burden but always a blessing since our primary vocation is to our family. Finally, the Lord's Day invites us to dedicate time to the mission of the Gospel and better equip ourselves as disciples who are being sent to bring God's mercy to others. Thus, works of charity, consideration of the less fortunate, and faith enrichment are other ways in which the Lord's Day is honored and sanctified.

---

19. John Paul II, Apostolic Letter *Dies Domini* (31 May, 1998), 21: *AAS* 90 [1998], pp. 713–776.

What does your Lord's Day look like? How do you try to sanctify the Lord's Day so it can be a day of encounter, mission, and discipleship?
What gets in the way of your ability to experience the Lord's Day as it is intended?
What can you do to better sanctify the Lord's Day for you and your family?
Why is it important for a disciple to honor the Lord's Day?
In our society, the Lord's Day is oftentimes seen as a day for recreation; God intends it to be a day of "Re-Creation" as His sons and daughters. How do you experience spiritual re-creation in your life?
What can we as a faith community do to help people enter more deeply into the celebration of the Mass so as to experience God's presence, peace, reconciliation, and mission?

Many times people think that the Scriptures represent humanity's search for God. In reality, the Scriptures tell us the story of God's search for humanity. In the book of Genesis, we read about Adam who sinned and was hiding from God. God came into the Garden searching for Adam who was hiding because he was ashamed. God's search for man continued through the writings of the Prophets in the Old Testament. Even the Exodus was an expression of the Lord's attempt to bring His people close to Him. In this Gospel passage, we see Jesus searching for the disciples while they are in hiding. Indeed, God is still searching for us while we try to hide in places of false security. Jesus first searches for the disciples who have locked themselves in the room out of fear. He goes to bring them peace and courage. Second, He goes to Thomas who has locked himself in a defiant stance of faith that demands empirical proof and wants to be convinced before he will believe. In each of these scenes Jesus is searching for His lost disciples. Even prior to this passage in John 20:11–18 we read of our Lord's search for Mary Magdalene who was in sorrow and distress because she could not find her Lord. All of these scenes show us that Jesus is the Good Shepherd who goes in search after His sheep. Sometimes we have a choice in whether or not we allow ourselves to be found by the Lord. Sometimes we can actually be more content to be alone in our fear and sorrow than to be united once again with God. Sin especially leads us to believe that we are not worthy of the Lord's forgiveness and love. This passage gives us hope and assurance that the Lord wants nothing more than our reconciliation and joy.

When have you not wanted to be "found" by God?
What causes people to hide from God today?
How does God try to knock on the door of our hearts so as to break into our lives?
How can you make yourself more open and ready to be found by the Lord?
What are the techniques we use to "hide" from the Lord— that is, what are the ways in which we try to lock God out of our lives?
What is it that people fear about God today?

Lastly, the Gospel writer tells us that Jesus said and did many other things that are not recorded in the Gospel. This is an interesting statement. Basically, it acknowledges that the Gospels do not contain everything that Jesus revealed. This passage of Scripture raises the question as to where we find the other things Jesus said and did that are not recorded in the Gospel. The answer to this question involves the role of Tradition, which includes the faithful passing on of other important things Jesus said and did. All of these actions and teachings of our Lord form the deposit of divine revelation, and many of them are not recorded in the Gospels (as stated in the explicit comment of Jn 20:30). In today's world, there are many people wanting to fill in the blanks of what Jesus said and did, but not everything is faithful to the Christian Tradition. Everything from the History Channel on television to pop culture is trying to interpret for us the Spirit of Jesus while oftentimes introducing unfounded and questionable elements into their presentations. Typically, these sources present someone who is labeled as an "expert" in one way or another. It is important to remember that virtually anyone can be interviewed and labeled an "expert", thus causing confusion in the minds of many people. This raises the question, how are we to know what is true and what is not true when it comes to resolving questions of faith that go beyond what is contained in Sacred Scripture?

What are your criterion for discerning what is truly revealed faith?

When has someone told you something about Jesus that you have not believed and what was it?

What was your process for discernment?

The ability to discern the truth is an important quality for disciples. What resources exist in the Church to help you discern what is true and what is not true about Jesus or the content of Christian faith?

When the New Testament was being codified (a process also known as the formation of the Canon), there were three primary criterion used to determine whether writings should be included or not: orthodoxy (that is, whether the writing was consistent with what was believed to be true faith), liturgical use (that is, was it already being used in a spiritually life-giving role for the Church), and connection to apostolic origin (that is, was its origin from someone who knew Jesus first-hand). Which of these criteria would best serve us today as we strive to resolve questions of faith?

When is it acceptable to believe something that is not contained in the Scriptures, and what is an example of such a belief?

Third Sunday of Easter

Our Scripture passage for this Sunday comes from the Gospel of Luke 24:13–35. In this passage, we read about the two disciples' journey from Jerusalem to Emmaus and of how Jesus accompanies them and reveals Himself to them. This passage offers us several points for reflection to help us recognize and respond to the presence of the Risen Christ in our midst.

The first thing to note is that Jesus walks with the two disciples even as they are going in the wrong direction and walking away from the others in Jerusalem. Nevertheless, Jesus accompanies them and listens to their story. They speak of their sadness at having lost a friend, their disappointment that things didn't turn out the way they had hoped, and their frustration that difficulties seem to continue, such as the news of the empty tomb. To them, everything was bad news, and they could not see the presence of God in the midst of such a terrible situation. These negative and erroneous perceptions caused the disciples to walk away from the others and pursue the wrong path. It is the companionship of Jesus that gained their trust and allowed them to be open to His Word. Had Jesus started to correct them or reprimand them immediately, they would not have listened to Him. Rather, Jesus first shows them that He is a friend who cares for them, and because of that the disciples will listen to what the Lord has to say. This dynamic is an important lesson for us as a Church. Oftentimes we see people going in the wrong direction because of tragedies, frustrations, misunderstandings or disappointments. Sometimes people pursue the wrong direction just out of human weakness. Whatever the reason, our response should be modeled on that of Jesus who shows us the importance of being a compassionate friend first and a challenging friend second. Rather than wait for the disciples to return to Jerusalem on their own, Jesus is the Good Shepherd who goes after the lost sheep by seeking out these two disciples. Jesus is present in us and through us when we become instruments of the Lord's mercy reaching out towards those going down the wrong path.

When have you gone down the wrong path in your life?
What negative experiences led you to do that?
Who befriended you and helped you see things from a new
perspective that made you want to be faithful?
What are some of the wrong paths that you see people
pursue today?
What are your common responses when you see people
going in the wrong direction?
How can a faith community better practice the mercy of
Jesus who seeks out the lost?
When have you relied on the presence of the Christian
community to help keep you on the right path?
One of the truths of this scene is that we experience the
hidden presence of the Risen Christ in the familiar presence
of one another (the Christian community). When have you
experienced the presence of Christ acting through someone
else and touching your life?

After Jesus has accompanied them for a time and listened to their story, He could then speak to them about the Scriptures and help them understand the necessity that the Messiah should suffer and die so as to enter into His glory. Suddenly, the disciples were able to see that the events of Calvary were not a sign of God's absence but rather the very fulfillment of God's promises. Indeed, God was present on Calvary after all. The empty tomb was not the tragedy of a stolen body but rather the good news of the resurrection. What the disciples thought was bad news has now become good news because they are able to understand the Scriptures through the lens of the death and resurrection of Jesus. It all made sense to them for the first time. This section of the passage tells us that the transformation of our intellect through the informed and interpreted Word of God in Scripture is an important step in the conversion process. We need help to see the events of our lives from God's perspective as well. The Scriptures offer us profound insights into how God has revealed Himself in history and acted in the lives of ordinary people. These insights speak to us. By properly understanding God's action in the life of Jesus we can correct our false assumptions and mistaken perspectives. The change of a person's mind is commonly called the process of repentance (Greek *meta-*

noia). This process takes time as we confront the many false beliefs that are communicated to us by a secular culture. Sometimes, too, we develop our own false beliefs because of insufficient or ineffective faith formation. Mature disciples are self-leaders who seek to understand God's will through the Scriptures and other sources of revelation including personal prayer, the teaching of the Church, and the witness of the Saints.

> *When has Scripture helped you to re-interpret an experience in your life?*
> *What has helped you understand the Scriptures in a personal and meaningful way?*
> *As disciples, it is important for us to know the Word of God so we can benefit from other people's experience of God's saving and revealing love. What resources exist to help you develop a deeper understanding of the Scriptures?*
> *Jesus did not tell the disciples anything from Scripture they did not already know. Rather, what Jesus did was help them interpret it through the lens of His death and resurrection. What are the various false lenses we can use to interpret Scripture that lead us to an incorrect interpretation such as the disciples previously had?*
> *One of the truths of this scene is that we can experience the Risen Christ speaking to us in the Scriptures. When have you experienced the enlightening voice of Christ speaking to you through the Scriptures?*

Finally, when they arrive at Emmaus, they invite Jesus to be their guest, but the Lord doesn't remain the "guest" of their lives for very long. Rather, at the meal Jesus reveals Himself as the one who is really the host of their journey. We see this self-revelation in the action of giving the bread, since the one who distributed the food at the table was always the host. By deferring this role to Jesus, the disciples were finally allowing Him to occupy His proper place as the master of their lives rather than their guest. Additionally, as they sit at table Jesus reveals something to them when He takes, blesses, breaks, and gives bread to them. Those are the verbs of the Eucharist and are used in the letters of Paul (1 Cor 10:16 and 1 Cor 11:23–24) and the other gospel accounts to describe the action of Jesus at the Last Supper (Mt 26:26–28, Mk 14:22–24, and Lk 22:17–19) and in the multiplication of the loaves and fishes (Lk 9:16). It is the revelation of Jesus in the Eucharist that opened their eyes and revealed the living presence of the Lord in their midst. It was also their realization of the living presence of Jesus that changed their lives and journey so that they no longer pursued the wrong direction but rather returned to Jerusalem. It's significant that mere knowledge did not change their lives, but the newfound relationship and personal encounter with Jesus in the Eucharist did bring about this change. The proper term for a change of life is conversion, which literally means "to turn around or change direction" (Greek *epistrephein)*. When we realize, acknowledge, and receive the living presence of Jesus in the Eucharist, then it is meant to be a life-changing moment for us as well. It is always a moment of conversion when we realize the need to live our lives in communion with God whom we have received and of whose presence we have become a living tabernacle. It is always a moment of relationship, adoration, and reverence when we humbly approach the Lord who has entrusted Himself to us in the Blessed Sacrament. It is a moment of surrender as we freely change roles and allow the Lord to be the Host, and we become the guests in His presence. The Word of God in Scripture may prepare us for this moment of conversion through the process of repentance, yet there is a superior grace in the Blessed Sacrament of the Eucharist that is meant to effect a lasting change in how we live. Saint Paul wrote poignantly of the necessary conversion that must take place in every disciple who shared in the Eucharistic Presence of Jesus (cf. 1 Cor 10 and 11). This Eucharistic conversion makes the assembly go from being a mere human congregation to become Christ's Church. The Eucharist is an intimate experience with universal repercussions.[20] After Mass, we leave the assembly with the firm conviction that the same sanctifying action that changed the bread and wine into the Body and Blood of Jesus can transform, through us, every person and every reality we encounter. Have you ever seen the bumper stickers that say, "If God is your co-pilot, then you need to change seats"? That is very much what happened when the disciples sat

---

20.   R. Cantalamessa, *The Eucharist, Our Sanctification* (Collegeville: The Liturgical Press, 1995), p. 16.

down to dinner with Jesus: they willingly traded places with the Lord. The disciples experienced so many graces when they shared that meal with the Lord and recognized Him in the Eucharist. These graces include revelation, consolation, adoration, conversion, and companionship.

> *What are some of the graces you have experienced through the Eucharist?*
>
> *When have you changed places with the Lord so as to consciously allow Him to be the pilot and you to become the co-pilot of your life?*
>
> *The disciples only realized in hindsight how Jesus was accompanying them and speaking to them on the Way. When have you realized the presence of God in your life through hindsight despite being blind to it in the moment?*
>
> *One of the truths of this scene is that we experience the Risen Christ present to us in a distinctive way in the Eucharist. When have you experienced the reality of Christ's presence in the Eucharist in such a way that it changed your life?*

This account of the disciples' journey to Emmaus is found only in Luke's Gospel. Luke uses it to address one of the primary concerns of his community: namely, how to experience the Risen Christ while we are on our Christian "Way". This passage is not just about two disciples and their own personal experience. Rather, it is meant to speak to all of us in our experience as a Church. The early Christians were called "Followers of the Way" and so it is important that Luke tells us multiple times that these things happened to the two disciples while they are on their "Way" (Lk 24:32 and Lk 24:35) (note: some translations use the word "road" but it should be more properly translated as "Way"). The Risen Christ is with us, too, in the community of the faithful who surround us (Church), in the Scriptures proclaimed to us (Liturgy of the Word), and in the "Breaking of the Bread" offered to us as food for the journey (Liturgy of the Eucharist). With the eyes of faith, we will see the presence of Jesus in the present, and through that faithful awareness we will be able to keep going in the right direction while encouraging one another to do the same.

How have you experienced Jesus present to you on your Christian "Way"?

How does the story of Emmaus change your understanding of the Mass?

How does the relationship between repentance and conversion as described in this passage inspire and challenge your discipleship?

Fourth Sunday of Easter

Our Scripture passage for this Sunday comes from the Gospel of John 10:1–10. In this passage we read about Jesus identifying Himself as the "Sheep Gate" for the flock. Our Lord further introduces Himself as the Good Shepherd who calls His sheep by name, and they follow Him. This passage offers several excellent points for our prayer and reflection.

One of the first things to note is how strongly Jesus stresses that being a member of His flock (the Church) is defined first and foremost by our relationship with Him. Thus, the Church is not primarily a social community of people who enter into a free association with one another; rather, the Church is a community of people whom the Lord has called by name and who have passed through Jesus as the Sheep Gate. Sometimes we can tend to understand our membership in the Church more on a social level than a spiritual level. The Church is first and foremost a community formed by the Lord and composed of those whom He has made His own. It is interesting to note that the doors of a church building are actually a symbol of Jesus as the "Sheep Gate" through which we (the flock) pass so as to enter into the sheepfold. This understanding of what it means to be Church has implications for the way we act towards one another and changes the motivation we have for coming to our local church building. First, it means that we accept and relate to one another, not out of our personal affections or common interests, but because we share the same foundational connection to Jesus who has called us. Sometimes we may not even like some of the people Jesus has called into the flock, but the same mercy of God that calls us also calls them. It's not up to us as the flock to decide whom the Lord calls. It is the responsibility of the flock to welcome and accept all whom the Good Shepherd places in our midst.

Second, this understanding of Church should also affect the reason we come to worship each Sunday. Namely, we come to be with the Good Shepherd, hear His voice, receive His protection and guidance, be nourished, and receive strength for the Christian journey. However, when people have a mistaken understanding of what takes place at Church, they can be motivated by the wrong attractions, which can easily become distractions. For example, sometimes we want to come because we like the music, we like the minister, we like some of the people there, we like the architecture, and so forth. These motivations may be interesting in themselves and may even bring us to the church, but they do not make us members of the Church nor will they sustain us during difficult moments. Only the love of the Good Shepherd and the personal connection to Him will keep us faithful despite the challenges we face.

> *When have you been annoyed by the presence of someone who is a member of the community with you, and how can this reaction be an opportunity to purify your faith?*
> *How can a faith community imitate the hospitality and acceptance of Jesus towards those we do not know so as to welcome them more effectively?*
> *How are people made to feel unwelcome when they come to church?*
> *As you pass through the doors of the church this Sunday and remind yourself that you are passing through Jesus as the Sheep Gate, how will that affect what you are seeking from the worship experience?*
> *How can a faith community help people to move beyond superficial attractions to discover an authentic encounter with the Good Shepherd when they come to church?*

Jesus stresses in this passage that His sheep both hear His voice and follow Him. This connection between hearing and following means that disciples must actively live out God's will in their lives and not remain passive in the reception of their calling. It is not enough that the Shepherd calls us by name or that we merely hear His voice. That experience of God's personal attention might be nice, but to truly be a disciple we still have to actively engage in the practical task of following Him. It's easy to want God's leadership in our lives when we get ourselves into trouble. That's when we call out for help saying, "What should I do?" Jesus wants us to seek and follow His guidance in our blessings as well as our burdens. That means we listen to His voice and follow His lead when the going is easy, as well as when the going gets tough. The Lord cares for each of us personally and individually. He knows our struggles, temptations, challenges, and burdens. The Lord desires that our prayer be a deeply personal encounter with Him as the one who knows better than we do how to respond to the dilemma of each day.

> *When have you sensed a truly personal rapport with the Lord and that God was calling you by name?*
> *How do you dispose yourself so you can hear the voice of the Shepherd giving you guidance and direction in your life?*
> *When does the personal attention of Jesus become uncomfortable for you, and how do you try to hide from the Lord so as to fade into the impersonal midst of the flock?*
> *Jesus goes before us as our Good Shepherd so we can follow. The reality is that the Lord will lead us to Calvary and ask us to carry the cross of faithfulness in a hostile world. When has being a disciple led you to take on a difficult or challenging situation of persecution or sacrifice?*
> *What are the ways in which we try to exempt ourselves from the need to follow Jesus so as to be content with merely hearing His voice?*
> *How can your faith community help people to be mature disciples who live out God's will in their lives?*

One other important element of this passage is when it warns us of the reality that there are those who try to be bad shepherds so as to lead us astray from Christ the Good Shepherd. These are shepherds who seek to use the sheep (us) for their personal gain and benefit. There's no shortage of people who try to use others for their personal gain. This passage implies that such bad shepherds try to take the place of Jesus in our lives so as to lead us away from the Lord. Jesus indicates that if we are intimately connected with Him, we will be able to distinguish the voice of the Good Shepherd from the voices of the bad shepherds and resist their destructive lead. To be intimately connected with the Lord means to live out a correct understanding of what it means to be Church and to be a mature disciple who hears, listens, and follows the voice of God. It also means becoming familiar with the Good Shepherd, knowing His teaching, learning His character, and sensing His presence. That requires spending time in prayer and study. Many of the great Saints reflected on the subtle tricks bad shepherds use so as to lure us away from Christ. Saint Ignatius of Loyola, for example, emphasized in his days (sixteenth century) the practice of "spiritual discernment"[21] that was so prominent in the first centuries of Christianity[22] and that continues to be an important exercise to ensure spiritual growth. These writings are worthy of our reflection because they will help us grow in our maturity and ability to discern the various influences that come into our life each day. Another guide that has proven to be a classic spiritual resource for such discernment of good and evil influences is the book by C.S. Lewis entitled *The Screwtape Letters*. This text provides an insightful and accurate understanding of how bad shepherds are alive and well in our world today and of the tactics used to lure us away from Jesus. You may be shocked at how real and effective are the subtle voices of these bad shepherds who attempt to corrupt, distort, and distract Christian disciples.

> *Who are some of the bad shepherds who have tried to influence you away from following Jesus or living Christian values?*
>
> *What are the influences of our culture and society that can lead us away from a Christian way of life?*
>
> *How do bad shepherds try to distort our understanding of Church so as to weaken the intimacy we share with the Good Shepherd, which causes us to become people who are less able to discern between good versus bad influences?*
>
> *How do bad shepherds try to distort our understanding of mature discipleship so as to make us content to only hear the Lord's voice but not necessarily to follow the Lord's lead in our lives?*

---

21. St Ignatius of Loyola, *Spiritual Exercises* (New York: Image, Doubleday, 1964).

22. 1 Corinthians 12:10; Evagrius of Pontus, *Praktikos* and *On Prayer* (Oxford: Faculty of Theology, 1987); A.D. Rich, *Discernment in the Desert Fathers* (Milton Keynes: Paternoster, 2007); L. Scupoli, *The Spiritual Combat* (Mesa: Scriptoria, 2012).

When evil cannot succeed in making us turn away from the Lord, then evil will try to distort our reason for being drawn to the Lord. What does that statement mean to you? What can a faith community do to help people discern correctly the voice of the Good Shepherd and reject the influence of bad shepherds?

Fifth Sunday of Easter

Our Scripture passage for this Sunday comes from the Gospel of John 14:1–12. In this reading we hear of Jesus preparing His disciples for His departure and the beneficial consequences it is intended to have for their lives and ministry. This passage from John's Gospel is particularly profound and presents some important teachings for disciples. There are several points for our reflection and prayer.

Jesus first says to His disciples, "Do not let your hearts be troubled." When He uses the word "troubled", He uses a word that expresses the trepidation a person experiences when confronted with the power of evil and death. Thus, He is saying to the disciples that they must stand firm even when it looks like evil and death have control over a situation. It is really a rallying cry for strength, confidence, courage, and perseverance in the face of such trials. Sometimes we need to be reminded to "let not our hearts be troubled" when we encounter seemingly hopeless situations. Think of how many people have faced the overwhelming conditions of war, systemic poverty, oppression, organized hatred, and so forth but have retained courage, confidence, and strength nonetheless. Jesus wanted to prepare His disciples for His imminent death on the cross, so He offers them this forewarning. Jesus wants to prepare us as well so we will remember that, through our Lord's death and resurrection, the power of evil no longer has the last word.

What are situations of evil that "trouble" you?
How does a disciple who is courageous, confident, strong, and persevering respond to such situations?
How does a disciple who is weak, afraid, doubting, and insecure respond to such situations?
How can we help people who are facing overwhelming situations of evil or death to persevere with faith and confidence?

Jesus then says to His disciples, "In my Father's house there are many dwelling places, and I am going to prepare a place for you."

The power of this statement cannot be underestimated. We often-times think of this statement as referring to a place in heaven, which is why this passage is so commonly used for funeral liturgies. However, we need to remember that throughout the Gospel of John, Jesus has been stressing the relationship He has with the Father in terms of "abiding" or "dwelling". For example, in verse 14 Jesus spoke about how He is in the Father and the Father is in Him. When Jesus tells us that He is going to prepare a dwelling place for us in the Father's house, what the Lord is really saying is that He will open to us the relationship He has with the Father so that we can share in it just as He shares in it. The place Jesus prepares for us in this passage, then, is about relationship, not location. It is about being given a part in a permanent life-giving relationship with God that allows us to experience heaven on earth through the indwelling Spirit of God in us. It is about accepting the gift of God's life in us and responding to that divine initiative by offering our lives to God in return. Through Jesus, we now have a "place" in that divine relationship because He has opened that indwelling presence to us.

> *When has someone opened a loving relationship and invited you to share in it?*
>
> *What is your response to the realization that Jesus is inviting you to become a co-participant in His relationship with the Father?*
>
> *The death of Jesus has many effects and beneficial consequences including the possibility of a new relationship with God. When you look at a crucifix, how does it change your appreciation of Calvary to know that Jesus died so that we could share in the life and love of God?*
>
> *Why do you think it was so important for Jesus that we share in the relationship He has with the Father?*

Next, Jesus tells His disciples, "I am the Way and the Truth and the Life." In first century Judaism, the word "way" was used as a metaphor to describe "life with God." Accordingly, Jesus is saying that He embodies life with God. He alone can reveal to us the face of the Father because He alone is the Word who was with God from all eternity and who is God. Those who seek heavenly realities must, in fact, seek Jesus who reveals them to us. The way of Jesus shows us that the Father is love and self-gift even unto death. If we are His disciples, then the way of Jesus must become our way so that we can share in that oneness of life with the Father. Jesus is Truth because He is the Word made flesh and reveals the truth of God to the world (Jn 1:14, 17–18, Jn 18:37). Jesus is Life because He brings God's gift of life to the world (Jn 3:15–16). Lots of people in the time of Jesus were looking for the "way" to God. Some sought it in philosophies, others in mystical religious practices, still others in pagan rituals and drunken orgies. When Jesus tells us that He is the Way, He is inviting us to accept discipleship and follow Him in His life of revealing, sacrificial, self-giving love. That, Jesus says, will lead us to God.

> *What are some of the erroneous ways people try to find God today (that is, how can people spend their time and energy "Looking for God in all the wrong places")?*
> *How do people try to discount or circumvent the call to accept the way of Jesus in sacrificial self-giving love?*
> *Jesus reveals Himself as the Way, the Truth, and the Life not to tell us about Himself but so that we can know what He is offering us. Which of these three aspects of Jesus' identity (way, truth, life) do you most desire to experience and why?*
> *How can a faith community better help people identify and choose the way of Jesus in their lives?*

In further clarification of His role as the Way, the Truth, and the Life, Jesus then says that, "No one comes to the Father except through me." This statement is the summit of the Gospel of John concerning the significance of Jesus. This is the truth that drives the entire Gospel; Jesus has decisively and permanently changed the relationship between God and humankind. He is the door to the Father. He is the only begotten Son. He is the eternal Word made Flesh. To reject Jesus is to reject the Father; to accept the Father requires that we accept Jesus in whom the Father is revealed. Pope St John Paul II reiterated this unique and necessary truth of Jesus as the sole means by which we can have access to the Father in the declaration entitled *Dominus Iesus*.[23] However, there are many people who have never heard of Jesus both historically and even in present times. The Church has taught that the Holy Spirit can, in a way known only to God, bring about the gift of salvation in such persons when they sincerely respond to the movement of God in their lives. In a sense, it is possible for a person to actually respond to the Lord Jesus without realizing it is He to whom they are responding. Still, such an uninformed response lacks clarity and is inherently weakened because of that lack of awareness. This central truth of the Gospel concerning the necessity of Jesus as the only way to the Father serves as the missionary impetus for the Church.

> *How do people today try to find God without seeking Jesus?*
> *What can distract spiritual people from seeking Jesus in their desire for encounter with God?*
> *What can we do as disciples to positively represent the message of Jesus so that others will want to learn more about Him?*
> *What opportunities exist for you to introduce someone to Jesus who does not yet know about Him?*
> *We live in a world of religious pluralism (meaning that people believe there are many valid ways to encounter God) and religious relativism (meaning that all ways are equal and no one way is better than the rest). How do these erroneous beliefs surface in your interactions with others, and how does the statement of Jesus in this Gospel passage affect the way you would respond in the face of such mistaken understandings?*

Finally, Jesus says to His disciples, "You will do greater works than these." We are then told that these greater works will explicitly take place because Jesus goes to the Father. This passage most likely refers to the missionary activity of the Church and the lived experience of disciples. Jesus was one person with one life to give. He lived in one time and in one place and died on Calvary by crucifixion. But there are millions of Christians throughout the

---

23. Congregation for the Doctrine of the Faith, *Declaration Dominus Iesus*, (6 August, 2000), 5: *AAS* 92, (2000), pp. 759–761.

world and throughout history. Many of these Christians have lived faithful and heroic lives showing us what communion with God looks like when it is pursued in the radical way of Jesus. Disciples are called to be people who are aware of God's many redeeming and powerful works in their lives. Indeed, through the lives of faithful disciples, the Church has done "greater works than these". Each Christian life presents a different nuance of how God's effective and real grace manifests itself. Each Christian life shows how the divine indwelling of God becomes visible in works of self-giving and loving sacrifice. The forgiveness of John Paul II for his would-be assassin, the gentleness and dedication of Mother Teresa for the destitute and dying, the heroic witness of 20th century Martyrs, the fidelity of a couple in a distressed marriage who seek to persevere in their vows, the courage of an alcoholic reaching out for God as his only strength, power and salvation are all examples of such manifestations of grace. The list can certainly go on. Through our sharing of life in relationship with God, we have provided the Lord with a myriad of ways in which God's works can be accomplished in us and through us. Jesus is pleased when we exercise our rights as children of God! He knew what the Father had in store for us and for the world through us. What an awesome mission! What a humbling love and confidence.

> *What are some of the works of God you see taking place in people's lives today?*
> *What work do you think the Lord wants to accomplish in you today?*
> *What is the work the Lord wants to accomplish through you for someone else?*
> *Whose Christian witness inspires you in such a way that you see the power of God shining through it?*

Sixth Sunday of Easter

Our Scripture passage for this Sunday comes from the Gospel of John 14:15–21. In this passage, Jesus promises to send us another Paraclete and assures us that He will return to be with us. This was an especially comforting and encouraging message for the disciples who were about to face Jesus' death on Calvary, and it continues to be an encouraging message for us today.

Jesus first instructs His disciples on the necessary relationship between love and obedience (faith) when He says, "If you love me you will keep my commandments." To believe in Jesus is to accept His word (teaching and instruction) as authentically from the Father. A disciple who loves Jesus will live out that relationship by holding fast to our Lord's commandments. There is an inherent connection between our love for Jesus and our actions. It is important to remember that the primary commandment Jesus gave is that disciples love one another even as our Lord has loved us (13:15, 34–35, 14:15a). Jesus demonstrated His love both in the washing of the disciples' feet and in the laying down of His life on the cross. It's easy to love the Lord when we define "love" to mean nothing more than an interior private emotion focused only on a spiritual relationship. It can be difficult, however, to love the Lord when it means loving Him in those around us and laying down our lives for them even as Jesus laid down His life for us. The challenge for us in this passage is to move beyond a spirituality that is focused on a cherished memory of the past or one that is based only on interior emotions. Instead, we are to become living witnesses of God's love for others so that the sacrificial love of Christ dwells in us and through us. By moving outside a merely private personal relationship with Jesus and living what He taught and demonstrated, we will find ourselves immersed in His love and enjoying even deeper relationship with Him in the present. It's easy to love those whom we like or those who are close to us, but it can be difficult to love those who need it most.

For whom do you find it difficult to love as Jesus loved?
Jesus clarified that authentic Christian love is necessarily manifested in lived obedience to His commands. This clarification was given to keep us from reducing love to a merely emotional experience. When have you been called to do something difficult or challenging because of your love of God?
When has someone's act of love for you reflected the self-giving love of Jesus shown to us on Calvary?
What can a faith community do to help people better understand how to live out their love for Jesus in the practical actions of their daily lives?

Next, Jesus tells the disciples that He will send another Paraclete for them. The word "Paraclete" is a strange term in English. It originally referred to a legal assistant who functioned in the capacity of a lawyer and who "called out" on another person's behalf (the term "Paraclete" comes from the Greek words *para kaleo,* meaning to speak on another's behalf). Over the course of time, the term took on broader meanings including "Intercessor" (one who prays for another), "comforter", "consoler", "guide", and "teacher of truth". Each of these terms expresses the very actions that Jesus performed for His disciples during His life and ministry. Thus, Jesus himself was the first Paraclete, and now He promises to send another Paraclete to continue His ministry to the Church when our Lord goes to the Father. That Paraclete is the gift of the Holy Spirit. The role of the Holy Spirit is not often well understood in Western Christianity, and as a result of that lack of awareness we can fail to appreciate the importance of passages such as this one. It is the Holy Spirit that animates the life of the Church, that inspires disciples, that draws us into the life of God to be in communion with Jesus and the Father, that unites us in the bond of love, and that continues to reveal the truth of Jesus in every time and place. The Holy Spirit teaches us what it means to be the presence of Christ in different situations—makes us the mystical Body of Christ on the earth, sanctifies us, and so forth. That is quite a list! In the gospel of John, we see how Jesus gave us the gift of the Spirit, both from the cross when He handed over His Spirit (Jn 19:30b) and in the upper room where the disciples were gathered and He breathed on them saying, "Receive the holy Spirit" (Jn 20:22).

> *If you were asked to tell someone about the Holy Spirit, what would you say?*
>
> *The work of the Holy Spirit in the life of the Church is varied and dynamic. Which of the effects of the Holy Spirit listed above have you experienced and how?*
>
> *Jesus gave the Holy Spirit to the Church at two moments (the crucifixion and the resurrection) and for two purposes (the gift of the Spirit from the cross was to form and guide the pastoral life of the Church caring for its members, while the gift of the Spirit from the resurrected Lord is to animate and empower the Church for its mission of evangelization). Which of these works of the Holy Spirit is most needed in the Church today?*
>
> *How is the Holy Spirit prompting you to become a more active member of the Body of Christ?*
>
> *What can a faith community do to help people learn more about the Holy Spirit?*
>
> *Why do you think Jesus wanted to share so many insights with the disciples into the spiritual nature of the Church (for example, the Flock who hears His voice, the Holy Spirit as the sanctifying presence, and so forth)?*

Lastly, Jesus assures His disciples of His own continuing presence among them when He says, "I will not leave you orphans; I will come to you" (Jn 14:18). Whenever Jesus uses the pronoun "you" in this passage, it is always in the plural. Thus, Jesus is telling us that the gift of His presence is first and foremost to the community of the Church rather than to us as individual Christians. This is a very significant teaching. Jesus' love for the Father was not private. It was public. The believer's experience of Jesus and witness of love for Jesus is to be experienced in the community of the Church as opposed to a merely private transcendental union. The promise of divine presence, including the gift of the Holy Spirit, is made to a community of believers and not to those who are living their faith apart from that community of faith. This passage, then, teaches us of the necessity of the Church for our relationship with God. The

Church is not primarily spiritual because we do spiritual things. Rather, the Church is essentially spiritual because of the gift of the Holy Spirit and the indwelling of Jesus that draws us into His life with the Father. The Christians of the first century experienced the return of Jesus primarily in the celebration of Baptism and the Eucharist. It is in these experiences of the worshiping community, and the other Sacraments, that we encounter and celebrate a continuing relationship with the Lord who is present to us. The reading for this Sunday teaches us that the absent one, the Lord Jesus, is truly present to those who believe His words, love Him in the fellow Christian, and keep His commandments. Jesus promises that when we live out our high calling as a Church, He will reveal Himself to us and we will experience communion of life with the Holy Trinity.

> *What are some of the ways today in which we tend to privatize the experience of Jesus and discipleship as opposed to understanding it as a communal gift?*
>
> *What are the ways in which people can try to exempt themselves from a personal response of faith by erroneously appealing to the communal response (that is, people can become content with just sitting in a pew rather than taking personal responsibility for their growth in discipleship)?*
>
> *How does this teaching of the spiritual reality of the Church challenge you?*
>
> *What are some of the other understandings of Church a person can have that differ from that of a primarily spiritual reality?*
>
> *No one likes to be abandoned (orphaned), and for this reason there are moments when we can sense God's presence with us in the midst of otherwise lonely experiences. What are some of your experiences of God that have assured you of our Lord's presence in your life?*
>
> *What circumstances or situations could cause you to doubt God's presence?*
>
> *People can come to church for a lot of different reasons. How should this understanding of Church—as the primary locus for the encounter with the risen Christ—change the way you prepare for and experience Sunday worship?*

SOLEMNITY OF THE ASCENSION

Our Scripture passage for this Sunday comes from the Gospel of Matthew 28:16–20. This scene tells us of Jesus' final moments before He ascended into heaven. As He goes to the Father, our Lord offers revelation, mission, and His continuing presence to the disciples. This passage offers several points for our reflection and prayer as disciples who are entrusted with carrying on the mission of Jesus.

When the disciples see Jesus, we are told that they worshiped Him but they doubted. That may seem like an unusual combination of responses, but it's probably descriptive of most of us. You see, "doubt" does not mean skepticism about who Jesus is. Rather, "doubt" refers to the hesitancy the disciples experienced when required to make a complete and irrevocable commitment to Jesus to the exclusion of other options. The reality is that the resurrection of Jesus didn't generate perfect faith in those who experienced it. The community of disciples was still wavering in their understanding and commitment to our Lord and to accepting His all-encompassing claim on their lives. Nonetheless, it is to that wavering community that Jesus entrusted His mission to the world. To re-phrase that insight, we might say that it is to us, as that community, that Jesus is entrusting His mission to the world even though we do not possess or express perfect faith. Most Christians have some areas of doubt with which they struggle, yet that does not diminish the faith they do possess. It is difficult to make a complete and irrevocable commitment when the slightest doubt exists. In such moments we like to keep our options open rather than reduce them. This is true with couples preparing for marriage and for Christians ratifying their discipleship. In Matthew's Gospel, we have previously heard Jesus address the little faith present in the disciples (Mt 14:31). We have also seen how Jesus is willing to work with the disciples to bring them to a deeper and more committed faith rather than abandoning them because of their weakness. This is good news for us! It tells us that Jesus will help us grow in our faith and commitment to Him, especially when we ask for His assistance. It is one thing to not understand a message of faith; it is another thing to not even try to understand it. This passage encourages us to not become complacent or uncaring (spiritual acedia) in our search for deeper faith. It also encourages us to know that God desires to work with us wherever we are in the journey of discipleship.

> *What are some of the doubts that people have today in their faith that make it difficult for them to make an all-encompassing and irrevocable commitment to the Lord?*
> *What can help a person persevere in their faith despite doubts?*
> *Jesus entrusted the worldwide mission of the Church to the hands of disciples whose faith was not perfect. When have you felt under-qualified to take on the work of the Gospel because you were unworthy or imperfect?*
> *Sometimes it's easy to think of the saints as perfect people who never struggled in their faith. How does this passage about the disciples help you to identify with them, and what encouragement does it give you?*

Jesus then tells the disciples that they, in turn, are now to "Make Disciples" of all the nations (that is, the Gentiles). Actually, Jesus uses a verb when He tells them to "disciple" the nations. We are more accustomed to thinking of "Disciple" as a noun that describes a person's character or religious affiliation rather than as a verb that describes the action by which one person mentors and forms another person as a follower of Jesus. The work of discipling requires that we pass on to others our own encounter with God and how we live our own life in Christ so that others can share in the same wonderful grace, which we have been given. Effective discipling doesn't usually happen in large groups. More frequently it occurs through one-on-one interactions within families and between friends. It requires mutual respect, trust, and sincerity to introduce others to Jesus Christ. Of course, we cannot give what we do not have, so the first stage of Christian discipleship is for ourselves to be deeply immersed and formed in the Christian way of life. However, that is only the first stage. The second stage of mature discipleship is for those who have been formed to now go out and form others so that they become missionary disciples. Thus, Christian discipleship reaches maturity in mission when the gift we receive becomes the gift we freely give.

Who has discipled you, and how did it happen?

We form others each day through our interactions with them. Are we forming Christian disciples, or are we forming disciples of secularism, hedonism, materialism, indifference, or self-preservation?

What do you need to do to prepare yourself to be a disciple who "disciples" others? Who has God placed in your life as an opportunity for you to disciple them?

What forums exist for you to invite others into discipleship? When Jesus told the disciples to "disciple the nations", He was really referring to the Gentiles who were generally looked down on as lesser people. Who are some of the less significant people in your world that the Lord may be asking you to reach out to so as to invite them into a life of faith?

This passage contains the one great lasting commission of Jesus for the work of the Church (it is our fundamental mission statement). How could the Church do a better job of forming disciples at each stage of life and preparing them for mission?

What tools and skills do missionary disciples need in order to accomplish this mission?

Next, Jesus specifies that discipling the nations will involve two actions: baptism and teaching. These are the ingredients of discipleship. In baptism we receive the great gift of eternal life in God and become members of the Church as the Body of Christ and the family of God. What a great gift! Yet like so many gifts, we need to know how to use it in order for it to really be beneficial in our lives. If we don't know how to live our Baptism, we will miss out on tremendous opportunities to let that grace become effective within us. Sometimes we can actually stifle the grace of baptism by our ignorance of Christ and the Christian way of life. To receive baptism without receiving teaching is like accepting a Christmas gift that we never open—it might be ours, but we can't really do much with it. That is why Jesus stresses the need for both of these ingredients of discipleship. Think of how many people are baptized but never taught either by formal instruction or by the lived example of others. Think of how many people misunderstand baptism more as a religious ritual, a social event, or a family tradition rather than as their sacramental initiation into the life of God. Baptism is the first step on a life-long Christian journey that will, hopefully, one day bring us into the very presence of the Lord. For a person's formation in faith to be relevant, they must see the connection between what they are learning and how they live. It is very significant that our Lord told the disciples that they should teach others to observe His commandments rather than teaching them to memorize what He said. There's a difference between memorizing what someone said and observing what someone commanded. To observe (or "carry out" as some translations say) what our Lord commanded means to live a life conformed to the Gospel and not merely acquire religious trivia. The teaching that Jesus commanded, then, implies communicating a lived witness of faith that manifests in daily action the life in Christ we receive in baptism.

> *What experiences of faith enrichment have most helped you to see the connection between belief and practice (discipleship) in your life?*
>
> *How can a faith community help people to better understand the gift of their baptism?*
>
> *How can a faith community help people to better understand the importance of their formation in faith so as to be disciples who are conformed to the Gospel?*
>
> *What is the difference between faith education, faith formation, and faith enrichment and why are all three important for a disciple?*
>
> *What are some of the various ways in which teaching occurs through word and example within your home, marriage, and office setting?*
>
> *What are some of the erroneous teachings that are carried out through word and deed that can actually deter people from living the commitments of their baptism?*

Lastly, the final words of Jesus in the Gospel of Matthew are a promise of His lasting presence with the Church when He says: "I am with you always, until the end of the age." At the very beginning of Matthew's Gospel, we were told that Jesus would be "Emmanuel". a name that means "God with us" (Mt 1:22–23). Now, Jesus promises to be "God with us" and thus reveals Himself as Emmanuel in this final verse. We are never alone when we carry out the mission that Jesus entrusted to us. The Lord always accompanies disciples who are living out this great commission. However, when we wander from the mission that Jesus has given us, we risk a certain spiritual distancing from the Lord. Instead of praying, "Lord, why aren't you with me?" maybe we should be praying, "Lord, how can I be with you in this moment?" The Lord promised us His presence earlier in Matthew's Gospel when He said, "Where two or three are gathered in my name, there am I in the midst of them" (Mt 18:20) and that we would serve Him in the hungry, the thirsty, the imprisoned, the homeless, and so forth (Mt 25:35–45). Indeed, the Lord is with us always in many and varied ways. As mature disciples, we must become self-leaders who know how to seek and find the Lord so as to do His will and faithfully carry out His mission.

> *What do you need to do in order to become a mature disciple who is a "self-leader" in your own discipleship?*
> *How have you experienced the presence of Jesus with you while carrying out His great commission?*
> *When do people tend to doubt the presence of Jesus with them, and how does this understanding of Jesus' promise shed light on those situations of doubt?*
> *How have you experienced Jesus with you in the Sacraments?*
> *How have you experienced the presence of Jesus in the work of ministry?*

Solemnity of Pentecost

Our Scripture passage for this Sunday comes from the Gospel of John 20:19–23. It is the scene of the Risen Christ sending the Apostles, breathing on them the gift of the Holy Spirit. It is an appropriate passage for this Sunday because in Pentecost we celebrate the moment when the first disciples were enlivened by the Holy Spirit and filled with enthusiasm to continue the mission of Jesus.

The word "Enthusiasm" comes from the two Greek words meaning "God within" (*en theos*). It refers to the experience a person has when they are "filled" with the Spirit of God. In the Greek world, it was originally perceived as an arbitrary invasion of God into the psyche that filled the individual with an indomitable energy.[24] This was the way the Greeks explained divine inspiration. In the Christian faith, however, to be enthusiastic is not only to be energetic; it is to be courageous, motivated, and committed. The disciples had that experience and thus began to carry on the mission of Jesus fearlessly as His witnesses even unto death. Because of their enthusiasm, they were able to do the things that Jesus did. The gift of the Spirit transformed their fear into faith, it motivated them from being self-preserving to become other-serving, and it changed the mission of the church from just a human organization into a holy endeavor. The Spirit can transform lives and communities!

When in your life do you experience "enthusiasm" in the religious sense of being "filled with God"?
What works of faith, that is Mission of Jesus, have you been led to do as a result of your enthusiasm?
What fears can cause people today to be "paralyzed" in their witness of faith and dampen their enthusiasm?

---

24. Plato, "Phedrus" in *Dialogues* [244] (Chicago: Encyclopaedia Britannica, Inc., 1952), p. 118.

*How can people fulfill their religious observances with a
"self-preserving" attitude rather than an "other-serving"
attitude?*

In John 19:22 we are told that Jesus "breathed on them". That is an
important statement for several reasons. First, it is a direct allusion
to the action of God in Genesis 2:7 when the Lord first created
humanity with an infusion of divine life. This connection to the
first creation is reconfirmed in Ezekiel 37:9–10 and Wisdom 15:11
and speaks to the power of the Holy Spirit in the transformation of
individual Christians. Jesus' action of breathing on the disciples is a
statement that a new creation is taking place in the life and mission
of the Church and that humanity is regenerated by the life-giving
action of the Holy Spirit. This life-giving spiritual regeneration
occurs in the Sacraments through Baptism (cf. Jn 3:5), through
the gift of the Holy Spirit in Confirmation, and in the Eucharistic
banquet where Tradition tells us that if we eat the Body of Christ
with faith, we eat "Fire and Spirit" because it is the Holy Spirit we
invoke over the gifts during the consecration.[25] Second, the gift of
the Spirit makes the community of believers, the Church, a fundamentally spiritual reality that carries out the works of God and
not just human efforts. When our Lord breathed on the disciples,
He gave them the Spirit so that they could continue to mediate His
divine presence even in His physical absence. The Church, then,
is the Mystical Body of Christ in the world through which Jesus
continues His ministry (cf. 1 Pt 2:5 for a similar understanding of
the Church as a "spiritual edifice"). Third, the gift of the Holy Spirit
draws the disciples into the communion of life and love, which
is the Holy Trinity. This incorporation into the divine mystery is
manifested by the ability to know the mind of Christ and speak with
a prophetic voice in our time (cf. Joel 3:1 [alt. 2:28], 1 Cor 2:6–16,
Jn 15:26–27 and 16:12–15).

*How is the prophetic ministry of the Church (that is, speak-
ing on God's behalf so as to interpret events from God's*

---

25. St Ephrem the Syrian, *Sermo IV in Hebdomadam Sanctam*: CSCO
413/Syr. 182, 55, quoted by John Paul II, *Ecclesia de Eucharistia*, (17
April, 2003), 17: *AAS* 95 (2003), pp. 449–450.

perspective) carried out today both in the lives of individual
disciples and through the institutional body of the Church?
What ministries in your faith community most clearly carry
out the work of Christ today?
What is a new work Christ wants to accomplish through
your faith community?
What prevents people from being able to fully receive and
live the spiritual regeneration of Baptism, Confirmation,
and the Eucharist?

The Holy Spirit's presence in Acts 2:1–11 was manifested by the
ability of people to hear the message of the Gospel despite "for-
eign tongues" (different languages). That means the Holy Spirit is
able to bring about a deep communion of faith that crosses the
divisions of language and culture. As Saint Paul teaches us, when
one member of the body suffers, the other members suffer with it;
when one member rejoices, all the members rejoice (cf. 1 Cor 12:26).
That is a statement of deep communion of life lived on a global
scale. Sometimes, however, we can have narrow vision and become
shortsighted when it comes to understanding and embracing the
universal communion of the Church. When we give in to a narrow
vision, we become selective and limited in our charity and concern.

When have you experienced your faith as something that
unites you deeply with those whom you have never met?
When do you most tangibly experience the "universal com-
munion" of the Church?
What are some of the attitudes or actions that can cause us
to lose sight of the universal nature of the Church?
How do you express your universal communion with those
whom you have never met?
Jesus sent His disciples to be witnesses to the world, and
that means they were to go beyond the safe confines of their
own community so that others could experience the joy and
peace they themselves had received from the Lord. What
parts of our world most need Christian witnesses today?

In Assisi, every year on the Feast of Pentecost, Saint Francis of
Assisi used to gather with his followers to pray for the Holy Spirit
to be with them and guide them. Francis believed that the power

of the Holy Spirit could change the world. Through Francis, the Holy Spirit indeed did change the world. The Holy Spirit is able to transform fear into courageous faith, anxious concern into peace, alienation into reconciliation, and disciples into missionaries! That's quite a powerful work!

> *When do you pray to the Holy Spirit?*
> *Through whom is the Holy Spirit working in a particularly powerful way to transform the Church and the world today?*
> *What do you feel prompted to do by the Holy Spirit in your own life of faith?*

In Paul's letter to the Corinthians (1 Cor 12:3b–7, 12–13), he specifies that there are many gifts given by the Holy Spirit to individuals, but that those gifts are for the benefit of everyone and not just the personal benefit of the one who receives the gift. Thus, God equips us and asks us to work together as one body (the Body of Christ) so that the ministry of the Gospel can be accomplished through the Church. Each of us is given some gift that we can use to help carry out that mission. Remember, there are no spare parts on the Body of Christ! If we are not actively engaged in the work of ministry, it is because we haven't found our place and not because there is no place for us.

> *What are some of the gifts or talents or skills with which you have been entrusted, and how can these be used for the common good and the mission of the Church?*
> *What gifts do we most need in the Church today to better carry out our mission?*
> *What gifts, talents, or skills would you like to use in the service of the Gospel?*

Jesus says to the disciples, "As the Father has sent me, so I send you ... Receive the Holy Spirit." The Spirit is given so that we can continue the mission of Jesus in the world. Jesus was sent to make God known, and in order to do that, He had to make love known (because God is love). To make love known, He died on the cross for us in an ultimate witness of self-giving and sacrificial love for others even in the face of hatred, rejection, and persecution. The Holy Spirit empowers us to carry on the mission of making God known in our world through the same demonstration of love. Others come to know God (who is love) through us. That is why Jesus was sent ... and that is the purpose for which He sends us.

> *Who in our time most needs to know the love of God?*
> *How have you come to know about the love of God through the witness of someone else?*
> *If Jesus appeared to your faith community this Sunday and said, "Receive the Holy Spirit ... as the Father has sent me so I send you," how do you think that personal challenge of Jesus would practically affect your community and its ministries?*

Take time this Sunday to pray for the gift of the Holy Spirit and to be accepting and responsive to that gift when it is given.

> Breathe into me, Holy Spirit, that my thoughts may all be holy.
> Move in me, Holy Spirit, that my work, too, may be holy.
> Attract my heart, Holy Spirit, that I may love only what is holy.
> Strengthen me, Holy Spirit, that I may defend all that is holy.
> Protect me, Holy Spirit, that I may always be holy.
>
> Saint Augustine

Solemnity of the Most Holy Trinity

Our Scripture passage for this Sunday comes from the Gospel of John 3:16–18. The Trinity is the revelation of God's identity as three persons in one God: Father, Son, and Holy Spirit. This teaching is relevant for us because we believe that we are made in the image and likeness of God. Thus, in learning about God, we also learn about who we are when we are true to our deepest identity. Our study of this passage will offer important insights for discovering that identity and understanding the challenges in living it.

The first thing Jesus reveals to us about the nature of God is that God is a communion (community) of persons in relationship. The very terms "Father" and "Son" are statements of relationship and they share a life of loving communion. That is the deepest nature of who God is. This relationship means, in a real sense, that we as a human community will express our deepest nature and identity when we mirror God's relational life of loving communion. It means that we can only become our truest selves when we give of ourselves to another in an act of complete selfless love. It means that we cannot be our truest self as long as we live lives of individuality, isolation, or self-interest. It means that humanity cannot realize its deepest nature until we love all people with equality and justice. It means that divisions of every kind are a fundamental sin against the unity of God. In short, the life of the Trinity is the model for our human lives and relationships.

What does that have to say about you, your family and your professional life?
When do you feel most connected to humanity on a profound level?
In what experiences do you feel that you are living your truest identity by your self-gift to another person?

*What are the primary sources of division that erode the
communion God desires in our families, communities, and
friendships?*

This passage tells us that the Father so loved the world that He
"sent" His only Son. Later, we are told that the Father "gave" the
Son to the world. Thus, God is known through His loving actions of
giving and sending. These are statements of God's great generosity.
The Father sends the Son; the Son later sends the Spirit when He
sends the disciples to continue His mission. The Father also gives
the Son to the world when Jesus, the eternal Word of God, takes
flesh and is born in time. Then Jesus gives His life on the cross and
continues to give His life for us in the Eucharist. John's Gospel is full
of statements that tell us how God "sends" and "gives". We believe
that we are made in God's image and likeness; therefore, in order
for us to truly be ourselves, we have to become active agents in
God's great cascade of love by not only receiving God's generosity
but by allowing God's generosity to flow through us to others.
When we become a conduit rather than just a container of God's
generous life and love, then we become active participants in the
divine life of the Father and the Son. The Father loves the Son; the
Son loves the Father and us; the Son sends the Holy Spirit to allow
us to receive that love and to return that love so that we can enter
into that life-giving relationship (Rom 5:5).

> *What is the difference between a disciple who is a "conduit"
> of God's life and a disciple who is only a "container" of God's
> life? For example, someone who receives but does not give?
> Who is an example of God's generous love for you?
> When have you received something freely as a gift of God
> and then passed that gift on to others?
> God is known through His actions. What have you come
> to know about God through His action in your life or the
> lives of others?*

This passage contains one of the most quoted statements of Jesus
in the entire New Testament. We see the verse of John 3:16 everywhere. "For God so loved the world that He gave His only Son, so
that everyone who believes in Him might not perish but might have
eternal life." However, when we take this text out of its context then

we risk misunderstanding its intended meaning. It is important to remember that in verse 14 Jesus was speaking with Nicodemus specifically about how Moses lifted up the serpent in the desert and of how the Son of Man will be "lifted up" so that whoever believes in Him will have eternal life. Thus, it is very clear that to "believe" in the Son means to believe in God present in Jesus crucified, that is "lifted up". To be "lifted up" in John's Gospel is always a reference to Calvary. The Father sent the Son with the specific mission of making God known in the world. In order to make God known, Jesus had to make love known because God is love. Thus, Calvary is Jesus' ultimate revelation of who God is. When we "believe" in the Son of Man, Jesus, "lifted up", then we believe in the love of God present and poured out for us on the cross of Calvary. When we say "yes" to that love, we are also saying "yes" to manifesting that love in our lives so others can believe in God through us—we are saying "yes" to living the cross every day. We can't accomplish that mission on our own; that is why at Pentecost we read that Jesus sent the Holy Spirit so we, as His disciples, could be "sent" just as Jesus was "sent" and so continue His mission of making God known in the world (Jn 20:19–23). Thus, the action of God's self-revelation involves the Father who sends, the Son who makes known, and Spirit who empowers us to continue that great work of divine self-communication.

> *What is the cross in your life that God wants to use so as to reveal His love to someone else through you (that is, in what way do you reveal God's selfless, sacrificial, self-giving love for others)?*
> *What other moments in Jesus' life and ministry can people focus on as the foundation of their belief of God in Jesus? What is the danger of founding our faith on a moment in Jesus' life other than Calvary?*
> *The Father sent the Son so that we might have life through Him, yet there are many temptations to find our "life" in something other than Jesus. What are the false ways in which people try to find life today?*

As we celebrate the Feast of the Most Holy Trinity, we remember that God is beyond our comprehension and that no matter what

God reveals to us, the Lord always remains a mystery. Thus, in faith we accept what God has revealed without needing to fully understand it and so reduce it to the level of human reason. St Bernard said that when we seek God, He provides the occasion, He creates the affection, and He consummates the desire.[26] Remember, God is not a problem to be solved but a mystery to be lived.

---

26. St Bernard of Clairvaux, *De Diligendo Deo*, 7.22, (3:137.18-138.2), quoted by B. McGinn, *The Growth of Mysticism*, vol. II (New York: Crossroad, 1994), p. 195.

Solemnity of the Most Holy Body and Blood of Christ (Corpus Christi)

Our Scripture passage for this Sunday comes from the Gospel of John 6:51–58. This is one of the most important Eucharistic passages in the New Testament. There are several important points to reflect on as we celebrate this great Feast with the Church throughout the world.

The first thing to notice is how strongly this passage stresses the realism of Jesus' presence in the Eucharist. In other passages of the New Testament (cf. Lk 22:19, Mt 26:26, Mk 14:22, or 1 Cor 11:23–26) the term *soma* is used to refer to the Eucharist which is best translated as "body". However, in this passage from John's Gospel, Jesus uses the word *sarx*, which means "flesh". Terms like "body" could have symbolic meanings, but the term "flesh" had no other meaning than the corporeal reality of one's very physical being. Jesus wants us to make no mistake about it—He Himself is really and truly present (flesh and blood) in the food and drink He gives us in the Eucharist. The second term emphasizing realism occurs when Jesus speaks of our need to "eat" His flesh and "drink" His blood. There were different words in Greek to describe the action of eating. The term Jesus uses in this passage is that of *trogein,* and He uses it four times (vv. 54, 56, 57, and 58), rather than the more respectable verb *phragein*. *Trogein* is important because it has no other meaning than the physical experience of "munching" on a piece of food whereas *phragein* could have a more figurative meaning of digesting something intellectually or assimilating something culturally. Thus, in this passage, Jesus is going out of His way to make His point very clear: He is giving us a real gift of His physical body and blood, and to receive that gift we must actually eat it. With the use of *sarx* and *phragein*, there can be no other interpretation. You see, in the prologue of John's Gospel, we were told that in the beginning was the Word and the

135

Word was with God and the Word was God. We were also told that
the Word became flesh (*sarx*) and was given to us for the life of the
world. Now in this passage we are told that the "Word made Flesh"
gives His flesh as food to us. Thus, when we receive the Eucharist,
we are receiving the very presence of the eternal Son of God. This
teaching in John's Gospel was probably meant to correct misunderstandings and doubts that were already developing in the first
century regarding the physical Incarnation of the Eternal Word
and true presence (reality) of Jesus in the Eucharist.

> *What is your understanding and belief in the reality of the*
> *Eucharist as the flesh and blood of Jesus?*
> *How does this teaching from John 6 challenge you in your*
> *faith?*
> *What can a faith community do to help people deepen their*
> *belief in the Eucharist?*

The next point for our reflection concerns why Jesus would give
such a tremendous gift of Himself. Throughout the chapter of John
6, Jesus has been drawing a parallel between the people of Israel
receiving manna in the desert and His gift of the bread of life. Just
as manna gave the people nourishment to continue their journey
on the way to the promised land, so, too, the gift of the Eucharist is
meant to nourish us in our Christian life. The journey of the people in the desert was a journey from sin to salvation, from slavery
to freedom, and from death to life. They had to be sustained and
encouraged in that process. The Hebrew people were guided by
the gift of the Law on Mount Sinai; so, too, the Christian people
are taught in John 6 that we are guided by the revelation of God in
the Word of Jesus and sustained by His Body and Blood. We are all
on that journey of moving towards God and away from sin, slavery
to self, and other false values. It is oftentimes difficult to break the
destructive patterns of sin in our lives, and so we need regular
encouragement to persevere in discipleship and conversion. That
process of growth is often our own experience of the "desert." It
can be tempting to stop on that journey of conversion and transformation so as to settle in a place of complacency with sin and
mediocrity of discipleship. In those moments, we have to turn to
the Lord and ask for His guidance and leadership. We can't do it

on our own; we have to rely on help from on high. Thus, Jesus says, "...whoever eats my flesh and drinks my blood abides in me and I in him" (Jn 6:56) and also, "...the bread that I will give is my flesh for the life of the world" (Jn 6:51). Our Lord is telling us that He alone can give us the necessary nourishment to get us through the desert. The Eucharist is manna in the desert, it is food for eternal life, and it is a sharing in the very body, blood, soul and divinity of Jesus. A disciple is not only someone who follows Jesus and obeys His teaching, but a disciple is someone who is actually transformed by the very presence of Jesus they receive and who grows into the likeness of God in whose image they are created. The Eucharist is our food for that journey of transformation and conversion.

> *What are the reasons we can come up with to justify our complacency so as to stop short on our journey of faith?*
> *How does the Eucharist challenge you to continue your Christian journey of discipleship each week?*
> *What transformation has taken place in your life as a result of your participation in the Eucharist?*

Over the past 2,000 years, our appreciation of, and devotion to, the Body and Blood of the Lord have expressed themselves in various ways. Mother Teresa, for example, began her day with one hour of prayer before the Blessed Sacrament, and it was that daily devotion that motivated her to carry out her great works of charity and mercy. Other great people of faith have similarly expressed how important the Eucharist is for them as the place of encounter with the revelation of God in the flesh and blood of the Son of Man (Jesus). There is a distinctive and real presence of Jesus in the Eucharist that is not available anywhere else. To help foster this awareness of the encounter with Jesus in the Eucharist, the Church encourages certain devotional practices such as genuflecting when approaching the Tabernacle, maintaining a prayerful silence in the sacred space of the church, and making the sign of the cross when passing by a church. Chapels of reservation are often made available so that people can stop by and pray throughout the day. Those parishioners who are homebound are brought the Eucharist when they can no longer physically come to Mass. All these expressions of devotion and piety are meant to remind us of the sacred encounter with God that awaits us in the Eucharist. Yet, like so many great opportunities, it can oftentimes be easy to let those opportunities pass without taking advantage of them.

> *How have you experienced the Eucharist as a privileged*
> *place of encounter with the Lord?*
> *What expressions of piety or religious devotion mean most*
> *to you in your encounter with the Eucharist?*
> *How can a faith community foster greater respect and devo-*
> *tion to the Eucharist?*

Finally, this passage of Scripture invites us to consider not only what Jesus is offering us in the gift of the Eucharist but to also consider our response to that gift. The text of John 6 tells us that the Jews "grumbled" at His teaching (6:52)—the same word used to describe the Hebrews and their response to Moses' leadership in the desert. Even many of Jesus' own disciples found this to be a hard teaching and left Him because of it (6:60–66). In response to this rejection and refusal to believe, Jesus does not alter His teaching in any way; instead, He challenges those who hear Him to believe and accept what God reveals rather than requiring that God's gift fit their desires and abilities to understand. Some disciples do accept Jesus' teaching, and their faith is voiced by Peter, who says, "Master... you have the words of eternal life" (6:68). Since the first years of Christianity, the Church has taken seriously the gift of Jesus in the Eucharist and of our need to respond with faith and readiness to be transformed by the gift we receive. By receiving the Body and Blood of the Lord, we are to become His living presence in the world. The gift of God, Jesus, is now given to us in the Eucharist, so that God can give the gift of His Son to others through us. When we receive Communion and say "Amen" to the Body of Christ, we are not only professing our belief in the reality of the Eucharist but are also stating our commitment to live that reality in what we say and do—to be the Body of Christ. Our response to the Eucharist, then, is not just in our prayer, beliefs, or statements but most of all in our willingness to "become that which we receive".[27] Our mission is to become a living tabernacle of God's presence every time we receive Communion.

---

27. St Leo the Great, *Sermo 12, De Passione*, 2, 7, PL54.

How do you experience the various responses to the Eucharist found in John 6?

How can we be tempted to accept only what we can understand, and why is that tendency destructive to faith?

What helps us to accept beyond what we can understand?

What are other teachings of Jesus that can be difficult to understand and accept?

Second Sunday in Ordinary Time

Our Scripture passage for this Sunday comes from the Gospel of John 1:29–34. In this passage we receive the testimony of John the Baptist concerning Jesus. It is an edifying profession of faith that provides the essential message of John's Gospel concerning the life and ministry of our Lord. There are several points worthy of our reflection.

With this Sunday we begin the liturgical season known as Ordinary Time. The designation of Ordinary Time refers to the majority of time each year that is not committed either for times of preparation (Advent and Lent) or special celebration (Christmas and Easter). The reality is that most growth in our lives takes place in ordinary ways every day. Certainly there can be exceptional moments of spiritual awaking when the "Heavens open" (as in last week's reading), but such situations do not represent the majority of our experiences. Many of the saints referred to the daily grind as the place where holiness and love are most commonly witnessed rather than in heroic or exceptional moments. It is important for disciples to know that God is working with them in the most mundane moments of each day as well as the grand moments of life. Sometimes we only recognize gradual growth when we compare ourselves with where we were one, five, ten, or twenty years ago.

What would you say is the most significant spiritual, professional, or personal growth that has taken place in your life in the past year?

What is the most significant growth during the past five, ten, or twenty years, and how has God motivated that growth?

What is the growth you want to take place in your personal, family, professional, and spiritual life this year?

What can you do on a daily basis to help foster that growth?

What can you do to become more aware of God's presence with you in the daily grind of ordinary time?

In the Gospel of John, the ministry of John the Baptist is primarily that of offering witness and testimony to Jesus. In fact, he is never referred to with the title "the Baptist" in John's Gospel. Bearing witness or giving testimony means that someone is verbally attesting to what is true based on their personal experiences. John was able to give his testimony about Jesus because of his knowledge and observation of the Lord. So, too, we are called to be witnesses in the same way—to be people who have come to know and recognize the movement of God in our lives and announce it to others so they can know and recognize God's movement in their lives as well. In fact, at the end of Luke's Gospel Jesus explicitly commissions His disciples to bear such testimony when He says, "You are witnesses" (Lk 24:48). This commission is repeated in the opening verses of the Acts of the Apostles (Acts 1:8). The ministry of bearing witness is an essential part of discipleship. Each disciple has a personal experience of Jesus, and thus, each disciple is called to offer a personal witness for others in his own unique way. We experience Jesus differently because of our own unique needs, expectations, and life situations. Perhaps we experience Jesus as our Savior in times of distress. Perhaps we experience Him as our Healer in times of illness. Perhaps we experience Him as our Peace when we need forgiveness. Perhaps He is our Brother when we need solidarity and companionship. Perhaps He is our Wisdom when we need understanding and guidance. Regardless of how we experience Jesus, every experience of the Lord can be an opportunity for us to bear witness so that others can be encouraged to seek the Lord's grace in their lives.

> *What is the testimony you would offer about who Jesus is in your life based on your experience?*
> *How have you heard other people express testimony about who Jesus is in their lives?*
> *How does the sharing of testimony and the act of witnessing help build up the Christian community?*
> *What can a faith community do to encourage its members to freely offer testimony and witness to Jesus?*

One of the very important titles John uses in his testimony about Jesus is that of "Lamb of God". This is a great title of faith and summarizes much of what Jesus will accomplish through His ministry of the cross. To be the "Lamb of God" means to be the lamb of sacrifice. Jesus will accomplish this sacrifice on the cross of Calvary. John points to Jesus as the Lamb of God on the cross by mentioning the hyssop branch and the phrase "break none of his bones", which are references to the Passover Lamb. The identity of Jesus as the true Lamb of God is also emphasized in John's Gospel by indicating that the crucifixion of Jesus took place on the Day of Preparation which means that our Lord was sacrificed on Calvary at the same time the Passover lambs were sacrificed in the Temple of Jerusalem (Jn 19:31).

Sacrifices in the Old Testament were a way in which people offered something of God's creation in return to the Lord as an expression of their desire to be in communion with God. There were different purposes for sacrifices. Some sacrifices were offered in thanksgiving. Some sacrifices were offered so as to establish communion with God and others through the sharing of a sacrificial meal. Still other sacrifices were for the forgiveness of sins in which the sacrificial victim paid the price for someone else's offenses. Finally, sacrifices were also offered to seal a covenant relationship between God and the people with mutual rights and expectations. Jesus fulfills all of these sacrificial meanings when He becomes the eternal and perfect Lamb of God. Jesus is our Thanksgiving to God (the word Eucharist means "Thanksgiving") for all the good God has given us in His Son. Jesus is the source of our Communion with God and others as we share in the Lord's Supper where Jesus offers His sacrificial presence in the form of Bread and Wine. Jesus takes our sinful condition on Himself and pays the price for our sins by dying on the cross in order to bring forgiveness and salvation to the world. Finally, Jesus offers us the eternal New Covenant in His blood at the Last Supper in which we enter into a new and enduring relationship of faith and love with Christ and others every time we share in the Lord's Supper. When the priest raises the Body and Blood of Jesus in the Eucharist at Mass and proclaims, "Behold the Lamb of God," he is proclaiming that Jesus is offering to us all these benefits of His sacrifice.

*Which aspect of Jesus' sacrifice means the most to you
(Thanksgiving, Communion, Expiation, Covenant)?*
*How does this understanding of Jesus as the "Lamb of God"
change your previous understanding of that term?*
*For which aspect of Jesus' sacrifice do you need to grow in
greater appreciation and understanding, and how can you
pursue this growth?*

John actually proclaims four titles of Jesus in this reading: Jesus as
the Lamb of God (previously explained), Jesus as the Pre-Existent
One (the Word of God who is eternally present), Jesus as the Vehicle
of the Holy Spirit (the Holy Spirit remains with Him and He freely
shares it with us both on the cross and after the resurrection), and
Jesus as the Son of God (the one who can show us the face of the
Father and lead us to Him). Each of these titles will be fulfilled in
Jesus' life and ministry. No one title can ever capture the full reality
of who Jesus is. As soon as someone thinks they have Jesus figured
out, they will see even greater things (Jn 1:50).[28] Titles of faith can
help us to describe God but can never fully define God. Throughout
the Gospel of John we will hear other titles attributed to Jesus as
well. These titles include the following: The Good Shepherd, the
Light of the World, The Living Water, The Resurrection and the
Life, and The Way, the Truth, and the Life. All of these titles help
us understand not only who Jesus is but also how we encounter
the Lord in practical ways through the events and circumstances
of our lives. Titles, then, serve to help us recognize and respond
to the presence of Jesus more readily and faithfully.

*Which of the four titles that John attributes to Jesus means
the most to you?*

---

28. To learn more about the contemplation of God's attributes, cf.
Pseudo Dionysius, "Divine Names" in *Complete Works* (New York:
Paulist Press, 1987), Chap. I, 1, p. 49. "When we say anything about
God, we should set down the truth not in the plausible words of
human wisdom but in the demonstration of the power granted by
the Spirit to the Scripture writers, a power by which, in a manner
surpassing speech and knowledge, we reach a union superior to
anything available to us by way of our own abilities or activities in
the realm of discourse or of intellect."

*What are other titles for God that have deep meaning for
you?*

*As we grow in faith, Jesus opens our eyes more and more
with each step of discipleship provided we are willing to take
the next step. When has the Lord shown you "greater things"
because you were willing to accept the risk of discipleship?*

*John risked disturbing the status quo of the religious, politi-
cal, and cultural world of his time in order to offer this testimony about Jesus. When are you called to risk disturbing
the status quo in order to offer testimony to the Lord as well?*

THIRD SUNDAY IN ORDINARY TIME

Our Scripture passage for this Sunday comes from the Gospel of Matthew 4:12–23. In this passage we read of how Jesus begins His public ministry and calls His first disciples. We also hear a summary of how our Lord carried out His ministry in Galilee. This reading offers several points for our reflection.

The Gospel indicates that the start of Jesus' ministry was prompted by the arrest of John the Baptist. In response to John's imprisonment, we are told that Jesus withdrew to Galilee, and in doing so He went to the very area where Herod Antipas reigned (Herod Antipas is the one who had imprisoned John). It seems odd that Jesus would go to the very place where Herod wielded power, yet that is part of the Gospel message. Jesus does not flee from evil; rather, He confronts it in a non-violent and non-retaliatory way. When evil and unjust acts were occurring, Jesus responded by manifesting the Kingdom of God as demonstrated in His healing ministry at the end of this passage. Our Lord also invites others to assist Him in carrying out that ministry. The wrongful imprisonment of John the Baptist triggered the rightful ministry of Jesus. This is an important message for us as disciples because we live in the midst of a complex and sometimes dangerous world. Sometimes we can think that the challenge of the Gospel is intended for those who don't face such daily threatening confrontations with evil. This passage causes us to reconsider that presumption and to realize that Jesus faced a complex and threatening world at least as much as we do. Our Lord responded not by shying away from those situations but by responding directly, effectively, and nonviolently so that the message Gospel would never be silenced no matter how great the intimidation. This passage also reminds us that we should be encouraged in our faith and discipleship both by the good examples of holy people and by the antagonistic actions of ill-willed people.

When have you seen an act of injustice actually become a motivation for people to do good?

When has a wrongful action motivated you to stand up for what is right?

Herod's tools were fear and intimidation. How are these tools used today in personal relationships, families, or professional settings to silence or control people?

Jesus would be not intimidated by Herod to remain silent but rather He actively proclaimed the Kingdom of God. What would it look like for you to do the same when you face a difficult situation?

What can a faith community do to help people become more aware of situations of injustice so as to motivate a Gospel-based response?

The passage continues with the call of the first disciples. When Jesus sees Peter and his brother Andrew, He calls them to follow Him based on the promise that He will make them "Fishers of Men". This phrase is not merely a play on words in that they were "fishermen" who became "fishers of men". Rather, it can be an indication that Jesus wants to use their natural talents and professional skills to accomplish an important work for the Gospel. We all have professional skills and talents, and Jesus calls us to be disciples who place ourselves at the service of the Gospel as well. When Jesus called the first disciples with these words, He was giving an important instruction on the nature of discipleship for all who would follow Him. In particular, following Jesus doesn't just mean that we focus on ourselves and are concerned only about our own personal prayer and way of life. Rather, being a disciple also requires that we become missionaries who are always bringing others to Christ. That is why the disciples are told that they will need to use their natural talents and human connections to draw others to Christ (Fishers of Men). For many centuries in the Church some people have mistakenly believed that missionary efforts were only for those who were engaged in missionary apostolates. As a result of that false assumption many people did not understand their baptismal calling to share in the missionary work of Jesus. This passage is an important wake-up call reminding us that when we follow Christ we have an immediate and essential responsibility to bring others to the Lord as well.

> *When have you been called on to use your professional skills and talents to aid in the Church's mission?*
>
> *What was your reaction to that experience?*
>
> *What skills or talents do you possess that you have not yet been asked to place at the service of the Gospel?*
>
> *How might you find a use for those skills or talents?*
>
> *What can your faith community do to better provide opportunities for its members to offer their skills and talents for the good of others?*
>
> *What is the mission field that you work in each day where you can use your skills and human connections to bring others to Christ?*
>
> *How does it challenge you to know that an essential part of being a disciple is the responsibility to be a missionary?*

When we hear the story of how readily Peter, Andrew, James, and John follow Jesus, we sometimes are tempted to think that it was easy for them to walk away from their daily occupations. This thought is sometimes mistakenly used to alleviate our own consciences for the many times when we have not followed the Lord's call in our own lives. Sometimes we can think that is was easier for the first disciples because they did not have as much at stake as we do, but that is not correct. Peter was married and operated a significant fishing industry with his brother Andrew. They were independent businessmen with assets, clients, business partners, liabilities, and all the other complexities that are part of our lives as well. To have a business like this in the time of Jesus was to be relatively affluent. Certainly Peter and Andrew had numerous responsibilities. Their lives were not happy-go-lucky adventures from one day to the next. They were far more like us than we may want to acknowledge. The fact that they could leave all that behind and follow Jesus demonstrates both the power and appeal of our Lord's message as well as the readiness of their response. When we exempt ourselves from responding to the call of discipleship because we mistakenly believe that we are too busy, we dismiss a graced opportunity to be close to the Lord. It is always our loss.

Peter and Andrew are presented to us as examples of readiness and freedom who recognize the day of the Lord's visitation to their lives and respond to the opportunities presented to them.

> *What busyness of your life makes it difficult for you to follow the Lord with readiness and freedom?*
> *What are some of the false presumptions you use to exempt yourself from the personal call to follow the Lord?*
> *Whose good example of faith challenges you in such a way that you say, "If that person can do it, then so can I"?*

It is interesting that in the call of Peter and Andrew we are told that they left their nets to follow Jesus. In the subsequent call of James and John, we are told that they left their boat and their father to follow Jesus. Thus, we see the first disciples having to leave behind both the resources of their lives and their closest relationships for the sake of following Jesus. It takes a lot of faith and courage to do that! However, such faith and courage were necessary for many early Christians if they wanted to remain faithful during the times of persecution and Matthew's Gospel is written during such a time. To be a Christian in the Early Church sometimes meant that a person might have their possessions and property confiscated. It also sometimes meant that they might be rejected or ostracized by their families and close friends. When people came to such a moment of sacrifice, they had to decide what was most important to them—Jesus or their possessions and relationships. To remain faithful required that a disciple be prepared for sacrifice. Sometimes our faith today calls us to sacrifice as well for the sake of following Jesus.

> *When have you experienced tension in your closest relationships because of your discipleship?*
> *Do you know of anyone who has experienced loss of a relationship because of a decision to be Christian or be Catholic?*
> *How can your faith community provide support for people who experience such stress in their relationships?*
> *How have you been called to sacrifice your possessions for the sake of following Jesus, or to let go of your material attachments in order to be a better disciple?*

Do you know of anyone who exhibits, expresses, or reveals detachment so as to be free to follow Jesus?

What happens to a person's faith life when they value possessions or relationships more than their attachment to Jesus?

The first disciples demonstrated a readiness to respond to the Lord's invitation with faith and trust. They didn't know where Jesus would take them or how long they would be gone. They didn't know what Jesus would ask of them or what the Lord would expect of them. They simply accepted the invitation and followed Him. Most of us like to know details before we make a commitment. We even praise hesitance and caution before making a decision. While such thoroughness may serve us well in our professional lives, it can become a detriment to our spiritual lives. God doesn't answer our questions or agree to our terms. The Lord asks us to trust Him and to follow without limit or condition wherever He leads us.

If Jesus called you to follow Him as He called the first disciples, what would be some of the questions you would want answered before you said "yes"?

What is the most trusting thing you've ever done based purely on faith?

Who is someone who stands out in your mind as a person of heroic response to discipleship?

What might Jesus ask you to do today as an act of trust and confidence in Him?

How will you respond?

One final note concerns the summary of Jesus' Galilean ministry contained in Matthew 4:23–24. We are presented with a list of ailments that afflicted the people of His time. Many of these ailments we are familiar with; we see Jesus healing these in various scenes (demonic possession, illness, paralysis, and so forth). One of these ailments is a bit unusual and warrants some further reflection. It is the ailment commonly listed as "epilepsy". The actual word in Greek means "lunatic" and in Matthew 17:15 we see a man present his son to Jesus with these words, "Lord, have mercy on my son for he is a lunatic and suffers sorely, for he often falls into fire and water." On a surface level we may understand this as the outdated belief of ancient cultures that the moon actually caused a person to develop mental illness and to act in a self-destructive way. While it is true that gazing on the moon (Latin *Luna*) was believed to have detrimental effects to a person's mental health, we should not so easily dismiss the destructive connection between what a person focuses on and the damage caused in that person's life. How many people today have caused great damage in their marriages, professional, and personal lives because they have become fixated on the wrong things? Being a lunatic can be as much about wrong priorities and destructive obsessions as it is about mental illness. Today many people have allowed themselves to become obsessed with or addicted to gambling, alcohol, the Internet, pornography, extra-marital affairs, materialism, the pursuit of pleasure, and all sorts of things that end up damaging their lives. When someone does these things, we may wonder what went wrong. While we may not refer to persons as lunatics, we do realize how easy it is for a person to focus on destructive and damaging pursuits that first affect the mind and then bear the bad fruit of destructive actions. Part of the ministry of Jesus was to heal such ill-focused obsessions and to redirect people's focus onto the healthy concerns of love of God and neighbor.

> *What are some of the destructive things people can focus on that damage marriages and family life today?*
> *How does the Word of God become a healing remedy for the ill thoughts that fill people's hearts and minds?*
> *How does the ministry of Jesus challenge the Church today to become more proactive in helping people avoid the temptation of harmful gazing?*
> *It is important for every disciple to periodically question if there are any harmful gazes taking place in their life. What do you find helpful in determining what harmful preoccupations may exist in your life and in overcoming those preoccupations?*

Fixing our eyes on the right thing is both a blessing and a challenge in our spiritual growth. In the XIV century, Blessed Henry Suso wrote this prayer to Christ crucified:

> O you charming Mirror of all graces in which heavenly spirits refresh their eyes lovingly, if only I had your dear countenance here as it was when you were dying that I

might wash it with the tears of my heart and might contemplate your beautiful eyes [...]. O gentle Lord, since a loving imitation of your meek way of life and your suffering from love is so very pleasing to you, I shall spend all my efforts from now on to imitate you joyfully rather than to lament with weeping.[29]

---

29. H. Suso, "Little Book of Eternal Wisdom" in *The Exemplar* (New York: Paulist Press, 1989), Chap. 3, pp. 216–217.

Fourth Sunday in Ordinary Time

Our Scripture passage for this Sunday comes from the Gospel of Matthew 5:1–12. We know this passage well because it contains a set of teachings known as the Beatitudes. For Christians, the Beatitudes serve as the defining characteristics we are to embody in our communal life. Just as Moses went up the Mountain and God gave the Ten Commandments to him, so we now read that Jesus goes up the Mountain and gives the Beatitudes to His disciples. That parallel between the actions of Moses and Jesus means that the Beatitudes are worthy of careful study and reflection because of the importance they are intended to have in forming us as Christian disciples.

Blessed are the Poor in Spirit

To be poor in spirit means that we realize our utter dependence on God for everything. The word for "poor" is actually "beggar". There are times in our lives when we have no choice but to rely on God. These are the times when we cannot do for ourselves. It can be difficult to experience these moments, but it's also a wonderful grace and a life-changing insight of faith to realize that the Lord is with us and that God can sustain us through difficult moments. In many ways, our strength and sense of false self-sufficiency can prevent us from realizing God's presence in our lives. Poverty of Spirit opens our eyes to know that presence. Every breath, every success, every accomplishment we experience comes from the Lord. Only with the eyes of one who is poor in spirit can that humbling truth be known. Our culture promotes self-sufficiency and independence; the Gospel promotes poverty of spirit instead. A beautiful statement accredited to Mother Teresa says, "I can do things you cannot, you can do things I cannot; together we can do great things." Only someone who knows and accepts with humility the reality of their human limitation can experience the joy and freedom of being poor in spirit. Such an attitude does not cause one to have low self-esteem but rather to know that their true dignity and self-worth comes from God and is neither enhanced by strength nor diminished by weakness.

> *When have you had to be completely dependent on God? Who have you known that has had to let go of their robust ego or strong sense of self-worth and had to find their only identity and security in God?*

Blessed are those who mourn

There are lots of things that can make us sad. It is important for us to remember that Jesus is not promoting sadness for its own sake. People can be sad because of a movie they watch or because they do not get their own way. Not all sadness is of a holy nature. There is a distinctive kind of sadness, however, that the Scriptures do esteem, and it is the sadness of those who mourn the sinful condition of God's people and resistance to God's plan for the world. Saint Paul teaches us that this "holy sadness" can lead to repentance (2 Cor 7:9–10). Jesus experienced this holy sadness when He wept over Jerusalem hoping and praying that the people would receive Him and cooperate with God's plan (Lk 19:41–44). The Psalms also express this holy sadness as a response to those who reject God's Law (Ps 35:13; 119:27–29). When someone submits completely to God's reign in their lives through poverty of spirit, then that person becomes increasingly aware of the presence of sin both personally and in the lives of others. It should be pointed out that there can be lots of reactions to the presence of sin that are different from holy sadness. Sometimes people can gossip about another's failings or have an unhealthy preoccupation with the wrongdoings of others. Jesus didn't say "Blessed are the judgmental" or "Blessed are the back-biters!" Sometimes sadness becomes the way in which others know that their actions are hurting themselves and others. In that moment of awareness they can experience the grace and invitation of conversion. Our responsibility as disciples is to demonstrate a holy sadness that invites and welcomes repentance both in our personal lives and in the lives of others.

*What is our reaction when we see other people's sinful con-
dition or read about it in the newspaper?*
*What do we do when the values of the Gospel are ignored
in individual lives or the decisions of governments?*
*When has sadness been a motivation for conversion and
repentance in your life?*

Blessed are the gentle

Note that this translation does not use the term "meek". Jesus will
use the same word to refer to Himself in Matthew 11:29 when He
says, "I am gentle and humble of heart." Gentle is a more accurate
translation and better conveys the virtue proper for a disciple who
is striving to carry out the will of God and promote the values of
the Gospel. To be gentle is not to be a wimp. Rather, it is the ability to accomplish what is right without harming someone or their
human dignity in the process. Aristotle taught that gentleness was
the mid-point between the opposing vices of spineless indifference
and rash anger.[30] When someone is gentle, they are persistent and
unwavering while being respectful and helpful at the same time.
It should be pointed out that being respectful of others does not
mean we do what they want but that we do what God wants for
them. Gentleness always includes such faithful respect. People
like Martin Luther King, Mother Teresa, and Mahatma Gandhi
are all examples of this Gospel gentleness and demonstrate this
beatitude in action. These twentieth century leaders changed the
world through their perseverance and determination, but they
did so in a way that respected the dignity of each person whether
that person agreed with them or not. Jesus was gentle in how He
treated the sinner and the saint so as to lead both of them in the
same path of discipleship. Those who are gentle trust in the power
of truth rather than that of violence or force.

*Who exemplifies for you the truth that "Gentleness is the
greatest strength"?*

---

30. A. Comte-Sponville. *A Small Treatise on the Great Virtues: The
Uses of Philosophy in Everyday Life* (New York: Picador, 1995), p.
368.

For whom in your life do you need to practice the Gospel beatitude of gentleness?

Blessed are those who hunger and thirst for righteousness

To be righteous means to actively do the will of God even in the midst of a world that is acting contrary to that will. One of the dangers of discipleship is that of complacency, which is the attitude that leads us to say to ourselves that we are "good enough" or that we have "done enough" or that we are "holy enough". Sometimes such temptations can cause us to excuse ourselves from the challenge of the Gospel and ever-deeper discipleship. When we give in to that temptation, we have stopped "hungering and thirsting" for greater righteousness. We are made in the image and likeness of God and only when we live out that identity perfectly and completely can we claim to be righteous. The problem is that we are often tempted to compare ourselves to others rather than to the example of Jesus. When we do so then we easily settle for just being "better than" someone else rather than being "better for" God. When we keep our crucified and risen Lord as the only standard for comparison in our discipleship, then we realize how far we have yet to go before we can reach the righteousness to which God calls us. While the lived example of our Lord may be a high ideal to live by, it is the daily striving (hungering and thirsting) for it that God desires.

> *How do you think complacency affects people's faith lives today?*
> *What are the excuses that you use to exempt yourself from the challenge of the Gospel?*
> *What can a faith community do to help people hunger and thirst for greater righteousness?*

Blessed are the merciful

Matthew's Gospel puts a lot of emphasis on the importance of mercy. Mercy is not just an inner emotional feeling; instead, it is expressed in concrete acts to alleviate the suffering of others. Our contemporary culture tends to reduce mercy to an interior sentiment, but the Gospel teaches us that mercy is to be a motivation for action. When Jesus had mercy on someone, He didn't just feel sorry for them or offer to pray for them, He actually did something to help them. As Christians, we are expected to be people who show the mercy of God to others through our actions. In a prayer accredited to Saint Teresa of Avila we say, "Christ has no hands or feet on earth but ours." Thus, Jesus now shows His mercy for the world through the works of His disciples. Our love of God is necessarily expressed in our love of neighbor whether they be next door or on the other side of the world. Mercy has no limits.

When are you most moved to respond to another person's suffering?
What is the most merciful thing you have done for someone else?
Who has shown you great mercy? Who needs your mercy today?

Blessed are the pure of heart

To be pure of heart really means to be focused on God with all our heart, mind, soul, and strength. Sometimes it is easy to have divided allegiances whereby we experience conflicting loyalties and mixed motives. In the ancient pagan world that divided allegiance was expressed by the multiple gods they worshiped. Today, many people compartmentalize their behavior believing that their faith has nothing to do with their professional life, their family, their politics, or their finances. When we separate our life like this, then we create a divided heart and make idols of our various endeavors. If we are pure of heart (that is, possessing singleness of heart), Jesus is the Lord of every part of our lives at all times. Being pure of heart means that in every situation and circumstance, we allow our decisions and actions to be guided by the Lord. It also means that while we may have mixed motives for our various actions we always allow our desire to do God's will to be the determining motive.

What are some of the conflicting loyalties that get in the way of being pure of heart today?
Who for you is an example of someone who is pure of heart?
What helps you grow in your purity of heart?

Blessed are the peacemakers

The Jewish understanding of *shalom* (Peace) referred to a person who experienced the fullness of God's gifts. Peace was the result of right relationship with God, others, the world, and ourselves. To be at peace was to be reconciled of all division and enmity. Thus, peace is not so much the absence of violence as it is the presence of justice. This connection between peace and justice was expressed by Pope Paul VI when he said, "If you want peace, work for justice." To be a person of peace is one thing, but to be a "peace-maker" is something else. That means we are people who not only experience reconciliation and right relationship in our own lives but that we become people who help others experience it in their lives as well.

> *When have you been an agent of reconciliation for others?*
> *When do you experience a deep faith-filled sense of peace?*
> *Who in your life needs the peace that is the fruit of right relationship?*
> *What can you do to be a peace-maker for them?*

Blessed are those who are persecuted for righteousness' sake

Jesus is not rejoicing in oppression. Rather, our Lord is encouraging us to be joyful when we are put down because of being a Christian disciple. When a person really lives the Beatitudes, they will act according to the values of the Gospel, which are often contrary to the values of the world. A person who lives the Beatitudes will be radically committed to following Jesus with all their heart, soul, mind, and strength. There will always be those who resist such a witness. A person will never experience rejection or ridicule so long as their faith remains a matter of mere attitude or interior beliefs. It is only when they attempt to live their faith in a visible and public way and to make a difference in the world that others will notice them and react to them with either acceptance or rejection. Persecution, then, is a confirmation that our faith is being lived in a visible way. Jesus blesses this lived expression of faith. One last thing should be noted about the beatitudes and that concerns the explicit qualification that such persecution must be for Christ's sake and must be false. This qualification exists to prevent disciples from mistakenly thinking they are blessed just because they are rejected. The reality is that there can be lots of reasons that can cause disharmony with others. Sometimes it's our personality, annoying habits, or poor people skills that cause difficulty in relationships. Jesus wanted us to distinguish between that rejection which is a part of the human condition and that rejection which is specifically caused by a witness of faith.

> *When has a visible witness of faith in your life brought about a negative reaction from others?*
> *Who do you know of today that is being persecuted for righteousness' sake?*

FIFTH SUNDAY IN ORDINARY TIME

Our Scripture passage for this Sunday comes from the Gospel of Matthew 5:13–16. In this reading, Jesus describes our identity and purpose as disciples. We are to be "Salt of the Earth" and "Light of the World". In giving us this identity and mission, Jesus is telling us that we are now to carry out the God-given role originally entrusted to the people of Israel through the Prophet Isaiah (Is 2:2–5, 42:6, 49:6). Let's look at each of these images for further insight to guide us we follow the Lord.

Salt had a variety of uses in the Old Testament and in the ancient world. Because of the many possible uses of salt, it is not clear if Jesus intended one particular meaning for disciples or if our Lord wanted to offer a variety of possible meanings depending upon the unique challenges each of us faces. We are probably most familiar with salt because of its use in cooking where it gives flavor to food. Today we refer to salted greens as a "salad", which comes from the Latin word for salt, *sale*. Salt was also used to preserve food from corruption. Once preserved, meats and other products could then be traded and exchanged for other goods. Such ability to preserve agricultural produce was essential in the creation of economies for those societies. Salt was a rare resource in the ancient world and was so valuable that it was considered as important as a person's daily wage. For this reason the English word "salary" is derived from the Latin word for salt as well. Roads were named after salt (Via Salaria), as were cities (Salzburg). Salt was also used to purify and for the offering of sacrifices in the Temple of Jerusalem. In the late first century, salt was even used in various parts of the world to build fires in earthen ovens (cf. Letter of Ignatius to the Magnesians).[31] In these ovens, chunks of salt were mixed with dung, which allowed the fire to start more quickly, burn more intensely, and last longer. Basically, salt served as a catalyst, which enhanced the fire but was not changed by the fire. With each application for the image of salt, there is a corresponding application for the identity and mission of disciples:

---

31. Ignatius of Antioch, *Epistle to the Magnesians*, p. 5:661.

- We are to be people who flavor all aspects of our world, relationships and situations we face with the values of the Gospel.
- We are to be people who pray and actively work to guard against temptation so as to preserve ourselves and others from the corruption of sin and human vices.
- We are to be people who constantly purify our world by removing what is contrary to the Gospel or distorted in our priorities.
- We are to be people who unite our difficulties and persecutions of faith with the sacrifice of Jesus so as to be offered with Him to the Father.
- Lastly, we are to be people who become catalysts of conversion in the world so as to allow the fire of faith to catch more quickly in people's lives, to burn more intensely in our hearts and theirs, and to endure. Sometimes this means that we are willing to put ourselves in the very messy situations of other people's lives (dung) so as to accompany them with compassion and love while facilitating their faith experience.

Which of these images of "salt" has special meaning for you and why?
Which image do you find to be the most challenging?
Salt does not lose its taste, but it can become adulterated with impurities, which weaken its effectiveness. What are the "impurities" that cause Christians to become weak in their mission to be "salt"?
While it is easy to apply the images of salt to our own personal lives of faith and spirituality, Jesus tells us that we are salt not for ourselves, or just for those around us, but for the earth, which means everyone around the world. Who needs you to be salt for them?

The image of light is also richly established in the Scriptures. Israel was called to be a "Light to the Nations" by the Prophet Isaiah. Paul spoke of his ministry as being a "light for those in darkness" (Rom 2:19). Luke's Gospel tells us that Simeon prophesied that Jesus would be a "light for revelation to the Gentiles" (Lk 2:32). All of these texts are important and deepen our understanding of what it means to be light in our own world. Light exists not for itself but so that others can see. As such, light has a purpose that benefits others and not just the one who provides it. That is certainly true for the people of Israel who were to be bearers of God's revelation so that others could come to know God through them. It was also true of Jesus who lived His life for others. It was true of Paul who carried out extensive missionary journeys so that others could be saved through the message of faith. Indeed, being light isn't meant to draw attention to ourselves but to help people see more clearly who God is and thus be drawn to the Lord. That is the ministry entrusted to us as disciples.

Matthew goes on to say that the good works of Christians are the way in which we bring light. Good works have the purpose of allowing others to see God's goodness and to praise God for His mercy. Good works are not for the benefit of the disciple who accomplishes them but to inspire others to recognize and respond to the presence and work of God in the world. Others will inevitably see good works, just as it is unavoidable that a city set on a hill would be ignored. Still, disciples do not take credit for the good they are privileged to do. Rather, disciples readily acknowledge that any good they have accomplished is nothing more than their cooperation with the grace of God who initiates all good works and brings them to completion.

Lastly, the image of light can also mean the ability to see clearly the world around us. The saints sometimes spoke about the clarity with which they could see the circumstances of their lives when the divine light illumined their hearts and minds. Sometimes it's more convenient to remain in darkness than to live in the light! When we see clearly our lives from God's perspective, then we realize the conversion and repentance that are necessary for growth in holiness. This light is a gracious gift that allows us to dismiss the lies that all too often cloud our thoughts and decisions when we are in darkness. Coming into the light in this way is much like stepping into a sunny day from a dark room and has the same overwhelming effect on our souls.[32] Jesus tells us in this passage that we are to

---

32. This experience known in the Christian spiritual tradition as "obfuscation" is the result of an excess of light that brings the soul to a more clear understanding of divine realities through the darkening of our own human insights. Pseudo Dionysius, "The Mystical

bring the light of the Gospel so as to illumine the misunderstood and darkened world of others' lives. In order to accomplish the identity and mission of being light, disciples must always remember that we are never the source of divine light. Jesus alone revealed Himself as the Light of the World (Jn 8:12). The Book of Revelation further reveals that in the Heavenly Jerusalem there will be no sun or moon, for the Lamb of God will be its light (Rev 21:23). Disciples are not called to be the origins of our Lord's light; we are called to be the windows through which that light shines in the world.

> *When have good works inspired and deepened your faith by opening your eyes to recognize the presence and work of God in our world?*
> *When has someone cast light on your life in such a way that you saw more clearly and chose to respond in a faithful manner?*
> *Who do you know that is in darkness now, and what can you do to be "light" for them? When have others been inspired to seek God because of a good work you did? Which aspect of light do you find most challenging?*

These two images of light and salt are meant to correct any misunderstanding of religion that considers faith to be only a personal or private experience. Because of our faith, we are called to be people who affect the world around us. Our "saltiness" and our "light" do not originate from within us; these qualities originate from God as gifts given to us. As Christians, we are simply called to live out those gifts so others can experience them. When we keep our faith private, we fail to affect the world around us and in doing so we fail in our identity and mission.

> *What situations are going on in your life or the lives of your family and friends that need your Christian influence?*
> *How can you be a better witness in order to inspire others?*
> *What leads people to sometimes think that faith is a merely private experience?*

Theology" in *Complete Works* (New York: Paulist Press, 1987), Chap. II, p. 138; St John of the Cross, *Ascent of Mt. Carmel*, prol. 5-6 (Washington: ICS Publications, 1991), p. 116.

How can a faith community provide opportunities for people to be "light" and "salt" for others?

Sixth Sunday in Ordinary Time

Our Scripture passage for this Sunday comes from the Gospel of Matthew 5:17–37. This text is part of our Lord's famous discourse known as the Sermon on the Mount, and it contains some of the most challenging teachings for disciples, as Jesus calls us to pursue greater righteousness and to not settle for conforming to the world around us.

Jesus teaches us that we can place our confidence in Him, especially when it comes to learning about the will of God for our lives. The Scribes and the Pharisees looked to Scripture (the Law and the Prophets) as the place where the revelation of God's will could be found. For Christians, this revelation is found in Jesus' life and ministry. In order to grasp what the Lord reveals about our lives, we must first know where to find that revelation. Jesus speaks to us especially in the Gospels, which relate His actions, interactions, and teachings. We also see Jesus guiding the life and ministry of the early Church through the Holy Spirit directing the apostles. We can experience the revelation of the Lord personally in moments of prayer, especially before the Blessed Sacrament. Finally, we see Jesus acting in the lives of holy men and women who embody the living Spirit of Christ.

What resources most help you to experience and know God's will?

Lots of people do things in the name of God. What are some of the indicators that someone is authentically following the will of God in their life?

For what situation do you need to seek the will of God at this time?

Commitment to Jesus means more than just confession of faith (v. Jam 2:18). Commitment to Jesus also involves a change of life that affects our actions. We have to do what we are taught. Jesus emphasizes this connection between professed and lived expressions of faith when He focuses on the practical ways in which the actions of disciples are affected by His teaching. When a person pursues religious studies they are accumulating interesting knowledge about the way in which people practice their faith. However, such an accumulation of knowledge does not necessarily affect the way a person lives. When someone seeks understanding of their faith in the context of a living relationship with God, then every insight serves to deepen their knowledge of the One whom they love and who loves them. Knowledge in a living relationship is never trivial. Rather, knowledge within the context of loving commitment becomes the motivation to change our lives in conformity to the will of the other. For disciples, any knowledge about God's will helps us understand the heart of Jesus so that we might know how we can mirror that heart, seek that heart, and make His heart our own.

> *When was the last time a realization of faith changed your actions?*
> *How do you teach others to seek and observe the will of God?*
> *When have your actions or example led others to act in a way contrary to God's will?*
> *When you are learning about your faith, is it more a matter of religious studies or a journey of deepened relationship?*

Our actions spring from our thoughts and the inner workings of our hearts; if we want to change our behavior, then we have to root out the thoughts that lead us to act in a certain way. Jesus wants us to go to the root of our actions so as to change our very thoughts. It is usually a sequential process from the time a destructive thought begins to the completion of a destructive action. By identifying and studying our destructive actions and the destructive actions of others, we can better understand the various steps that led a person to that painful moment. It is this honest study of our lives that allows us to recognize the various moments in the process where we could have and should have acted differently. Such changes may include seeking the council of a trusted and faith-filled friend, turning to prayer at a decisive moment, or openly acknowledging our destructive temptations in the graced-filled healing Sacrament of Reconciliation. Our actions will rarely change until we understand the events that lead to those actions. A mature disciple includes periods of reflection throughout their day so as to examine the various states of consciousness. This daily examination of conscience will help a person recognize and pursue those thoughts that are in conformity with God's will and to dismiss those thoughts that are contrary to God's will.[33]

> *With whom do you share your thoughts so as to seek cor-*
> *rection before they develop into destructive actions?*
> *Counselors oftentimes ask their clients to look at their lives*
> *and ask three questions: What happened to you? How did*
> *you respond? What did you believe about yourself as a*
> *result of that experience? These questions are meant to*
> *help people see the connection between false thinking and*
> *harmful doing. How has your growth in maturity allowed*
> *you to better understand the reasons for your actions so as*
> *to find greater freedom to act differently?*
> *When can you take time to practice a daily examination of*
> *consciousness and what do you think would be the practical*
> *benefits of such a practice?*

Each of the following four sections of this Gospel passage demonstrates how the great commandment (Love God and Love Neighbor) is expressed in concrete ways. It is by fulfilling the Love Commandment that we exercise greater righteousness than the Scribes and Pharisees.

- If we treat our neighbor as ourselves then we will not harbor anger towards them; thus, love shows no hostility. In those

---

33. In the IV century, Evagrius of Pontus, following the Alexandrian interpretation of Scripture, proposed the concept of *Logismoi* or "Assaultive Thoughts" that threaten the inner dignity of those who seek perfection. These thoughts need to be identified and refuted with the power of God's word (cf. *Praktikos* and *Antirrhetikos*). In more recent years, Henri Nouwen, following the teachings of the Trappist monk Thomas Merton spoke of this process of discernment as "to unmask the illusion of our life experiences," that is, to submit our perceptions to a divine consideration of the facts, cf. *Discernment* (London: SPCK, 2013), p. 92; T. Merton, *Contemplation in a World of Action* (South Bend: Notre Dame University Press, 1999), pp. 154–155.

times when we do find ourselves in situations of conflict due to human weakness then we are to seek reconciliation. Sometimes we learn to become comfortable with conflict and do not even desire reconciliation.

When have you allowed anger to grow too much in your heart and what has been the effect?
When have you reached out to reconcile with someone else?
What are the excuses you use to justify your anger or resentment towards someone else?
If you laid bare your thoughts before the Lord, what would God say about your hostile feelings?
With whom do you need to reconcile at this time and how can you do it?

- If we respect one another as fellow human beings, then we will not covet them with lustful thoughts; thus, love is not predatory. In those times when we do find ourselves filled with lustful thoughts, Jesus counsels us to place safeguards in our life to guard against acts of weakness. In today's world, there are a multitude of temptations when it comes to sexuality.

What are some of the prevalent ways in which lustful thoughts or behaviors cause damage in people's lives today?
What are some of the safeguards that could be used to remove or overcome the occasion of such temptations?

- If we are faithful to our life commitments and the promises we have made before God, we will persevere in fulfilling those promises; thus, love is faithful in marriage. In those times when we are distressed due to the challenges of fulfilling our life commitments, Jesus reminds us to seek God's intention for our lives rather than settling for culturally accepted ways of handling problems.

What can couples do to deepen their love and commitment to each other?
What are some of the tools that can help couples successfully grow together through difficult moments in their marriage?

If you could offer one important piece of wisdom or advice for others on how to live a happy and lasting marriage, what would it be?

What can a faith community do to better help people who experience the pain of divorce?

- If we relate with one another in an honorable way, we will speak what is true at all times; thus, love is unconditional truth. Taking an oath has typically been used as a means of ensuring the truth of a person's testimony. In the absence of an oath, the obligation to be truthful was substantially lessened. Jesus wants to remove the distinction between the words we say and intend to fulfill and the empty words we don't mean or intend to fulfill. When a Christian speaks, their "yes" is to mean "yes" and their "no" is to mean "no" without conditions, qualifications, caveats, and so forth. For a disciple, all communication is to be truthful—not just some communication.

Who is a person for you that exemplifies the consistent truthfulness Jesus is calling for?

What is it like to be in a situation where you can't trust what someone says?

When has someone placed extraordinary trust in your word with no external guarantee of truthfulness?

When have you been let down by another person's lack of truthfulness?

Jesus gives us these examples of destructive actions that have their origins in harmful thoughts. Our Lord was addressing the prevalent ways in which He saw violations of the commandment to love your neighbor. Our world is different from that of Jesus, yet human weakness remains the same.

What examples do you think Jesus would point out in our current world as ways in which we violate the commandment to love our neighbor, and what would He recommend we do to overcome our contemporary destructive behaviors?

Seventh Sunday in Ordinary Time

O ur Scripture passage for this Sunday comes from the Gospel of Matthew 5:38–48. In this passage, Jesus continues His radical teaching on Christian discipleship with the final sets of antitheses. He summarizes this section with the call to "perfection". These antitheses and the summary call to perfection offer deep insights into the challenge a Christian disciple faces so as to live in the Kingdom of God.

The first teaching stresses that love does not retaliate. It is a natural and human tendency to retaliate when others have wronged us. Efforts were made in the Old Testament to limit retaliation so that retribution did not exceed the original injury (Ex 21:24, Lv 24:20, and Dt 19:21). These previous regulations of the Law were an attempt to prevent the cycle of violence from escalating. Jesus offers a different way of breaking the cycle of violence that is based on non-retaliation rather than limited response. In these five situations, Jesus addresses a variety of ways in which disciples are called to be people who consider the interests of others above their own. The examples that are used are somewhat extreme but follow the same pattern. First, a situation is presented in which another person is perceived as an aggressor who interrupts one's own personal endeavors. Second, the solution Jesus offers calls for disciples to respond, not by insisting on their own rights but by considering the needs and interests of those whom they perceive to be the aggressor. Thus, there is a clear movement in this teaching away from simply not retaliating (passive resistance) towards actively reaching out and doing good for the one who has wronged us (turn the other cheek, give the cloak, go the extra mile, and so forth). Each of us has people in our lives who sometimes appear to be aggressors when it comes to laying claim to our time, attention, energy, resources, affection, effort, and so on. As disciples, Jesus expects us to consider their needs first rather than asserting our

rights or retaliating for any perceived infringement on our lives.
This Christian response is not easy and requires that we rise above
our natural human responses so as to mirror the supernatural love
of God. Such love is not a sign of weakness or intimidation but
rather a decision to seek the good of the other no matter what the
circumstances.

> *Who lays claim to your time, energy, attention, resources,*
> *affection, or effort so as to require sacrifice from your life?*
> *Whose needs do you put before your own?*
> *When have you put a stranger's needs above your own*
> *interests?*
> *Who puts your needs before theirs?*
> *What is a situation you are facing now in which you need*
> *to move from a passive response of non-retaliation to an*
> *active response of reaching out and doing good for the other?*

The second teaching stresses that love knows no limits. All of us
find it easy to love those who love us. Those are the people close to
us, and we readily call them our neighbors. The challenge of discipleship is to love those who are not close to us or even those who
are at odds with us. The term "enemy" could mean national enemies, competing religious groups, corporate adversaries, or those
against whom you have interpersonal ill feelings. Jesus reminds us
that God provides rain and sun for everyone including the good
and the bad. He then challenges disciples to see others as God sees
them and have the same love and care for them that the Lord does.
To love someone is to seek what is good for the other person in the
eyes of God and not merely to do what the other person wants.
The reality is that people do not always, or even often, desire what
is holy for their own lives. Doing good for someone means that we
help them in their journey to God and seek their eternal salvation.
When we do that, then we act like God and can be called "Sons
of God" or "Children of your Heavenly Father" (Dt 14:1). It is this
quality of love and charity for one's enemies that distinguishes a
Christian from someone who is merely a nice person. Christians
are called to witness a heroic and faith-based love that goes beyond
what a non-believer is capable of. It is only by understanding the
universality of God's love and choosing to demonstrate uncondi-

tional love in our lives that we can be such distinctively Christian witnesses. Our Christian tradition declares, "Love joins the lover to the beloved and of the two makes but one thing."[34]

> *Who loved you when you didn't expect it or deserve it?*
> *Love forms us into the people we are. Who are the three primary people whose surprising acts of love have formed your life (even acts from a stranger)?*
> *Who are the people who most need your love now to form them?*
> *When have you shown kindness towards those who are your "enemies"?*
> *When have you been called to do what is good for another person even though they didn't want it? What are some of the excuses you use so as to dismiss yourself from the obligation to show selfless love for others in their time of need?*

Finally, when Jesus tells us that we should be "perfect" as our Heavenly Father is perfect, He is not telling us to seek perfectionism in the way our contemporary world understands it. Rather, He is summarizing the entire message of Matthew 5:21–48. Jesus knows that we are people who live in the midst of a broken and fallen world. Things will not always be as they should be or as we want them to be. Our situations require us to discern the relative values at stake in every moment and to respond as best we can while being guided by the teachings of the Gospel. Sometimes Christians can think that living a life of holiness requires that they remove themselves from the world, but that's not the message of Jesus in this passage. Christians are called to be deeply immersed in a fallen world and to act in a God-like way in the midst of that messiness. The command to be "perfect" really means to be "whole" in the sight of God. It means to serve the Lord with single-minded devotion in everything that we do and to whole-heartedly carry out the Lord's will in difficult situations. By living this single-minded

---

34. The premise is accredited to St Augustine and well developed by XVI Century Spanish mystics such as St John of the Cross, *Spiritual Canticle*, XXVIII, 1 and Diego de Estella, *Meditaciones devotísimas del amor de Dios*, vol. I (Barcelona: Subirana, 1886), p. 73, Chap. LXXVI.

devotion to act as God would act in every situation, we will fulfill the commandment of Deuteronomy 18:13, "You must be altogether sincere with the Lord, your God." Christians are called to imitate Jesus who immersed Himself in a very imperfect world yet witnessed the values of the Kingdom of God in how He dealt with the situations He faced. Christians live their lives manifesting the same values as God who re-defined what is "great", "honorable", "powerful", "loving", and "admirable" in the life, ministry, death, and resurrection of our Lord. The Greek word *teleos* is used to describe the perfection to which Jesus calls us. This term really means the fullness of what God intends for our lives. To be "perfect" in this sense of the word is to live our lives so that we become who God has destined us to be in Christ. The beauty of our Christian identity is that through our baptism, Christ dwells in us. Our "perfection", then, is to let Christ reign in each moment of our lives. By becoming who God has destined us to be in Christ Jesus, we allow His life to be perfected in us. The Greek word *teleos* can also be translated as "accomplished", "completed", or "fulfilled" instead of "perfect". We could easily translate this final verse of this passage using any one of those previous alternate meanings and so gain a complementary understanding of our Lord's teaching.

> *How do you evaluate situations in the light of the Gospel?*
> *When do you find yourself wanting to be removed from a messy situation rather than addressing it in a God-like way? What are the temptations you face to handle situations in a non-God-like way?*
> *What distorted value in your life does God want to re-orient so as to help you conform more perfectly (wholly) to the person of Jesus?*
> *How is your understanding enriched by considering the alternative translations offered in this reflection of our Lord's final commandment to be perfect?*

EIGHTH SUNDAY IN ORDINARY TIME

Our Scripture passage for this Sunday comes from the Gospel of Matthew 6:24–34. In this reading, Jesus teaches His disciples the necessity of making God the priority of their lives and of trusting in the Lord's goodness, providence, and care. Having clear priorities and trusting in God are perennial challenges for all disciples.

Jesus begins His teaching by presenting the impossible scenario in which a person allows two competing masters to govern their life. Such a situation would obviously be absurd because of the conflicting demands that would necessarily follow. The extremes of love and hate are biblical expressions meaning that a person would eventually need to choose between one or the other master in such a conflicting situation. By presenting this scenario, Jesus is asking us to consider what masters we are following by looking at the choices we make. This is especially true when the values and guidance of the Gospel differ from the expedient possible solutions for each situation. The question for disciples is not whether we will serve something or someone, but rather what or who we will serve. The ultimate master we are serving will be revealed through our daily decisions. The term "mammon" refers to that in which we put our trust for security (it actually comes from the same root word as our faith expression "amen"). In the time of Jesus, people found their security [mammon] mostly in wealth, positions of honor, human relationships, and property. Whenever we give mammon the same attention and priority that we give God, then we have allowed the mammon of our lives to become a competing "god" and have given in to idolatry. As you look back on your day or week, it can be easy to recognize situations in which you know Jesus would have acted differently. That awareness can help reveal which values or priorities were governing your life and motivating you to act in a way different from that of our Lord. These values and priorities reveal the mammon (security) that took the place of God in a particular moment. Sometimes we allow other priorities to infiltrate our lives without even thinking about it. This practice of periodic review can help us become more aware of when we are serving mistaken priorities. Our lives are given meaning based on what or whom we serve.

> *What is the mammon in which people trust or believe today that gives them a sense of false security or meaning and takes their attention away from God?*
> *It's sometimes jokingly stated, "when the going gets tough, the tough go shopping". Where do you look for security or comfort when the going gets tough?*
> *When has mammon failed to give you the security or meaning you expected and what was your response to that disappointment?*
> *What practices help you to have an undivided heart and maintain single-focused devotion to the will of God in your life?*

Anxiousness over possessions can affect everyone. For those who have possessions, anxiousness can be manifested as a false sense of security, self-worth, even competition based on who has more. For those who do not have many possessions, anxiousness can tempt them to believe the myth of materialism that teaches "wealth equals happiness" and become preoccupied by the endless pursuit of what they do not have. Jesus is not telling us to be lazy by telling us to be unconcerned about the matters of daily life. We need to remember that He is speaking directly to people who are actively involved with the tasks of production, industry, farming, and other business ventures. As such, He is reminding them that life is not based on these things and that these pursuits should never take the place of God or become our primary goal. Life is something greater than what we do or what we have. Life is a gift from God. Human work and accomplishment has its proper meaning when it is understood as our participation in God's creative and redeeming effort in the world rather than just a way for us to get ahead of someone else or to better our individual lives. When we know and understand that God is with us and cares for us, we can let go of the need to dedicate timeless energy, attention, and anxiety into securing our own lives and begin to consider what God wants to do in us and through us each day. This teaching is meant to place human endeavors into proper and faith-filled perspective. It is also meant to ensure that we are seeking an encounter with God in all things and at all times. Lastly, it is the only way in which we can serve the Lord with all our mind and all our strength. A person who is pursuing the Kingdom of God and trusting the Lord in their daily endeavors is every bit as productive, and even more so, than the person who is pursuing lesser goals through their work. When a person knows that they are doing God's work, then they are more enthusiastic and diligent in their endeavors because they are trusting God and not chasing after temporary reward.

> *What helps you to understand, from God's perspective, the meaning of your daily work?*
> *What is the good that God is able to do through your work?*
> *How has your work given you a deep sense of meaning and satisfaction in your life?*
> *How is the myth of materialism promoted in our culture and what has been the destructive effect in the lives of those who believe it?*
> *Who is someone you know who lives his or her life with unwavering trust in God?*
> *When have you had to trust in God in order to discover the Lord's caring providence in your life?*
> *How has that experience changed the way you live?*

The Kingdom of God and His Righteousness is revealed in Jesus' teaching and ministry. By telling us to seek first these things, Jesus is reminding us that disciples are people who "follow" where He is leading us. Sometimes we can pray for God to follow us where we want to go rather than praying to follow where the Lord is leading. In order to follow faithfully and to do the will of God, we have to first know that will and then have the courage, self-sacrifice, and trust to be disciples in all situations of our lives. Jesus addresses us as disciples who are already trying to follow Him but need encouragement to persevere during difficult times or moments when we experience little faith. He wants to help us identify our obstacles and give us the confidence necessary to overcome them. All of us have moments of crisis when we are tempted to reach for false security.

In these moments, Jesus wants us to remember that God, who created us and calls us, will bring us into His Kingdom. Ultimately, that goodness of God is the only thing we can really count on. With that assurance, we can then be generous and selfless instruments of God's goodness to others.

One other note should be made about the nature of the command to seek. This seeking is not just a spiritual endeavor or intellectual exercise. Jesus manifested the Kingdom through His active works of healing, forgiveness, and charity. When we are told to seek first in all things the Kingdom and righteousness of Jesus, we are being challenged to allow God's reign to be visibly manifested through our active serving as well. Sometimes people can think that the Kingdom and righteousness refer only to interior dispositions or qualities. The life and ministry of Jesus shows us a different understanding, which requires conforming our life to the will of God in all things.

> *Do you pray for God to follow your will or for you to follow God's will?*
>
> *What teaching or ministry experience of Jesus (His righteousness) can speak to a particular crisis (moment of decision) in your life right now?*
>
> *When do you most experience "little faith" and need encouragement to keep going in your discipleship. What can a faith community do to help people in moments of "little faith"?*

Jesus ends His instruction with the comment that tomorrow has enough concerns of its own. It would be an interesting exercise to look at our concerns and recognize how many of them are outside of our control. The Lord expects us to use our reason and to prepare for the future while at the same time trusting in God's ultimate care and providence. Our future planning is to be in cooperation with God's will and not a rejection of it. We all know situations in which someone has made great plans and preparations only to have tragedy strike at the last minute. Tragedy can take the form of illness, accident, or other catastrophic events that cause us to change our plans in an instant. Regardless of our planning, things don't always work out the way we want or expect them to be. The Lord wants us to experience a certain detachment and freedom from the need to control the outcomes of our lives. Ultimately, we need to trust our belief that God is in control of history and that God loves us, is with us, and forgives us. It is within the context of this act of faith that our other pursuits can properly take place with peace and calm. The benefit of this loving surrender is reflected, in the words St Gregory of Nyssa, in the cloud that led the people of Israel into the Promised Land by which God eased the unpleasantness of being out in the open, forming a shelter from the heat.[35] The greatest joy for a disciple is not when they accomplish their own will but when they cooperate with the will of God so as to help bring the Lord's Kingdom to fulfillment.

> *What preoccupations about tomorrow fill your mind? How have you come to realize that God is ultimately in control of history?*
> *How does this challenge to focus on today and the opportunities that lie before you challenge and inspire your discipleship?*

---

35. St Gregory of Nyssa, *The Life of Moses* (New York: Paulist Press, 1978), Book I, 41, p. 41.

Ninth Sunday in Ordinary Time

Our Scripture passage for this Sunday comes from the Gospel of Matthew 7:21–27. This section concludes Jesus' Sermon on the Mount, which began with the Beatitudes in Matthew 5:1. It stresses the importance of not only listening to our Lord's instruction, but also living our Lord's instruction. This emphasis on practical discipleship is of enduring importance for us as we strive to follow the Lord as well.

The section begins with Jesus cautioning those who would follow Him that being a disciple requires more than just religious knowledge. He stresses this point by explicitly saying that it will require more than just saying "Lord, Lord" to enter the Kingdom of Heaven. Later in Matthew's Gospel Jesus will relate the Parable of the Ten Maidens in which those who call out "Lord, Lord" are specifically excluded from the wedding feast (Mt 25:11). These two passages correlate to each other and caution us on the necessity to integrate our Lord's teaching into the practical aspects of daily life. It can be good for a disciple to acquire accurate religious knowledge. Our Lord never instructs someone to not advance their religious education. In this passage Jesus is reminding disciples that knowledge of faith always incurs the obligation to live that faith. This is the necessary relationship between orthodoxy (right faith) and orthopraxy (right living). The title "Lord" was used by early Christians to identify and proclaim Jesus as the divine Son of God. As such, it is a very accurate and right title of faith. However, if Jesus is proclaimed as the Son of God with the title "Lord", then there is a corresponding obligation to accept His teaching as the Word of God and not just the opinion of a wise teacher. This is where faith can become challenging. Oftentimes it is easier to profess our faith than to live our faith. Jesus is reminding us that having a right understanding of faith does not benefit us unless we are also seeking to live that faith. This instruction on the need to accept and live our Lord's teaching brings to a close the previous two-chapter teaching entitled the Sermon on the Mount. It is in these two chapters that Jesus offers His most challenging insights on discipleship and reveals the values of the Kingdom of God. These are difficult teachings to put into practice and include such things as loving our enemies, doing good to those who persecute us, uprooting sinful desires from our hearts, trusting God with our future, and so forth. While we may agree with these teachings in concept, it is often difficult to live them out in practice. Faith is more than just saying, "I agree"; faith is also saying, "I will do."

> *What are other examples of settings in which increased knowledge brings increased responsibility?*
> *What happens when a person emphasizes orthodoxy (right faith) without a corresponding emphasis on orthopraxy (right living)?*
> *What happens when a person emphasizes orthopraxy without a corresponding emphasis on orthodoxy?*
> *How would your day be different if you were to truly allow Jesus to be the Lord of every aspect of your life?*

Jesus then goes on to specify the objections people will raise when they are excluded from the Kingdom. In particular, they will claim that they prophesied and did mighty works in Jesus' name. It is their implicit belief that those spectacular accomplishments should be considered the same as doing the Father's will. Jesus mentions these objections and mistaken criteria because He wants us to be clear about the difference between doing great things for God and doing God's will. Indeed, those are different things. We can do a lot of great things for God ("in Jesus' name"), but that doesn't necessarily mean we are doing God's will. In fact, one only has to read the newspaper to see how many mistaken and hurtful actions take place in the name of God each day. Sometimes people do indeed accomplish great things like building churches, starting ministries, writing books, teaching classes, and so forth, but sometimes those efforts can be a reflection of their own desire or need for accomplishment rather than a pure-hearted fulfillment of God's will. Of course, God can bring about grace through any situation, but the Lord wants disciples who have a docile, prayerful, and obedient spirit that seeks first and foremost to know the will of God and to do it. The Lord does not want disciples who do their own will and disguise it with God's name. The decisive question of our judgment will not be, "Did you do great things?" but rather, "Do the great things you did really reflect the will of God?" While we may be able to point to very successful lives, it is only the parts of our lives that are faithful, which will matter in that most important moment.

> *How have you seen people use the name of God to disguise their own actions?*
> *How do you know when you are doing the will of God versus doing something for God?*
> *What great works of faith do you feel inspired to accomplish at this time in your life and how can you do that in a faithful and selfless way?*
> *If you were to be judged before the Lord today, what is the great work of your life that you would claim as proof of your faith?*

Jesus then summarizes His teaching with an analogy contrasting how wise and foolish men build their houses. The first analogy concerns that of a wise man who builds on rock because he anticipates the storms that will necessarily come some day. This foundation on rock is identified as the practical integration of our Lord's teaching in daily life. The person who builds on this foundation does so not because it is necessarily convenient in the moment but because it can withstand the trials of the future. The wise man, then, is the one who acts now with the future in mind. That future can be the trials and tribulations of this life, the challenges and pressures of faithful witness, or the moment of eternal judgment. Of course, those reasons are not mutually exclusive and a combination of reasons provides ample motivation for choosing such a solid foundation. The writings of the Old Testament previously established this necessary connection between hearing and doing the will of God (Dt 31:12). What is distinct about this passage is that Jesus identifies His own words as revealing the divine will.

The second analogy of these final verses relates the story of the foolish man who decided to build his house based only on present conditions without taking into account future realities. He builds on sand during the dry season without considering the storms to come. The region of Palestine, in which Jesus taught this parable, was accustomed to a rainy season and a dry season. During the dry season there are large flat areas of sandy ground that require no leveling. However, during the rainy season these same areas become subject to flash floods. A person who was familiar with the weather patterns of that area knew to plan for the rainy seasons and would never build in such a dangerous area. Even today we read periodically of desert areas where flash floods occur and people are swept away in horrific disasters. How much worse is the tragedy of a disaster when a person knew the danger and ignored it? The man is described as foolish not because he didn't know he was building in a dangerous area or because he didn't know the rains would come; he was foolish because he knew both of those things and still did not exercise the necessary precautions to anticipate them. The foolish man built his house only for the moment and not for the future storms that would surely come. In the same way, Jesus relates this contrast of perspectives to the disciple who knows the criteria for future judgment and lives his life now in preparation for that moment, versus the disciple who knows the criteria for judgment but lives his life now with disregard for it. One is building on a solid foundation and is wise while the other is building on sand and is foolish. It is certain that the storms will come and that the storms will be intense for each disciple. Whether they be the trials and tribulations of this life, the challenges and pressures of faithful witness, or the moment of eternal judgment, those storms will come. The time to prepare is now. The way to prepare is by living a life conformed to the will of God as expressed in the words of Jesus. This preparation is an active response to the faith we profess. As an act of hope and confidence in God, Saint Claude de la Colombière prayed,

> My God, I believe most firmly that you watch over all who hope in you, and that we can want nothing when we rely upon you in all things. Therefore I am resolved for the future, to cast all my cares upon you.[36]

---

36. St Claude de la Colombière, "Act of Hope and Confidence in God" in *Hearts on Fire,* Ed. By M. Harter (Chicago: Loyola Press, 2004), p. 49.

What are you doing now to live in such a way that you are preparing yourself for the trials and tribulations of this life, the challenges and pressures of faithful witness, or the moment of eternal judgment?

When are you tempted to make decisions of faith based only on present conditions rather than inevitable future challenges?

What are other natural occurrences that can be used as instructive analogies for the life of faith?

What can a faith community do to help people make right decisions in the present so as to be prepared for future challenges?

What aspect of this analogy means the most to you and why?

Tenth Sunday in Ordinary Time

Our Scripture passage for this Sunday comes from the Gospel of Matthew 9:9–13. This is the famous story of Jesus calling Matthew the Tax Collector to be His disciple. Our Lord's gracious initiative was not celebrated by everyone, however, as we hear of the Pharisee's objection and disapproval.

The call of Matthew occurs at an interesting place in the Gospel narrative and this context may help us understand the importance of the passage. First, Jesus is already well into His public ministry by this point. He called His first disciples (Peter, Andrew, James, and John) five chapters previously in Matthew 4:18–22. From those whom He has called, Jesus will choose Twelve and send them on mission as His special messengers (Mt 10:1–25). Matthew is the last disciple called by Jesus who will be among this group of Twelve carefully selected and commissioned messengers (Mt 10:3). This late call in the Gospel narrative may also reflect a certain lateness in the life of Matthew himself. Matthew undoubtedly heard about Jesus and of the disciples He had gathered around Him. Matthew also knew that up until this point Jesus had not called him. Perhaps he felt both safe and un-chosen at the same time. All that changed when Jesus stepped into His life this day. Our Lord may have waited to call Matthew, but eventually He did do so. Matthew now realized that being a disciple wasn't something just for the good people or for the innocent people, or the holy people, or the perfect people. Even people with sinful pasts and complicated histories could be called to follow Jesus. Matthew probably wondered if Jesus had meant what He said when He preached non-judgmental love of neighbor (Mt 7:1–5), and now he knew it was true. If Matthew, a publicly regarded sinner, could be called so late in the ministry of Jesus and late in his own life (he obviously had a successful career already established), then who couldn't be called? This was good news for Matthew and it is good news for us because sometimes the Lord issues a personal call to us late in life after we have spent years of attending church and raising families. Sometimes we can feel like the Lord has passed by us while we see others growing in their faith and deepening their relationship with God. The point of this passage is that it doesn't matter when God calls us; the important thing is that we are ready to respond when He does. Matthew had that readiness, was looking for that change, and hungered for that relationship. When it was offered to him, he readily abandoned his tax collector's stand and followed Jesus. Saint Brigid tells of a spiritual insight she received when she prayed at Matthew's tomb at Malphi. In Saint Brigid's prayer, the former tax collector turned Apostle explained:

> It was my desire at the time I was a publican to defraud no man, and I wished to find out a way by which I might abandon that employment, and cleave to God alone with my whole heart. When, therefore, He who loved me, Jesus Christ, was preaching, His call was a flame of fire in my heart; and so sweet were His words unto my taste, that I thought no more of riches and honors than of straws. Yea, it was delightful to me to weep for joy, that my God had deigned to call one of such small account, and so great a sinner as I to His grace. And as I clung to my Lord, His burning words became fixed in my heart, and day and night I fed upon them by meditation as upon sweetest food.[37]

In what ways do you identify with Matthew?
How can people be tempted to think it's too late to begin a life of intentional discipleship?
What virtues or qualities do you think Matthew needed to have in order to accept our Lord's call at this point in his life?
Why do you think Jesus waited to call Matthew?
When do you feel passed by when it comes to an experience of faith?

Second, it is important to note that the call of Matthew immediately follows Jesus' healing of the paralytic whose sins were forgiven (Mt

---

37.   See St Brigid, Lib. 1 Rev. c 129. See also *The Holy Gospel According to Saint Matthew. The Great Commentary of Cornelius a Lapide.* Volume one; translated Thomas W. Mossman, revised and completed by Michael J. Miller (Fitzwilliam: Loreto Publications, 2008).

9:2–8). In many ways, Matthew was like that paralytic who was immobile and bound by sin until Jesus freed him with the call to discipleship. It is important to note that Matthew is not described as a tax collector but rather as "a man sitting at the tax office". This phrasing tells us that Jesus sees Matthew first and foremost as a human being and only secondarily as someone who was collecting taxes. Certainly the Lord sees each of us in the same way: first and foremost as human beings who have the potential to become disciples despite our current sinfulness. Jesus saw something in Matthew that Matthew probably didn't see in himself, just like our Lord saw in the paralytic a man who was capable of walking. Jesus called Matthew to follow Him, and we are told that Matthew stood up and followed the Lord. Although this Gospel passage does not use the more common word for "rise" that can mean resurrection (Greek *egeire*), the term for "stood up" (Greek *anastas*) is also sometimes used to describe the resurrection in the writings of Saint Paul (see Eph 5:14, "Awake [*egeire*], O sleeper, and arise [*anasta*] from the dead, and Christ shall give you light"). Paul used that word to describe the necessary moral transformation of life (Christian walk) that takes place in disciples who receive the grace of the Risen Lord in Baptism. To "stand up," then, implies a certain moral conversion in Matthew's life. No one is beyond this possibility of conversion even late in the Gospel and late in life. Following Jesus involves more than just memorizing what the Lord said or imitating what He did. Following Jesus means to embrace His teaching with all our heart, mind and soul and to let our Lord's instruction and example guide every action of our lives so as to be conformed to the Gospel in everything we say and do. We are told that Matthew did, indeed, follow Jesus in such a way. Matthew's story gives us all hope that it is never too late to receive and respond to the grace of Christ calling us to stand up and follow Him. In his polemic, *On the Genealogy of Morals*, German philosopher Friedrich Nietzsche observed that the sense of guilt is based on the primitive relationship between a debtor and a creditor—a seller and a buyer by which we measure person against person.[38] If we used such a principle to understand our worthiness before God, it would be easy to think that the merit

---

38. *On the Genealogy of Morals and Ecce Homo*. trans. W. Kaufmann and R.J. Hollingdale (New York: Random House, 1967).

of our vocation depends on our own moral accomplishments, but Jesus shows us that the relationship between God and man can only be measured by the rule of mercy. Jesus also shows us that we can only stand up in our life after He invites us to friendship.

> *What leads people to think they need to do something in order to earn God's mercy?*
> *What kind of actions do people tend to do so as to obtain God's favor for themselves?*
> *What is the value of human merit in our relationship with God?*
> *How does divine mercy compensate our human poverty?*
> *What moral transformation (stand up) has occurred in your life as a result of your friendship with Jesus?*
> *Jesus was able to see the inherent dignity in every human person regardless of their sinful actions. How does our Lord's respect for each person challenge you to reconsider the way you see others?*

The narrative then goes on to tell us that, when He was at table in the house, many tax collectors and sinners came and joined Jesus and His disciples for the meal. To sit at table and share a meal in the ancient world was an important setting that indicated a sharing of life (fellowship). Our English word "companion" actually comes from the Latin words *cum* (with) and *panis* (bread) meaning "someone with whom we break bread" and captures this sense of communion formed around the table. People in the ancient world paid great attention to those with whom they shared meals because of the necessary relationship implied by that action. Because we were previously told that Matthew stood up and followed Jesus, it would seem reasonable that our Lord shared a meal with him to celebrate his reconciliation and newly established relationship. However, the text indicates that many others came and joined in that meal as well, which prompted the condemnation of the Pharisees. It seems that Matthew's friends wanted to meet Jesus, and the Lord welcomed them to the celebration. This is an important insight for us in our lives as disciples. Like Matthew, when we "stand up" through the grace of Christ, others tend to notice it and can become curious to learn more about how the Lord has changed us. It is important to share our story of how God's grace has transformed us because our personal witness may be the invitation others are waiting for and which will draw them to the Lord. As Saint Peter says, "Always be ready to give an explanation to anyone who asks you for a reason for your hope" (1 Pt 3:15). Matthew gave that answer, and his friends wanted to meet Jesus for themselves as a result of it. For that reason, they came to the meal. This passage teaches us that one person's conversion can and should have a ripple effect in the community that affects all those around them, from their family, to their friends, to their professional relationships. When God moves in our lives, it is never only for us to experience but so that God can affect others through us. By sharing our stories of faith, conversion, and discipleship, we can help lead others to Christ so the Lord can transform their lives even as He has transformed ours.

> *How can we erroneously think that some people are incapable of becoming disciples of Jesus because of their sinful past?*
> *When has your personal transformation of life inspired others to want to learn more about your experience?*
> *Who do you think Jesus wants you to invite to the Lord's Supper so they can be drawn into friendship with Him?*
> *What can make a person hesitant to share their experience of God with others, and how does the quote from 1 Peter 3:15 challenge that hesitancy?*

The passage ends with the challenge of the Pharisees and Jesus' proclamation that God desires mercy rather than sacrifice. When the Pharisees saw that dinner in the house, they did not see human beings gathered around their Lord and Redeemer but rather sinners who were not worthy to share in a meal with a holy teacher. Their objection prompts the corrective response of Jesus who clearly defends this event of reconciliation and conversion while clarifying His mission. The saying regarding physicians being in the company of the ill was somewhat common in the ancient Greek world, and even the Old Testament contained passages that stressed the healing work of God (Jer 8:22 and Ex 15:26). Jesus summarizes His ministry as that of a divine doctor who brings healing and salvation to those who most need it rather than focusing His mission on those who think they do not need it. Jesus defends His presence among sinners since they are the ones who hunger for the healing gifts of forgiveness, reconciliation, and conversion. Our Lord has nothing to fear from associating with those whom society deems outcasts. Because we are all human beings in the eyes of Jesus, He wants us to stand up and fulfill our dignity as disciples who follow Him. He will accept anyone who responds to His invitation, and He calls each of us by name even as He knew the name of Matthew. Discipleship is a deeply personal invitation to experience God's mercy and then to be merciful in welcoming everyone else who accepts that invitation. The early Church had many converts who came from sinful and difficult pasts. It was, and still is, important for the community of faith to welcome one another without judgment as brothers and sisters regardless of a person's previous sins. The final saying of Jesus instructs us that our sacrifices to God mean little if we are not merciful towards one another. Acceptance at the Lord's Table of the Eucharist is certainly such a setting that warrants this welcoming and encouraging response.

> *How can an exclusive or judgmental attitude manifest itself in faith communities today?*
> *How does the phrase, "...our sacrifices to God mean little if we are not merciful towards one another", challenge you?*
> *How is the Sign of Peace at Mass intended to heal the divisions that wound the Body of Christ (the Church)?*
> *Who do you know who is hungering for the gifts of forgiveness, reconciliation, and conversion?*
> *What leads a person to believe that God values religious sacrifices more than mercy towards others?*

Eleventh Sunday in Ordinary Time

Our Scripture passage for this Sunday comes from the Gospel of Matthew 9:36 to 10:8. This is a decisive moment in our Lord's ministry when Jesus sends the Twelve out on mission to continue His works and announce the Kingdom. There are several elements of this passage that are meant to be informational for us as disciples who continue to carry on the mission of Jesus today.

When Jesus looked out at the crowds, we are told that our Lord had compassion on them for three reasons: they were harassed, distressed (or torn apart), and like sheep without a shepherd. All of these elements are important. First, we should note that Jesus' response was one of compassion. There are certainly lots of other responses our Lord could have had when He looked out and saw the crowds. The description implies that the crowds were difficult at best and errant at worst. Our Lord could have expressed frustration, anger, antagonism, or a range of other reactions towards such a group but His noted response was that of compassion. That's because Jesus saw in the crowds not occasions of error, but potential for greatness. Our Lord wanted to see the crowds as potential disciples and wanted to help them develop and grow rather than wither and waste away their lives. In order to accomplish this growth, they would need direction (shepherding), and so Jesus is moved to satisfy that need. Our Lord could have been motivated to send His disciples on mission out of a desire to confront the bad leadership that was misguiding the crowds, or to correct their errant ways, or to fill a power vacuum in the society of that time. While any of those motivations would have resulted in the same action, it is clearly stated that Jesus' ministry was motivated by compassion. That motivation implies a heartfelt empathy for the plight of others and the willingness to help alleviate their suffering. The compassion of Jesus should challenge us to consider how we respond to difficult moments with other people and whether we can see in those moments an opportunity to invite someone to discipleship or just a chance to correct a wrong situation. Second, when we are told that the crowds were harassed and torn apart, we must wonder what the origin was of those destructive influences. In the Old Testament, Israel is oftentimes described with the image of lost sheep when their religious and political leaders led them into error resulting in destruction or calamity (Num 27:17, 1 Kg 22:17, 2 Chr 18:16, Ez 34:5, Zec 13:7). Certainly the people of Jerusalem were scattered during the time Matthew was writing his Gospel because of the Roman military campaign to suppress the Jewish revolt of AD 70. This distressed state is presented as the natural consequence of inadequate or unfaithful leadership. In such a setting of poor leadership, the common crowds are the ones who suffer. Jesus sends His disciples on mission to provide that leadership, which will care for the people's needs and lead them to God.

> *How do you typically respond when you see someone who is harassed by the circumstances of their life, torn apart by the malice of others, or lacking clear guidance?*
> *Who has helped you develop your potential as a disciple and become great in some way and what motivated their influence in your life?*
> *Who is someone God has placed in your life and who has the potential for greatness of faith? How can you be an instrument to help that person become a better disciple?*
> *What circumstances typically harass disciples today?*
> *How can members of the Church be torn apart from their commitment of faith?*
> *In what ways do people today pay the price for the bad decisions of their leaders?*

Jesus then describes the leadership (shepherding) He will provide as being part of a great harvest. The image of the harvest is both powerful and deeply rooted in the prophetic books of the Old Testament (Is 18:4, Is 27:12, Jer 51:53, Hos 6:11, Joel 3:13). In the writings of Joel 3:13 and Micah 4:11–14, the harvest was a metaphor for the time of judgment. Jesus uses the harvest in this passage to describe the work of the Gospel and the mission of the Church. By using the image of the harvest, Jesus is communicating a sense of urgency and the need for everyone to do their best. The harvest waits for no one, and the magnitude of the work is seemingly greater than the workers can ever handle. It requires the committed efforts of those involved, each in their own capacity, for the harvest to be successful. If we delay or if we choose to not take advantage of opportunities, then the ripe harvest will be in jeopardy and what was intended to be a bumper crop could become a lost crop. The harvest requires commitment, but sometimes we find it easy to dismiss ourselves from the task while waiting for others to step forward in which case the opportunity of the harvest is oftentimes lost.

> *What are some of the "harvest" moments you run across in your daily life (family, profession, and other social encounters) when situations are ripe for a message of faith or an expression of Christian compassion?*
> *What are some of the excuses we use to exempt ourselves from working in the harvest?*
> *By using the image of the harvest, Jesus is stressing that there are opportune moments of faith that do not last forever in people's lives. What is the harvest the Church is missing out on today, and who are the workers the Lord wants to send into that harvest?*

In the face of such great need, it would have been easy for the disciples to think their first action should be that of organizing, planning, and travel. However, Jesus is very clear about what their first action should be. After explaining the huge work they have to do, the Lord simply commands them to Pray. Prayer is essential in the life of a disciple and is necessary before we begin any effort of ministry so that whatever work we do may be in accord with God's will and guided by the Holy Spirit. It does not matter what we accomplish if it is not in accord with God's will. In fact, disciples sometimes act with good intentions but can end up working against the Gospel rather than for it. Prayer keeps us focused on our purpose, open to the Lord's inspiration, and aware of the sacredness of our efforts. Without prayer, we risk doing our own will rather than God's will. Jesus sent the disciples to proclaim the Kingdom of God, and in order to do that, the disciples had to know clearly what the Lord wanted to occur in every situation they faced.

> *What prayer do you use to start your day so you can be guided by the will of God and responsive to the harvest you will encounter?*
>
> *Reflect on the following prayer, "Lord, may everything we do begin with Your inspiration, continue with Your saving help, and come to completion in Your Kingdom." How does this prayer speak to you? What happens when we begin doing something without first praying about it?*

When Jesus sends the disciples on mission, He tells them to basically do three things: communicate the Good News (the Kingdom of Heaven), alleviate suffering (works of healing), and confront evil (cast out demons). These actions summarize the basic ministry of Jesus Himself and show that the disciples were sent to continue that ministry. For this reason Jesus shared with them His own authority and power. These are the actions that are intended to provide guidance to the crowds and protect them from undue distress and errant distractions. These actions continue to be essential elements of the mission of the Church today. First, the message of the Gospel forms the heart and soul of our ministry as much as it did when Jesus first sent the disciples on mission. Individual disciples, and the Church in general, must never lose sight of this mission. Christianity is not a self-help organization whose mission is to esteem the power of the human person so that they can determine their own individual life. Christianity is the unwavering committed belief that the world, created inherently good by God, is wounded by sin but that God sent His Son as our Savior to restore us to grace and reveal to us the divine plan for our lives. That is the Good News of the Kingdom of Heaven. No matter what else the Church proclaims, or individual disciples communicate, if we are not telling the story of salvation through the message of Jesus (*kerygma*), we are not fulfilling our mission. In fact, we can actually begin to lead people astray from God rather than leading them to God and end up becoming bad shepherds.

Second, the mission of the Church and individual Christian disciples must always include works of charity that seek to alleviate human suffering. Jesus stressed this important work by healing the sick, raising the dead, and cleansing lepers. Human suffering is not limited to physical illness but can also extend to social exclusion and destitute poverty. Just as Jesus manifested His compassion by caring for those whom He met, so too He sends us as His disciples to continue His compassionate ministry in the world today. Disciples who are not actively involved in alleviating human suffering on any and all levels are failing to fulfill an essential part of their mission in Christ. The charitable works of the Church are actually another way in which we are called to proclaim the Good News of God's love and mercy to the world. A maxim commonly attributed to Saint Francis of Assisi says, "The deeds you do may be the only sermon some persons will hear today." There is an authentic evangelization that takes place anytime the love and mercy of God is shown in the world. Jesus did not want His disciples, or us, to ever lose sight of the importance of this witness.

Third, Jesus commanded the disciples to cast out demons. This is a way of saying that they are to confront the presence of evil and never become complacent or tolerant with it. Indeed, there is no place for evil in the Kingdom of Heaven. The work of confronting evil happens on personal, communal, and societal levels. It can mean everything from helping disciples grow in freedom from oppressive and sinful attachments to addressing systemic prejudice, poverty, or indifference on societal and communal levels. It can also mean addressing cultural values that oppose the Gospel or the dignity of the human person. The confrontation with evil is a necessary part of the Church's mission (and every individual disciple's mission) because the Kingdom of Heaven cannot coexist with evil.

If you were to summarize the basic message being communicated by the Church today, what would be that message?
What messages can actually be in contradiction to the kerygma (story of salvation) of the Gospel?
What part of the kerygma is most overlooked in communication by Christians today?
Why do you think Jesus included works of mercy and compassion (alleviating human suffering) as an essential part of the disciples' mission?

What situations of human suffering do you encounter every day?
What evils most threaten marriages and families today?
What evils most threaten a disciple's individual moral integrity?
What societal evils most need to be addressed, and how can a faith community be part of that confrontation?

The last part of our Lord's instruction is the simple command to give without cost. This teaching on the necessity of gratuitous ministry was present in rabbinic writings of the ancient world. Saint Paul reiterates this same principle when he reminds the Corinthians that he preached the Gospel to them "without cost" (2 Cor 11:7). Jesus preached the Gospel, healed the sick, and cast out demons without charging for His services, and legitimate disciples will do the same. The reward for a true disciple is the joy and honor of sharing in God's work in the world. Other miracle healers in the ancient world did make a personal profit from their healing ministries. This teaching of Jesus was meant to distinguish the Christian disciple from those miracle workers. It is challenging to realize that every gift God shares with us still belongs to the Lord. As Christian stewards of God's gifts, we are responsible and accountable for how we use the Lord's blessings according to His will. This is true both with the authority for ministry and the resources of ministry. Jesus has given us the tools we need to continue the ministry of the Gospel in our time. It is up to us to use those tools to build the Kingdom of Heaven and not only to build our own personal kingdoms. After having given the disciples so much power and authority, it was important that Jesus also remind them of the great responsibility they receive along with those gifts. This command, too, is one of the ways in which we effectively preach the Kingdom of Heaven. When we use our gifts, talents, and resources freely and generously for the mission of the Gospel (proclaiming faith, alleviating suffering and confronting evil), we become more authentic witnesses of Jesus. Sacrificial generosity and good stewardship will always be distinguishing characteristics of a true disciple.

In what way does this reflection challenge you?
How can disciples be tempted to use their God-given gifts
and talents for their own gain rather than for the Kingdom
of God?
How does a disciple's witness of generosity and selflessness
render credibility and authenticity to the Gospel?
In what ways can the mission of the Gospel be impeded by
the self-seeking actions of Christian leaders?

For those who teach the faith the Church prays with these words:

We thank you and bless you, Lord our God. In times past you
spoke in many varied ways through the prophets, but in this,
the final age, you have spoken through your Son to reveal to all
nations the riches of your grace. May we who have met to pon-
der the Scriptures be filled with the knowledge of your will in all
wisdom and spiritual understanding, and, pleasing you as we
should in all things, may we bear fruit in every good work. We
ask this through Christ our Lord.[39]

---

39. USCCB Liturgy Committee, "Order of Blessing for a Catechetical
    Meeting" in *Book of Blessings* (Collegeville: The Liturgical Press,
    1992), p. 171.

Twelfth Sunday in Ordinary Time

Our Scripture passage for this Sunday comes from the Gospel of Matthew 10:26–33. In the verses immediately preceding this passage, we heard of Jesus sending the Twelve on mission to continue His ministry. In this Sunday's Gospel passage, we hear our Lord's instruction to the Twelve to sustain and encourage them in their missionary efforts. As disciples who are sent on mission each day, this instruction has much to offer us as well.

The first thing to note is how many times Jesus counsels the Twelve to not be afraid. In fact, the phrase "do not fear" appears three times in this short section (verses 26, 28, and 31). The first obstacle the Twelve will have to overcome in order to be courageous witnesses of Jesus is that of fear. People were not afraid to follow Jesus, so we must wonder why fear can prevent people from being an effective witness of Jesus. There are lots of fears that we can experience and which can paralyze our witness of faith as well.[40] For some it is the fear of failure, rejection, inadequacy, insufficiency, irrelevance and so forth. For others it is the fear of persecution or the fear of social inappropriateness by creating an uncomfortable situation. Sometimes it can be the fear of breaking a rule in the workplace or public sphere. Still others can be afraid of the commitment and sacrifice involved in being a Christian witness especially when the challenge of discipleship requires our own

---

40. The Catechism of the Catholic Church in N. 1828 says, "*The practice of the moral life animated by charity gives to the Christian the spiritual freedom of the children of God. He no longer stands before God as a slave, in servile fear, or as a mercenary looking for wages, but as a son responding to the love of him who "first loved us (1 Jn 4:19).*" This reminds us of the two basic types of fear identified by our Tradition: *Servile Fear,* which is a selfish fear of punishment without the consideration of love; and *Filial Fear,* which is fear of offending the one who is feared, based on reverence and love.

conversion of life. Fear can prevent us from becoming missionary disciples as much today as it did nearly two thousand years ago. These words of Jesus, then, are directed to us and to each of the personal fears that are an obstacle to our missionary outreach and witness. Jesus knows that the human heart is influenced by fear, so He not only tells us to "be not afraid", He also tells us that if we are going to fear someone it should be the Lord of Heaven and Earth who has power over both body and soul rather than some earthly power who can only affect our life and wellbeing for a short time. All these instructions are meant to help us overcome the obstacles that can prevent our effective Christian witness.

> *What are some of the fears that can hold you back from being a witness of Jesus in your marriage, family, friendships, and professional world?*
> *When was the last time you had the opportunity to share your faith but fear prevented you from doing so?*
> *When have you overcome fear in order to be a witness of Jesus?*
> *How does the counsel to fear only God help you put in perspective the various obstacles you experience?*

The second thing Jesus teaches is that the Gospel is meant to be the public property of all people and not the personal possession of only a few. Everything that the disciples have heard "whispered" is to be proclaimed from the rooftops. The disciples have received much personal instruction from Jesus, and these privileged insights are not only for their own enrichment. The Gospel is meant for all creation, and every insight the disciples received is to be shared with everyone they meet. When a message is shouted from the rooftops, it inevitably falls on open ears as well as deaf ears. The Gospel is not diminished by those who reject it, and so disciples should not hesitate to generously and freely share the message of our Lord with everyone. Some will respond and some will not. That is the reality of faith and the mystery of human free response. One thing is for certain, however, and it is this: a person cannot accept the Gospel if the Gospel has not been communicated to them. Our failure to proclaim the message of Jesus is what will definitely prevent others from receiving it. For this reason, Jesus instructs the Twelve to proclaim His message far and wide for all to hear in the hopes that many will respond. Sometimes we like to budget our energy and efforts so that we share ourselves only in situations that have a high probability of success. Sometimes, too, we can mistakenly believe that our personal experience of Jesus and insights of faith will somehow be diminished if we share them with others. That is simply not true. Faith grows only when we do share it with others. Jesus wants the Twelve to become stronger in their own faith, and for that reason He sends them out to share it with others. They may not have all the answers or understand all the mysteries, but that's okay. They do have an experiential knowledge of Jesus, and the Lord wants them to give to others what they have received.

> *How does it challenge you in your discipleship to know that your personal experience of God is actually public property that others have a right to receive?*
>
> *When do you find yourself budgeting your faith witness to others based on the probability of successful reception?*
>
> *When has another person surprised you because they responded to an experience of faith that you did not think would affect them?*
>
> *What percentage of your faith efforts do you think are successful?*
>
> *What do you think are the criteria Jesus uses in determining whether or not we are successful witnesses?*

The third thing Jesus teaches the Twelve concerns their need to trust in God's providential care. To communicate this instruction, our Lord uses examples of two relatively insignificant things in order to demonstrate that if God cares about things of such small value, He will care even more about disciples who are of greater value. The first example concerns a sparrow, which was eaten by the poor and was among the cheapest meat a person could purchase in the market. An *assarion* was worth 1/16 of a denarius, the wage of a day laborer. If God cares about something as insignificant as a sparrow, then how much more does God care for a missionary disciple of Jesus Christ? God created every follicle for an individual strand of hair, which emphasizes the enormous care and concern the Lord has for every human person. If God is attentive even to the many follicles on our head, then how much more must God care for the well-being of His faithful disciples? In each case, the argument is from smaller to greater and is intended to give the Twelve confidence of God's presence with them even when they experience difficult and painful situations. This is a challenging teaching for us because it calls us to trust the Lord with our lives and to firmly believe that God will take care of us no matter what we experience so long as we do His will and continue His mission. It is this confidence that allowed the Martyrs to embrace their deaths with peace and even joy. It is this confidence that motivated the first missionaries to carry the message of the Gospel to the far corners of the world having no idea what awaited them when they arrived. It is this confidence that can inspire us each day to face each situation as an opportunity to be a friend of Jesus who introduces others to Him. Indeed, God gives us a hundred circumstances every day to be His witnesses. Sometimes we are blind to such opportunities because we fail to realize that God is the Lord of History and that every moment is a manifestation of God's grace and an opportunity to be a faithful disciple.

> *When has a relatively insignificant event opened your eyes to help you realize that God is truly the Lord of History and to help you trust more?*
> *In what do you typically place your trust?*
> *Who has most inspired you by their trust in God?*
> *Why do you think Jesus needed to encourage the Twelve to trust in God before they could begin their missionary journey?*

The last part of our Lord's instruction reminds the Twelve that their temporal efforts will have eternal consequences for good or for ill. The language of "acknowledge" or "confess" had certain legal overtones to it and indicated that the Twelve were on trial even as they were carrying out their missionary responsibilities in the world, and this trial would continue in Heaven at the Final Judgment. If the Twelve were faithful in acknowledging Jesus before others, Jesus would be faithful in acknowledging them before His Father (Mt 10:33). However, if the Twelve were unfaithful in their missionary efforts, then they would be denied before the Heavenly Father (2 Tm 2:12–13). This fidelity is not so much to a message as it is to the person of Jesus Himself. This is a significant development in our Lord's instruction to the Twelve and indicates that they are being commissioned not only to communicate a message of faith but to actually confess their deep, abiding friendship with Jesus Himself. It is actually easier to communicate a message we have heard than to share the relationship with which we have been blessed. Suppose that someone asked you why you acted with integrity in your professional life. Would your answer be based on principles of business or on your relationship with Jesus? As disciples, we are called to introduce others to the person of Jesus and not just to His message. In fact, many people may not be open to the message until they have been introduced to the Person! When we readily acknowledge Jesus as the source of our life, faith, and confidence, we prove ourselves to be His faithful friends who are not ashamed to bring Him into our marriages, families, friendships, and professional life. What a powerful message! To be a friend of Jesus means to introduce all the other people in our lives to the Lord. We can't do that if we are afraid or if we think our relationship with Jesus is private. We can only do that when we are concerned with fulfilling God's will more than anything else in this world, when we know that God cares for us, and when we know that our eternal salvation depends upon it.

> *How successfully did you pass your trial of faith this past week?*
>
> *How does it change the way you approach your day to understand it as a trial of discipleship?*
>
> *What situations give you an opportunity to bear witness to Jesus in your life?*
>
> *When are you tempted to communicate a Christian message rather than your relationship with Christ?*

Thirteenth Sunday in Ordinary Time

Our Scripture passage for this Sunday comes from the Gospel of Matthew 10:37–42. In this reading Jesus continues to instruct the Twelve about the obstacles they will inevitably encounter while on mission. In last week's Gospel passage, we read of how Jesus cautioned them to not be intimidated. In this week's passage, Jesus cautions them to not be unduly influenced or deterred by those closest to them in their families. We all know how effectively intimidation and influence can be used in our world to control the actions of others just as these methods were used in the world of Jesus and the early Church. Our Lord not only wants to caution the disciples to anticipate such influences, He also gives them instruction on how to persevere through those influences. Let's study this passage in greater depth to see how it can encourage and enlighten our lives as disciples.

The Twelve have been blessed with the opportunity to hear Jesus teach, watch Him reach out to the poor and suffering, and learn about the mysteries of the Kingdom of God. Now that they are being sent on mission to bring that message of Jesus to others, they must have been filled with optimism that everyone would receive it with joy and excitement even as they had. Oftentimes we presume that those who are closest to us will share our joy and values, but that's not always the case. Sometimes those closest to us can be disturbed by God's movement and resistant to the Lord's grace acting in our lives. Jesus wanted to caution the disciples that not everyone would welcome their message and that the Gospel will inevitably bring about division. If the disciples were seeking a superficial peace with those around them, then they might be tempted to acquiesce in the face of rejection. That could especially be true when their message of faith brought disharmony into their family relationships. The disciples need to clearly understand that their relationship with Jesus must be the most important foundational relationship in their lives and that all other relationships must be based on it. If they do not love Jesus more than anyone else, they cannot be effective missionary disciples who are willing to embrace the rejection of others. The reality is that many Christians in the early Church were rejected by their families because of their decision to follow Jesus. They failed in their discipleship if they did not love the Lord first and foremost. Sometimes we can be tempted to acquiesce or compromise our beliefs in order to keep the peace as well. It happens in both our professional and personal worlds. We know instinctively when others disapprove of our actions and statements. When those actions or statements are communicating the message and values of the Gospel or a way in which God has worked in our lives, then our silence or compromise prevents our effective witness. We need to remember that the peace of Christ is different from the peace of the world. Those who have experienced the Lord's gift of peace want to share it with others. For someone who has not experienced it, that gift of peace born out of a relationship with Jesus can actually seem threatening because it challenges their values and presumptions. Disciples who are living witnesses of Jesus have a way of disrupting the values of a secular world. Such a conflict of values can actually be a sign that a person is an authentic witness.

> *When have you experienced the resistance of others because*
> *of a faith experience in your life?*
> *When are you tempted to acquiesce or compromise your*
> *stated beliefs for the sake of keeping the peace?*
> *Who has tried to influence you to not continue your growth*
> *in faith and to not take the next step of discipleship?*
> *What are examples you know of where a person's decision*
> *to follow Jesus has caused significant disharmony?*

Next, Jesus informs His disciples that they must be willing to take up their cross and follow Him or they are not worthy of Him. The cross represents all the sacrifice, intimidation, rejection, and negative influence a person may experience as a consequence of a decision for discipleship and faithful witness. The image of the cross should not be trivialized or reduced to minor inconveniences. Crucifixion meant a horrific and painful death that was familiar to people of Jesus' time. Jesus gave the disciples power to carry out His ministry, and now He promises them a sharing in His cross as well, but they must be ready for it and accept it when it comes. Christians of the first century sometimes faced horrific deaths because of their decision to follow Jesus. If they were not willing to accept sacrifice, they would not persevere in their commitment of faith. Even today we read about people who experience great persecution and sacrifice because of their commitment to follow Jesus. Such accounts of martyrdom remind us that discipleship is a serious commitment and requires unwavering dedication to the Lord. The mission of continuing the work of Jesus is entrusted to the Church, and our Lord's promise of both authority and the cross continue to be relevant for us. We receive authority and power so we can be courageous witnesses who know that it is God who works through us. We receive the promise of the cross so we will not be surprised, silenced or deterred when we encounter forces that oppose the Gospel. In the mystical poetry of St John of the Cross, the disciple's determination is beautifully captured in this stanza, "Seeking my Love I will head for the mountains and for watersides, I will not gather flowers, nor fear wild beasts; I will go beyond strong men and frontiers."[41] When we are called to accept the cross, we must remember our Lord's words in last week's Gospel where Jesus said to fear not the one who can kill the body but who cannot kill the soul (Mt 10:28–31). Rather, trust in God who cares more for us than a flock of sparrows or the hairs on our head. The cross was used by the Romans to intimidate the populace into conformance with imperial rule. For Christians, the cross becomes the confirming sign of faithful discipleship and the fulfillment of our Lord's promises.

What methods are used today by our secular world to intimidate disciples into conformance with secular values? What do you think the Twelve disciples thought when Jesus told them about the necessity of the cross, and why do you think our Lord wanted them to know about it before they ever set out on mission?

---

41. St John of the Cross, "Spiritual Canticle, Stanza 3" in *The Collected Works* (Washington, D.C: ICS Publications, 1991), p. 471.

Who is bearing the cross today because of their commit-
ment to Jesus, and how can a faith community assist them
in carrying it faithfully?
Why is the cross a necessary part of a disciple's witness?

Jesus ends His missionary instruction to the Twelve disciples by
speaking about the incredible blessings people will experience
through their ministry. Indeed, not everyone will respond positively
to their message. However, some people will respond positively
to the disciples' message, and our Lord wants the last word of
His instruction to remind the disciples of how much others will
be blessed through them. The knowledge of these blessings and
benefits is meant to encourage them to persevere through every
moment of resistance and rejection. The ultimate reason for their
missionary activity is the salvation of peoples. Those who positively
receive the apostles' message will also receive Jesus and the Father.
They will receive the reward of the Prophets and righteous ones as
well. The realization of how much others will benefit because of
our ministry should motivate us to continue the mission of Jesus
because we now have something wonderful to share with others
that will bless their lives. How could we not want to do that? The
sure and certain knowledge of how others will be blessed makes
it worth the sacrifice (cross), resistance (family relationships),
and hardships (fear) that may come our way. One thing is certain,
though: people cannot be blessed unless we become the messengers of that blessing. Some people may resist the message of faith
for years before finally receiving it. Disciples who are faithful will
persevere in their efforts to bring others to Jesus because they
never lose hope in God's gracious mercy and because they never
want anything less for those whom they love. Jesus never gave up
on the people He encountered. Rather, He prayed for them and
loved them to the end. Even as He was being crucified, He prayed
for those who were driving the nails. He wanted them to experience the reward of the blessed rather than the condemnation of
the cursed. The perseverance of discipleship, then, is motivated
not by our determination or desire for success but by our love for
others in the example of Jesus. It's never too late for someone to
receive the Lord, or to welcome the message of a prophet, or to
become a righteous one. Inspired by that hope, disciples are willing

to overcome every obstacle for the sake of others and in witness
to their love of Jesus.

> *Who do you think God wants to bless with His presence,*
> *and how can you be an instrument of that blessing?*
> *How does the vision of a world blessed by God inspire you*
> *to want to persevere in your Christian witness?*
> *What motivates you to keep going when faced with failure*
> *or rejection and how can that source of motivation inform*
> *and inspire your discipleship?*
> *How can a faith community help people understand that*
> *it's in their best interest to commit their life to Jesus?*

Fourteenth Sunday in Ordinary Time

Our Scripture passage for this Sunday comes from the Gospel of Matthew 11:25–30. In this passage, we hear Jesus offering a prayer of thanksgiving to the Father in the midst of a difficult ministry experience. Jesus also issues an invitation to discipleship by appealing to the hungers of the human heart. Let's study this passage more to see how it might speak to our lives as disciples.

It is interesting to note that Jesus offered His prayer of thanksgiving and invitation to discipleship immediately after facing rejection from the two towns of Chorazin and Bethsaida. That is an interesting response to an otherwise negative experience. Perhaps our Lord is trying to tell us something by the timing of His prayer and His invitation. First, let us consider the prayer of thanksgiving. By pausing to reflect on an experience of failure, and seeking God's will in the midst of it, Jesus is giving us an example to follow. None of us are successful in all of our efforts. Failure happens in ways large and small. It is important that we take time, like Jesus, to bring our experiences to prayer and ask the Father to help us understand how our moments of difficulty fit into His divine plan. Only then can we be accepting of failure in a healthy way such that we learn from our mistakes, strengthen our resolve, and recommit ourselves to fidelity in the future. God always has something to teach us. To those who have ears, let them hear it! Prayer is the way in which we open ourselves to hear and understand the Lord interpreting our experience for us. Saint Paul reminds us that Christians should be able to thank the Lord for everything we experience in our lives (1 Thes 5:18 and Eph 5:20). It is easy to thank the Lord for the blessings we receive, but it can be difficult to be thankful when we are given trials and difficulties. By offering His prayer of thanksgiving immediately after an experience of rejection, Jesus was teaching us by example how we are to respond as Christian disciples when we experience difficulties in our efforts to carry out the work of God.

Second, we can now better consider the call to discipleship. Jesus wants us to follow Him wherever He leads us. By issuing the call to discipleship after a moment of rejection and failure, Jesus was reminding any would-be followers that being His disciple will not bring them popularity or success. There are very few leaders who ask people to follow them after a moment of failure. Jesus wants disciples who will not only be faithful when the crowds applaud their message but who will also be faithful when others jeer at their message. Our Lord wants disciples who are so deeply committed to following Him that they are not unduly motivated by the pursuit of success or deterred by the disappointment of failure. Only someone who is profoundly drawn to the Lord Himself would accept the invitation in light of these circumstances. That is a disciple who will remain faithful in good times and in bad and who will truly thank the Lord for all things.

> *When have you had to stop and go to prayer with a particular failure in your life so as to seek God's direction and consolation?*
> *When is it difficult for you to thank the Lord for all things and not just some things? What virtue has been fostered in your life because of an experience of failure? How can the fear of failure paralyze disciples today?*
> *How does the desire for success and fame prevent you from accepting the sacrifices of discipleship?*
> *What do you think went through the minds of the would-be disciples when they heard the Lord's invitation?*

In addition to the rejection of the towns of Chorazin and Bethsaida, Jesus also experienced rejection from the Scribes and Pharisees. They were the ones who claimed to be scholars and have understanding of religious matters, yet they could not see God acting in Jesus. They were also the ones who tried to tell people that access to God is difficult, complicated, and takes great effort. For that reason, they believed that access to God was only for a privileged and skilled few rather than for all people. Jesus teaches us something very different. Our Lord praises the "Little Ones" and shows how they are able to see God with pure receptivity and effortless simplicity. The "Little Ones" (also translated as "infants" or "babes") are those who are unpretentious, trusting, open to direction, not concerned with status (or ego), and who don't put others down to make themselves look better. They are open to the gift of God in Jesus and want to receive the Lord in any way possible. The ability to know God isn't a matter of shrewdness that requires complicated spiritual gymnastics or restricted to only a few accomplished and well-educated disciples. Rather, knowing God is a gift freely given to those who ask for it in humility, openness, and sincerity. Those who know they have no claim on God can truly receive the Lord as a gift. They are the "Little Ones". Those who believe they already have God figured out will miss countless opportunities to experience the God of surprises and unpredictability. To be "little" in the eyes of the gospel is to trust in God and to live by faith. In the spirit of her "Little Way" (Fr: *petite voie*), St Thérèse de Lisieux wrote, "The only way to arrive to the furnace of divine love is to abandon ourselves like a child in his father's arms."[42]

> *What does a complicated spirituality look like to you?*
> *What does the spirituality of a "Little One" look like in practice? What characteristics of childhood (infancy) make for a good disciple?*
> *Jesus' prayer implies that God withholds His presence from the wise and the learned. When have you felt the presence of God being withheld from you in your life?*
> *How can you learn more about how to pray as a little one?*

Finally, after stating that He alone knows the Father, Jesus invites all people to come to Him and put on His yoke so as to find rest. This invitation makes some very important claims that would have appealed to people in Jesus' time because they searched for Wisdom as a valued asset. It is important to remember that knowledge of the Father is the source of Wisdom (Sir 24:23) and Jesus is now announcing Himself as the revealer of that knowledge. In the Old Testament and other Jewish writings, it is written that Wisdom can be found in a variety of areas including the Law of Moses (Sir 24:23), the larger universe (Wis 7:24–26), and even the Jerusalem Temple (Sir 24:8–12). In this passage, Jesus claims that He alone

---

42. Thérèse de Lisieux, "Manuscript B, 1r" in *Oeuvres complètes* (Lonrai: Cerf, DDB, 2011), p. 220.

is the source of true Wisdom. Because He is the Wisdom of God
incarnate, He doesn't just tell us about the Father. Rather, Jesus
actually shows us the Father! This is an important message for disciples who are trying to figure out the circumstances and events of
their lives. It teaches us that we can only correctly understand and
interpret the situations we face through the person of Jesus. Our
Lord then invites us to take on His "yoke". A yoke was a wooden
crossbeam that was laid across the necks of two oxen and attached
to a cart or plow; it also makes the oxen responsive to the direction
and discipline of the Master. It's that responsiveness to direction
and discipline that allowed the yoke to make the efforts of the
oxen more productive and effective. Thus, when we take on the
yoke of Jesus, we are not just following Jesus' teaching but are also
entering into a personal relationship of openness, dependence, and
surrender to the Lord. We are actually asking Jesus to give our lives
direction and to correct our faults and weaknesses. We are also
asking Him to guide our efforts so that we can cooperate with His
will and become more effective disciples.

The Lord wants us to have a relationship with Him by which
we willingly put on His yoke and seek His guidance and direction.
All we have to do is ask for it with sincerity, humility, and openness. When we allow our lives to be bound to the Lord in loving
trust, then we will cling to Him and follow His lead through our
successes and failures. What we face is not nearly as important as
with whom we face it. Everyone's life is influenced by something
and someone. For a disciple, relationship with Jesus must be the
primary influence (yoke) that gives guidance, direction, and discipline to us each day. Saint Paul taught in the New Testament that
wisdom was to be found in the Church (Col 1:18), which he could
say because he also taught that the Church is the Body of Christ
(1 Cor 12:27). This teaching means that the yoke of Jesus is communicated through the Church, empowered with the Holy Spirit,
to be Christ's instrument in the world.

> *What are some of the false yokes people are willing to put
> on today that lead them into error?*
> *When you think of following Jesus, do you think more of
> obedience to a set of teachings or to a deep trust in a com-
> mitted relationship with the Living God?*

Committed disciples are usually very active people. What is the "rest" you think Jesus offers us if we accept His yoke? Sometimes we seek the yoke of Jesus most readily when we are tired and disappointed by the misguidance of false yokes. What has that moment looked like in your life? When and why did you decide to seek God's direction rather than the direction of others trying to lead, guide, and discipline you?

Fifteenth Sunday in Ordinary Time

Our Scripture passage for this Sunday comes from the Gospel of Matthew 13:1–23. This reading contains the familiar parable of the Sower and the Seed and includes an extended reflection on the various types of soil that possess differing degrees of fertility, receptivity, and potential for growth. This parable offers a challenging teaching to us as disciples so that we might strive to be the good soil in which the Word of God can take root and grow to maturity.

Jesus begins the parable by describing the action of the sower who scatters seed in all types of soil. There are various ways to understand this action of the sower. Some would consider it wasteful or careless to toss seed where it has little or no chance of growing. However, that action is one of the important points Jesus wants to make. Our Lord wants to emphasize that God is so generous with His Word that He offers it everywhere and to everyone, even when there is little hope of it taking root, growing to maturity, and producing a harvest. Indeed, God is generous and merciful in ways that far exceed our human capacity to understand or our ability to imitate. Most of us would not waste our time or effort on causes that have little chance of success, but God's ways are not our ways. The Lord is willing to invest deeply in each of us regardless of our hardness of heart, resistance to cooperate, or lack of receptivity. God's surprisingly generous action invites us to reflect on how often we have been the recipients of grace even when we were least prepared for it, wanted it, or thought we deserved it. Yet God gave it anyway. Think of how many times God has planted His Word in us through the reading of Scriptures, the Eucharist and other sacraments, personal prayer, and graced moments in life, yet we were not open to receive it or give it a place in our hearts and souls. Think, too, of how often we have refused to imitate the generosity of God by reaching out to others and sharing with them the Word of God that has been planted in us.

> *How does God's generosity and mercy inspire you to recon-*
> *sider the ways in which you budget your efforts based on*
> *the probability of success?*
> *When were you least receptive to God's grace in your life,*
> *and how did the Lord continue to offer that grace to you*
> *despite your lack of receptivity?*
> *For whom is God asking you to be the sower of His Word*
> *at this time?*

The parable then continues to tell us about the different types of soil. This assessment invites us to consider how we have been each of these types of soil at various moments in our lives and what we can do to eagerly make ourselves "Good Soil". One thing to remember is that when the parable speaks about the seed being God's Word, we need to recall that Jesus is Himself the Word of God incarnate (John 1:1). Thus, the Word of God refers to the self-gift of the Lord in a variety of ways: Scripture, sacraments, spiritual communion in prayer, and so forth. With that understanding in mind, let's reflect on each of these types of soil.

The first type of soil is that of the pathway where the seed remains on the surface and is taken away by the birds. Jesus later explains privately to the disciples that the footpath is that person who hears without understanding. Therefore, the Word (seed) cannot enter into their worldview and is quickly rejected. The image of a footpath is a good one to describe this type of person. The reality is that there are lots of obstacles that can prevent a person from being able to receive and understand God's word. Sometimes it can be their own arrogance that prevents them from considering that God has a better plan for their life or a better answer for their life questions. Sometimes, too, it can be a person's life experience. The footpath is an area that is well-worn and hardened from years of people walking on it. Sometimes people's lives can become hardened and insensitive from years of being walked on by others as well. This experience can harden a person's heart and lead them to be distrusting of God and others in such a way that they are unreceptive to what is offered or unwilling to become vulnerable even to God. The good news is that the most hardened of soil still has potential if someone will cultivate it and protect it from being trampled underfoot. It is the responsibility of disciples to care for those who are being hardened by the circumstances of life and the indifferent actions of others. By caring for those who are being walked on, we demonstrate that we are credible witnesses of God's mercy and earn the trust of others. It is that trust that will allow them to become open and receptive to the Word of God. This is an important instruction that can guide us in the missionary work of evangelization. Sometimes we have to cultivate receptivity in the lives of others before we can effectively share the Word with them. Sometimes, too, we must conduct an interior assessment of our own presumptions and prideful attitudes so as to become aware of the ways in which we can be resistant to God's Word in our own lives.

> *What do you think causes hardness of heart in people's lives today and renders them unreceptive to God's Word? How can we as disciples help transform the "footpath" soil into good soil by tilling and protecting it?*
> *When in your life have you been the footpath, and what helped transform you from resistance to receptivity of God's Word?*

The second type of soil is that of the rocky ground where the soil is shallow. The seed may take root quickly but it is unable to survive the heat of tribulation and persecution. The word "root" is used in the New Testament as a metaphor to mean internal stability (v. Col 2:7 and Eph 3:17). Thus, the rocky soil represents that disciple who is eager and enthusiastic about things religious but lacks the internal stability to persevere in commitments of faith when those commitments require sacrifice. As Jesus said to His disciples at the Last Supper, "The spirit is willing, but the flesh is weak" (Mt 26:41). The challenge for this type of disciple is to grow in the virtues of perseverance and fortitude. These virtues require practice and maturity so as to perfect them in the Christian life. The first step in acquiring greater depth is to recognize that a person is shallow in their faith. This can be a humbling and even painful realization, yet it is the starting point for any real personal growth. This realization usually occurs when we meet someone who is a mature disciple and who shows us what an authentic life in Christ looks like. It is crucial that this humble awareness of a shallow faith be accompanied by the loving encouragement and acceptance of others so as to motivate a person to desire growth rather than to shy away from that growth due to insecurity, fear of inadequacy, or lack of guidance. As long as we pursue a faith based on external attractions, emotional rewards, or personal satisfaction, we will not be able to persevere in the face of sacrifice or persecution. The rocks that exist in the soil of our souls need to be removed so that the seed can take deeper root and we can gain an unshakable internal stability. Rocks are those things that lie beneath the surface and are resistant to the penetrating power of God's Word. These rocks can be complacency with sin, attitudes of selfishness or self-preservation, need for immediate gratification, desire for reward and recognition, or the need for others' approval. We will always be shallow disciples when we allow these attitudes and actions to remain in our lives.

> *What is the "heat" people experience today because of their faith, and how do you see people wither in their discipleship during difficult moments?*
> *What can a person do practically to remove the "stones" in their souls?*
> *When have you faltered in a commitment of faith because it required sacrifice or risked persecution?*
> *What can a faith community do to help people grow in fortitude and perseverance?*
> *When have you realized your own shallowness of faith, and who accompanied and encouraged you to pursue more profound mature growth?*
> *What resources helped you in that growth?*

Next, Jesus speaks about the seed that was sown among the thorns, which choked it as it grew. The thorns are then identified as those competing forces, which cause spiritual death, and include worldly anxiety and the lure of riches. In order to properly understand what Jesus is saying when He describes the thorny ground, it is helpful to remember the teaching of the 20th century theologian

Paul Tillich when he summarized faith as the experience of being grasped by an ultimate concern.[43] Tillich's insight cautions us that our ultimate concern will determine our life priorities and guide our decisions. If our ultimate concern is something other than God, then the message of the Gospel, the Word of God, will be perceived as a threat and eventually rendered powerless by our self-exemption from discipleship. Worldly anxiety and the lure of riches can include such things as social positioning, career climbing, materialism, consumerism, hedonism, and so forth. These attitudes describe a disciple whose greatest concerns are for the things of this life. Jesus teaches us that the values of the Kingdom of God are eternal, whereas the things of this world are temporary. When we make temporary things our ultimate concern, the seed of God's Word will be prevented from growing within us. That is because the values of the Gospel are oftentimes incompatible with the values of this world. In the Beatitudes, Jesus praises the poor in spirit, the merciful, the gentle, the peacemakers, the pure of heart, and those who hunger and thirst for righteousness (Mt 5:3–12). These are not the qualities that help a person get ahead in this life, but they are the qualities that witness the values of eternal life.

> *What ultimate concerns dominate people's lives today in such a way that those concerns can choke the Word of God (the message of the Gospel)?*
>
> *What teachings of the Gospel are most challenging to someone who is focused above all on the values of this world?*
>
> *What distracts your prayer at Mass causing you to be inattentive to the gift of God being offered in the Eucharist?*
>
> *Sometimes people try to find meaning for their lives through worldly anxiety and the lure of riches, but these things inevitably leave us feeling empty and unsatisfied. How can the Word of God be presented in a more attractive way for someone who is trapped in the addictive cycle of worldly pursuits?*
>
> *Who is someone you know who may be getting tired of the endless pursuit of worldly anxiety and the lure of riches?*

43. P. Tillich, *Dynamics of Faith*, Introductory Remarks (New York: Harper & Row, 1957).

Lastly, Jesus uses the image of the good soil that receives the word, understands it (that is, internalizes it and applies it to lived experience), and bears a harvest. The real focus of the good soil is not so much that it receives the seed, but that it bears fruit in an abundant harvest. The only verification that the soil is good is in the quality and magnitude of the harvest. This is a challenging insight for us as disciples because it is tempting to think of ourselves as good soil or to presume we are receptive to the Word of God. This teaching challenges us to consider that the real test for the quality of our discipleship is not so much in what we receive but in the quality and quantity of the harvest we are producing for the Lord. When asking ourselves the question, "Am I the kind of disciple described as being good soil?" we should first look at our lives and ask a different question, "What is the harvest I am producing?" The answer to that question will tell us what kind of soil we are like. Discipleship is not just about our openness to the Word of God or to how well we allow that Word to grow in us. Authentic discipleship is ultimately about the harvest we are producing for the Lord. To answer this question, we might reflect on the difference we are making in people's lives, the people we have inspired to grow in their faith, and how we have generously used God's gifts to us for the mission of the Gospel (Stewardship). How the Word affects us personally may be good and comforting, but how the Word affects others through us is ultimately the reason God sends His grace into our lives. Good soil returns a hundredfold harvest to the Lord from all that the Lord has done for us. Indeed, this is a very challenging teaching, which captures the import of the message Jesus wanted to share with those who would be His followers.

How does the emphasis on the quality and quantity of the harvest change the meaning of this parable for you?
What is the harvest you are returning to the Lord?
What does it look like in lived experience when people think that faith is only for their personal enrichment?
What does it look like in lived experience when people understand that an encounter with God is given to us so that through us it can be shared with others and multiplied?
How can a faith community help people become "good soil"?

Sixteenth Sunday in Ordinary Time

O ur Scripture passage for this Sunday comes from the Gospel of Matthew 13:24–43. In this section of Matthew's Gospel, our Lord continues to teach us about the Kingdom of God through the use of parables. As with all parables, the intended meaning is often found in the unexpected elements of surprise. Although these stories may seem like simple accounts from an agrarian culture, they are instructive and challenging for disciples of all times and offer several points for our prayer and reflection.

The first parable concerns that of a man who planted good seed in his field but while he slept an enemy came and planted bad seed. Rather than have his servants pull up the weeds, which might result in pulling up the wheat as well, the man instructs them to be patient and wait until the harvest time when the harvesters will be entrusted with the task of separating the good from the bad. There are distinct and precise details in this parable that will help us unlock its meaning and significance. First, it is interesting that the planting of the bad seed occurred while the man was asleep. In the New Testament, "sleep" is a metaphor for neglect (Mk 13:36, 1 Thes 5:6–8, and 1 Pt 5:8). This is an important caution for disciples. When we are not vigilant and discerning of what we allow to influence us, then bad seeds can get planted in our lives, our families, our marriages, our relationships, and so forth.

Second, when the parable goes on to speak about weeds, Jesus uses a term that specifically refers to a type of weed that looks very similar to wheat in its early stages of growth. Therefore, it is legitimately difficult to distinguish which one is a good plant and which one is a bad plant. That is a very good image for how evil works itself into our lives; it masks itself to look like something "good" in the moment and only reveals its devastating impact when we have complacently tolerated its growth for some time.

Third, the workers want to separate the good from the bad while the field is still growing, but the master commands them to be patient and tolerant. A time will come for separation, judgment, and punishment, but it is not their responsibility to carry out those actions in the present. Rather, it will be the responsibility of the harvesters (angels) to carry out this action in the future. This is an insightful teaching for us as disciples and reminds us that we are not given the power of judgment over others. As long as the field grows, there is always hope for conversion. The definitive separation of good and evil will occur only at the harvest. Thus, patience and tolerance are Christian virtues that teach us how to live in a world that does not always embrace or accept the Gospel. This parable is a timeless reminder to the Christian community that the Church will never be completely pure. Although we see the ongoing presence of evil in the world (and in our own world), this parable assures us that there will be a final judgment.

> *What are some of the evil seeds that get planted in people's lives and relationships today when they sleep and are not vigilant?*
> *When have you seen some evil tendency, desire, or intention mask itself to look like something good?*
> *How do we see today the tendency to make the Church a pure community of saints by removing anyone who sins?*
> *How do you reconcile the teaching against intolerance with the teaching on active Christian witness?*
> *It's interesting that Jesus never gave the Church the power to condemn or curse but only to forgive and bless. When do you feel tempted to condemn or judge others?*
> *How does this parable challenge you?*
> *Why do you think Jesus thought it was important to tell His disciples this parable?*

The second parable is of the mustard seed that becomes a tree. This is a really strange image to describe the Kingdom of God! The mustard bush was a common herb in the gardens of Palestine. It was never a tree and only grew to a moderate height (maybe 10–12 feet). That's what is so surprising about this parable. We must wonder why Jesus would use the image of a mustard bush to describe the

Kingdom of God. You see, kingdoms in the time of Jesus did use the image of trees for self-description, but they always referenced trees that were perceived as symbols of power like the Cedars of Lebanon or the mighty Oak. To use the image of a mustard bush would have been a joke. Perhaps that's precisely the point. Namely, what the world considers insignificant and powerless is, in fact, God's work that will grow to greatness. The Kingdom of God may be overlooked now because it is small and ordinary, but it will grow into a glorious reality. Oftentimes we accept God's reign in our lives in very small and relatively insignificant ways. By doing so, the Kingdom grows within us until we eventually accept God's reign in large ways. If we wait for great challenges before responding to the small challenges of faith, then greatness will never come. By responding to the small challenges and relatively insignificant moments of faithfulness, we are encouraging the Kingdom of God to grow to maturity.

> *What are some of the small ways in which you can allow faith to grow in your life today?*
> *What are some of the small ways in which you see God's will being accomplished in the world around you?*
> *What are the ways in which people are tempted to look for the great manifestations of the Kingdom of God such that they end up overlooking the small manifestations?*
> *Why do you think Jesus needed to remind the disciples of the importance of seeing the Kingdom of God in small ways rather than expecting it to always be manifest in great ways?*
> *In what ways can disciples in the Kingdom of God be tempted to imitate the standards of power and glory manifested by secular kingdoms in the world?*

Jesus may have had other reasons why He chose the image of a mustard tree for this second parable. The mustard bush was also a common wild plant along the Sea of Galilee where it grew to a relatively small height of four to six feet tall. It was known as being a hardy plant, good for the health that germinated quickly and was capable of taking over an area.[44] Certainly there are reasons why this plant would be an apt description for the Kingdom of God. Aside from the small beginnings and enormous growth referenced in the first explanation of this parable, the mustard bush was also an image of perseverance (hardy) in adverse situations, good for people (Gospel), spread quickly and was difficult to destroy or eradicate. Lastly, Jesus points out that the mustard bush also bears a certain harvest because its branches provide shelter for the birds. Sometimes we think of this image as referring to birds' nests elevated above the ground in the branches. However, the mustard bush more commonly provided shelter for birds that lived on the ground and sought protection under low-lying branches. These birds were considered to be more vulnerable than others because they could not fly away in time of danger. This final insight points to the fruit the Church bears when it cares for the poor and vulnerable in our world as well. It is the harvest of charity that is a necessary sign of authentic faith and mature discipleship. The mustard bush may look healthy and vibrant, but it is only of value as it provides protection, security, and benefit for others. Such charity may not mirror the powerful kingdoms of the world, but it is a manifestation of God's reign.

> *What quality of the mustard seed do you think most motivated Jesus to use it as an image of the Kingdom of God?*
> *How can disciples be tempted to be content with their growth and stop short of producing a harvest of charity?*
> *In what ways do you think the description of a mustard bush by Pliny the Elder most accurately describes the Christian disciple (for example, "hardy", "good for health", "spreads quickly", "invasive", and "tenacious")?*
> *Most people today are not very familiar with mustard bushes; if Jesus were to use a more contemporary image to communicate to us the same analogy for the Kingdom of God, what do you think it would be and why?*

The third parable is about a woman who hides leaven in three measures of flour. Three measures of flour is a huge amount. It would

---

44. Pliny the Elder, *Natural History*, 78 AD. See the edition of Baldwin and Cradock, London, 1928.

be the equivalent of about fifty pounds! She is preparing a meal for a lot of people. Actually, she's preparing food for a great banquet: the banquet of the Kingdom of God. The surprising element of this parable is that she uses leaven in a positive way. Leaven (yeast) in the Jewish tradition and in the New Testament was traditionally a symbol for corruption, arrogance and pride (Ex 12:15–20, 23:18, 34:25, Lev 2:11, 6:10, Mt 16:6, 1 Cor 5:6–8, Gal 5:9). By using this image, Jesus is teaching us that God can even use human weaknesses to bring about His Kingdom. That is a powerful message! God used, for example, the ambition of Ignatius of Loyola to lead him to seek eternal greatness in God's glory (Lt: *Ad maiorem Dei gloriam*). God used the youthful arrogance of Francis of Assisi to lead him to detachment from worldly concerns. God was even able to transform Paul of Tarsus from one who was filled with zeal to persecute Christians into someone who was filled with zeal to promote the Gospel (cf. Acts 9:1–19). Also, note that the woman hid the leaven in the flour. People are usually described as placing it in flour rather than hiding it. Our Lord is very clear in telling us that she hid it. That is because the Kingdom of God remains hidden to those who do not seek it, but to those of faith, the Kingdom of God is visible and active in the world and will grow to produce a huge result from a small beginning. Indeed, in the Kingdom of God, the Lord can use even our arrogant, prideful, and corrupt actions to accomplish His will. Saint Paul captured this truth well when he wrote, "Where sin abounds, grace abounds much more" (Rom 5:20).

How have you seen God use tendencies of human weakness, failure, or corruption as the means of accomplishing His grace and rule in people's lives?

When have you turned to the Lord in a moment of personal failure to surrender to God's will in your life?

When have you been surprised to discover God in unexpected places and circumstances of your life?

Why do you think Jesus needed to remind the disciples that the Kingdom of God is both present in the form of "leaven" and "hidden"?

Seventeenth Sunday in Ordinary Time

Our Scripture passage for this Sunday comes from the Gospel of Matthew 13:44–52. In this section, Jesus teaches three more parables to communicate the mystery of the Kingdom: the Buried Treasure, the Pearl of Great Price, and the Dragnet. Each of these parables offers us a challenging teaching on discipleship and is meant to encourage our total irrevocable commitment to the Lord, as well as govern and focus our missionary outreach to others.

The first parable concerns that of the man who accidentally finds a treasure buried in a field. This was territory that he had most likely walked over many times without realizing what was right beneath his feet. Then one day he suddenly discovers the treasure that has been there all along, and when he does, he commits all his resources to acquiring that treasure as his own. The experience of stumbling upon buried treasure continues to happen in our world today as we occasionally read stories of people discovering a treasure trove of ancient coins buried in various locations. These discoveries occur because the practice of burying valuables was a common method of protecting them in the ancient world especially during times of political or military uncertainty. This is a wonderful teaching for all of us who can so easily take our blessings for granted. All too often, we pass by buried treasure every day in the many blessings of family and friends that surround us. Sometimes we only appreciate the treasure we have when we lose it. Every now and then we are given the grace to see things in our lives in a new way so as to appreciate the extraordinary in the ordinary. When these moments occur, we sometimes wonder how we could have missed, overlooked, or taken for granted such a valuable blessing. Suddenly, all our priorities change and we understand what is really important. The greatest treasure we can rediscover is that God loves us, God is with us, and God forgives us. That is the Good News Jesus came to bring through His life and ministry. When we discover the reality of God's love, we will do whatever it takes to have that loving relationship. In such a relationship, we treasure what God treasures and so the Kingdom becomes realized in our midst. The man's action of selling all he has in order to acquire the field with the buried treasure exemplifies the total commitment God desires of all disciples who pursue the Kingdom. It is important to note that we are told the man was joyful when he made that total commitment. This response means that the man focused his attention on what he had gained rather than on what he had sold in order to acquire the treasure. Joy is not always our response when we are asked to make an encompassing commitment to God that requires sacrifice. The man's joy invites us to examine those inordinate attachments that prevent us from making an all-encompassing commitment to God and willingly, even joyfully, sacrificing for the sake of that Kingdom.

> *What are some of the treasures that people overlook in their lives today?*
> *What familiar things in your life have you come to see in a new way and to value as great treasure after having taken them for granted?*
> *What experiences led you to this realization?*
> *The man in the parable committed everything in his life to obtain that treasure. For what have you sacrificed most everything in your life?*
> *When and how have you come to realize God's love for you, and when have you made a complete and irrevocable commitment to the Lord in response to His love?*
> *When has a commitment of faith caused you sadness because of what it cost you?*

The second parable concerns that of a man who is specifically looking for, and finds, a really valuable pearl. Like the previous parable, the finding of the pearl requires that the man sell all he has in order to purchase this one, really valuable pearl. Unlike the man in the previous parable, however, he does not stumble upon the pearl by accident. Instead, he is specifically searching for something and knows it when he sees it. That, too, is like the Kingdom of God. It is helpful to know what we are looking for in order to recognize it and respond to it. The Gospels relate various scenes in the life of Jesus to help us see what the Kingdom of God is like and so to better recognize opportunities and experiences of the Kingdom in our own lives. Because the Kingdom of God requires our total commitment, we cannot have the Pearl of Great Price unless we are willing to let go of all competing priorities and values. That means we cannot obtain the Kingdom unless we are willing to let go of sinful attitudes or actions of greed, selfishness, and so forth. Letting go of what we are holding on to is a necessary requirement to obtain what we are searching for.

> *What is the treasure you are looking for in your life right now?*
> *What treasure do you think Jesus wants you to seek?*
> *What is worth the commitment of your whole life?*
> *When have you found what you were looking for and made a radical commitment to obtain it?*
> *What is the Lord asking you to let go of in order to whole-heartedly accept His reign in your life?*
> *What parts of your life do you try to separate from God's reign?*

The final parable concerns that of the Dragnet being swept in the sea that is filled with all kinds of fish. Only when the net is full is it time to separate the good from the bad catch of fish. When Matthew tells us that the bad are to be thrown out, he uses a word that really means "rotten" and is used elsewhere in his Gospel to describe the evil deeds (rotten fruit) of people (Mt 7:17–18 and Mt 12:33). Thus, the "bad fish" are known to be such based on their deeds.

There are two points for us in this parable. The first point is that judgment and condemnation are not our responsibilities. Like the parable from last week's Gospel passage about the weeds among the wheat, the role of judgment and condemnation is always reserved to the Lord and His angels. The responsibility of the Church, and of disciples, is to welcome and encourage all people to grow deeper in authentic faith and to pray for conversion, reconciliation, and repentance.

The second point is that judgment is based on whether we have become rotten in our deeds (bearing bad fruit) or whether our deeds are good in the eyes of God. It is difficult to remain pure when we are surrounded by corruption and rotten deeds. Sometimes we can wonder if it's worth the effort to live a life of faithfulness and sacrifice when others seem to be doing well while living a life that is contrary to the values of the Gospel. This parable is for us in those moments of question or doubt. The challenge for disciples is to live in a world filled with corrupt deeds but not to be corrupted by what surrounds us. Rather, we are to show to those bearing rotten fruit an attractive life of focused discipleship that is willing to commit all to the person of Jesus and that finds joy in the Gospel.

This is the same joy of the man who buys the field with the buried treasure. By doing so, we clearly distinguish what is "good" from what is "bad" while inviting others to discover the same treasure we have found. That treasure is the gift of an enduring, committed, loving relationship with God. When the net is raised out of the water, what a great thing it would be for all the fish to be good! The parable of the Dragnet reminds us that the basis of judgment will not be appearance or words or external religiosity; rather, the basis of judgment will be whether or not we have allowed ourselves to be caught by the Lord and whether our deeds are found to be good in His eyes.

When have you seen otherwise religious people do rotten things?

What thoughts delude people into thinking their actions don't matter when it comes to God's judgment?

Sometimes we are focused more on who is next to us in the net than our own lives and how we will be judged before the Lord. How does this parable cause you to reconsider your own need for conversion?

When have you been tempted to follow the example of others who seem to get ahead by their rotten deeds?

How can a faith community help people want to persevere in good deeds when there are so many bad examples around us?

Jesus ends this section on the Parables of the Kingdom with an instructive teaching concerning what it means to be a wise and a learned scribe. He wants us to be disciples who are able to appreciate what is good about both the "old" and the "new" regarding matters of faith. When it comes to God's action in the world, we can anticipate that the Lord will always be consistent with His previous self-revelation, but we should not expect that God will always conform to previous self-revelation. That is a complicated way of saying that the same God continues to reveal Himself in new ways. The example of the learned scribe encourages us to be people who are always looking for God's presence in new ways while not losing sight of what the Lord has already revealed. Thus, we are to be people deeply rooted in Scripture and Tradition yet open to the Lord's presence in surprising and enlightening ways. It was specifically a lack of openness to the Lord's presence in new and surprising ways that caused the Jewish leaders of Jesus' time to reject Him and His teaching. On the other hand, it was the openness of the disciples that allowed them to recognize, accept, and respond to the revelation of God in Jesus. Our Lord wants us to follow the example of the first disciples who were always open to God's revelation however the Lord wished to accomplish it.

> *What temptations exist in the Church today to value only what is "old"?*
> *What temptations exist in the Church today to value only what is "new" and to dismiss what is old?*
> *How do we try to protect our own comfort, control, and security by resisting new challenges in life?*
> *What values or qualities do we need in order to embrace our contemporary challenges without compromising our Christian principles and ideals?*

EIGHTEENTH SUNDAY IN ORDINARY TIME

Our Scripture passage for this Sunday comes from the Gospel of Matthew 14:13–21. This is the famous scene of the multiplication of the loaves and fishes, and it was obviously an important teaching in the life of the early Church because there are six similar accounts in the four Gospels (Mt 14:13–21, Mk 6:35–44, Lk 9:12–17, Jn 6:1–15, Mt 15:32–39 and Mk 8:1–10). Indeed, this passage has much to say about the life of discipleship and how we cooperate with the Lord's grace so as to meet the overwhelming needs we face each day.

When reading any biblical text, it is always important to place it in the context of what preceded it. If we look at the verses immediately before this passage, we read the account of the beheading of John the Baptist at Herod's banquet. This context tells us that the banquet of Jesus (feeding of the 5,000) is meant to be understood in stark contrast to the banquet of Herod. Herod's banquet was a manifestation of arrogance, conspiracy, and murder. Jesus' banquet was a manifestation of healing, faithful obedience, and caring for others through the sharing of food. What dramatically different experiences! Indeed, the Christian banquet of the Eucharist, of which the multiplication of the loaves and the fishes is a foreshadowing, is always meant to be a counter-cultural sign of the Kingdom in the midst of the world. When we come to Mass, we do not seek to replicate the experience of secular society (egoism, materialism, consumerism, and so forth) but to replace it with the Christian experience of the Kingdom (communion, fraternal caring, surrender to God's grace, and so on). Instead of wanting the Church to be like the world, we should want the world to be like the Church.

How does the Church today witness the counter-cultural values of the Kingdom of God?

*What influences or attitudes of secular society can infiltrate
and negatively affect our celebration of the Mass?
What situations exist in the world today, which are des-
perately lacking a Christian response, and what should be
that response?*

Notice also how Jesus and the disciples respond differently to the
needs of the crowds. When the crowds approach Jesus with the
burden of their suffering, Jesus responds by helping (healing) them
and so they remain close to him. When Jesus meets people in
need, He establishes communion with them. The disciples, on the
other hand, wanted to send the crowd away and let them care for
themselves. Our Lord corrects the disciples' errant desire and by
caring for the crowds Himself is offering us a lesson in discipleship. This is one of the first lessons of this passage, and it invites
us to reflect on how we respond to those in need around us. Jesus
saw people in need as opportunities for ministry; the disciples
saw people in need as burdens to be avoided and dismissed. The
Acts of the Apostles teaches us that charitable outreach for those
in need was a distinguishing quality of the early Church (cf. the
relief efforts in Acts 4:32–37, 6:1–6, and 11:27–30). The first lesson
of this passage, then, is that disciples should welcome those who
come to them regardless of their need and not turn them away. For
the Church to reflect the hospitality of Jesus, we must learn to see
the needs of others as opportunities for our ministry rather than
burdens to be avoided or dismissed. Saint Paul teaches that we are
all one in Christ (Gal 3:28) and that the sufferings of one become
the sufferings of all, just as the blessings and joys of one become
the blessings and joys of all (1 Cor 12:26).

*How can we be tempted today to turn away those in need
because we see them as burdens rather than as opportunities for ministry?
How can we be tempted to rely on our own limited resources
rather than faithfully trust in God's eternal greatness working through us?
What are the common responses we experience when we
see others in need?*

Who has reached out and freely chosen to establish communion with you in your moment of need?

Next, the disciples present their small, inadequate ability to satisfy the crowd's hunger. They only have five loaves and two fishes. Had the disciples tried to feed the crowd with their own resources (separate from Jesus' action), then they would have been able to feed only five people. When they offer their meager, inadequate, and limited resources to Jesus, our Lord can do great things with them. Remember the expression: "The great temptation is to do nothing because we can only do a little." Don't give in to that temptation! When we offer to the Lord whatever small capability we have, God can do great things with it. The problem is that we oftentimes don't offer the Lord much to work with because we feel inadequate. This passage makes it clear that a life of discipleship is not focused on what we can do on our own but rather on what God can do with the life we offer Him. In her Nobel Prize lecture, Mother Teresa said,

> If we could only remember that God loves us, and I have an opportunity to love others as He loves me, not in big things, but in small things with great love, then Norway becomes a nest of love...[45]

God wants us to be His co-workers in ministry. God wants to act in and through us as His instruments. The Lord is always the source of a disciple's success, but the Lord works through the human resources we offer Him. The disciples needed to better understand that they are only instruments of God but not the source of God's gifts. The ministry of the Church depends upon God and is not defined or limited by the resources we muster. When disciples understand themselves as instruments rather than origins of all good gifts, then disciples will become more generous towards others and more trusting of God's providential grace. What God can do through us is infinitely greater than what we can do by ourselves.

When have you been presented with a need that you felt totally inadequate to fulfill?

---

45. Mother Teresa, "Nobel Prize Lecture" in *Nobel Lectures*, Peace 1971–1980, Editor-in-Charge Tore Frängsmyr, Editor Irwin Abrams (Singapore: World Scientific Publishing Co., 1997).

How do you identify with the disciples who present the small gifts they have?

When have you seen someone's simple efforts grow to have a huge impact?

In the celebration of the Mass, the moment of the Offertory (when the bread and wine are brought forward to the altar) is meant to be the moment when we prayerfully offer to the Lord our lives (symbolized by bread and wine) to be transformed so that we can become His presence in the world (just as the bread and wine become His presence, Body and Blood, in the Eucharist). What do you think God would do with your life this week if you really offered Him your heart, mind, soul, and strength?

How can a faith community fall into the trap of believing that the effectiveness of its ministry relies only on its physical resources rather than on the Lord?

Finally, we reflect on the interesting and often misunderstood statement of Jesus when He says, "Bring them here to me" in Matthew 14:18. This statement immediately follows the disciples' summary of their limited resources, so it is easy to presume that Jesus is speaking about the loaves and fishes when He says, "bring them here to me". However, the very next statement that follows our Lord's command says that Jesus ordered the crowd to be seated on the grass. This context has led some Scripture scholars to interpret the phrase "bring them here to me" to refer to the crowd rather than the loaves and fishes. While this point may seem insignificant at first, it is really a rather profound dynamic of discipleship in Matthew's Gospel. Discipleship is first and foremost based on the encounter with Jesus. Our Lord calls people to Himself and asks His disciples to bring others to Him. Jesus can effect great changes in people's lives when He meets them personally and directly. The disciples can't feed the crowds on their own, but Jesus can, and so the best thing they can do is bring the crowds to the Lord. The disciples can't heal the crowds on their own, but Jesus can, and so the best thing they can do is bring them to the Lord. This is a lesson in missionary discipleship. Instead of only telling people about Jesus, we are to bring people to Jesus. It is that personal encounter and connection that allows the Lord to work directly and intensely in people's lives. Disciples are to be intercessors and facilitators to help that encounter take place; they are not to insert themselves in the process as intermediaries who obstruct or prevent that encounter. Every time we meet someone who has spiritual hunger or spiritual need, we need to be reminded of the words of Jesus directing our efforts just as He did the efforts of the disciples in this passage: "Bring them here to me."

> *How can it be tempting for disciples to insert themselves in other people's faith journeys and end up becoming obstacles?*
> *Who is someone you know that is spiritually hungry or in spiritual need, and how can you bring them to Jesus?*
> *Who has introduced you to Jesus?*
> *Why is the personal encounter with Jesus such an important element in authentic discipleship?*
> *How do you foster your personal encounter with Jesus each day?*

As we close this reflection, we should remember some inspiring prayers that capture this teaching on the need to offer the Lord our lives so that He can work through us.

> *Take, O Lord, and receive*
> *All my memory, understanding,*
> *And entire will.*
> *All that I have and call my own,*
> *You have given it to me.*
> *To you, Lord, I return it.*
> *Everything is yours;*
> *Do with it what you will.*
> *Give me only your love and your grace.*
> *That is enough for me.*
>
> —St Ignatius of Loyola

Let nothing disturb you.
Let nothing frighten you.
All things pass.
God does not change.
Patience achieves everything.
Whoever has God lacks nothing.
God alone suffices.
Christ has no body on earth now
but yours;
no hand but yours;
no feet but yours;
Yours are the eyes
through which the compassion of Christ
must look out on the world.
Yours are the feet
with which He is to go about doing good. Yours are the hands
with which He is to bless His people.

— Attributed to St Teresa of Avila

How do these prayers challenge you in your discipleship?
What do you find attractive about praying these prayers?
How do you see each of these prayers as exemplifying the
teaching of this Gospel passage?

Nineteenth Sunday in Ordinary Time

Our Scripture passage for this Sunday comes from the Gospel of Matthew 14:22–33. It is the story of Jesus walking on the water towards the disciples in the boat and of Peter's faltering faith that causes him to sink into the stormy waves. This passage has much to teach us about discipleship and correct faith.

It is an interesting detail when Matthew tells us that Jesus forced the disciples to get in the boat and go without Him to the other side. This is the first time the disciples are sent without Jesus accompanying them. Note, too, that we are told Jesus was alone and by Himself on the land while the disciples were far from land. All these details emphasize the separation from Jesus being felt by the disciples. Then things get worse, as if mere separation isn't bad enough! In the midst of their aloneness, we are told that they are harassed (literally "tortured") by the sea and fighting contrary winds. These terms are very specific and refer to the situation the early Church faced when it was tortured and persecuted by pagan Rome as well as the struggles early Christians faced when they fought against the contrary forces of pagan culture. These details, and their relationship to the situation of the early Church, tell us that this is no ordinary storm. The fact that they are in a boat is symbolic as well since the boat was an early symbol for the Church itself. Today we still refer to the central part of a traditional church building as the "nave", a Latin word that means "boat". Then things still become worse! They come to the fourth watch of the night, which is the darkest hour of the entire night. It is then, in the darkest hour, at the most difficult time of struggle when they feel utterly alone and distanced from the Lord that Jesus comes to them. He has not abandoned them after all. He is with them just as was promised in Matthew 1:23 when He was announced as Emmanuel, a name that means "God with us". The situation of the disciples was no accident or error of judgment. Remember, Jesus forced them into it. Sometimes the trials we face teach us a lot about ourselves and God. Sometimes we only discover our potential when we have to utilize every resource for our survival. Sometimes it is in the midst of our darkest night and greatest feelings of abandonment that we realize God has been with us all along. The storms we face are both communal and personal. Sometimes we can actually blame God when we feel a sense of isolation and separation from the Lord's presence. Sometimes, too, we can feel like God has forced us into a situation where we are vulnerable and at risk. All these elements are present in this Gospel passage and should give us profound cause for reflection without dismissing such questions with superficial answers. Indeed, we cannot understand the meaning of this passage until we understand how these elements have taken place in our own lives as well.

> *What do you think is the good Jesus intended when He forced the disciples to get in the boat and face this situation while He remained on the land?*
> *When have you felt most separated from Jesus in your life?*
> *How are Christians tortured and harassed today?*
> *What are the contrary winds of our culture that fight against the values of the Gospel?*
> *How can the Church give people strength and encouragement in the midst of the storms we face?*
> *What has been the "darkest hour" in the Church's history?*
> *What has been the "darkest hour" in your life? Where was the Lord in the midst of it?*
> *How has Jesus come to you and given you strength when you least expected it? The disciples must have wondered why Jesus let them go through such a trial. For what painful trial or vulnerable situation in your life are you searching for a divine answer?*
> *It's interesting that the disciples cooperated with Jesus' command and actually got into the boat without Him; so often in our lives we refuse to follow when the Lord leads us into vulnerability. What risk of faith is the Lord asking you to take in your life now?*

The second significant element of this passage is in the experience of Peter. Peter first expresses his doubt when he hears Jesus announce Himself by stating "I Am", which is the revealed divine name of God in Exodus 3:14. Peter responds to our Lord's revelation with an element of doubt when he said, "Lord, if it is you..." Peter doubted that Jesus could be present to him in such a troubling moment of life and expresses his doubt by using an expression similar to that employed by Satan when tempting the Lord in the desert ("if you are..." Mt 4:3). Peter's statement, then, is an effort to make the Lord prove Himself. Peter believed that God's presence should be manifested by a calm environment when our lives are peaceful and we are happy, secure, and carefree. Peter did not think that God's presence would be manifested in the midst of being tossed about, tortured, and our lives placed at risk. Peter doubted that the voice of Jesus could really be speaking to him in the midst of that boat caught in the storm. Peter then asks to walk on the waters like Jesus is doing. This is Peter's second doubt. He wants to do something that only God can do (walk on the waters). To "walk on the waters" was a symbol of triumph and a demonstration that one could overcome the forces of chaos. Rather than endure faithfully the storm he is facing, Peter reveals his desire to walk on the waters and show that he can conquer them and be unaffected by them. In response to Peter's doubtful question, Jesus says, "Come." This is not so much an invitation as it is a challenge. You see, Peter wanted to be "like God" and walk on the waters that were threatening him. Jesus wants Peter to realize his dependence on God rather than trying to be like God, and so Jesus invites Peter into a vulnerable state so he can know his need for a Savior and stop trying to be like God. It was not that Peter took his eyes off Jesus that caused him to sink but that he wanted proof of the presence of Christ and that's why he left the boat in the first place. Jesus calls this "little faith". Sometimes we can be like Peter and ask God to prove Himself because we doubt His presence in the midst of our life struggles as well. Sometimes we can think that we should be able to overcome all our life challenges and problems in spectacular ways as a witness of our discipleship. The reality is that our lives are filled with weakness, tragedy, and uncontrollable circumstances that sometimes make us feel like we are sinking. That's not a sign of our lack of faith, or of God's absence, but can be the motivation for us to call out to God as our Savior. Remember, Jesus can't be our Savior if we don't acknowledge our need for a Savior. Peter had to be brought to a desperate state before he called out to the Lord to be his Savior, and sometimes so do we.

> *When have you asked God for an opportunity that turned out to be a situation of distress rather than blessing (like Peter walking on the water)?*
> *When do you find yourself asking God for proof of His presence in your life or doubting God's presence in the midst of challenges?*
> *In what ways can we fall into the temptation to believe that being a disciple means we should be able to "walk on water" and be preserved from the challenges and weaknesses of human life?*
> *How has Jesus led you to need Him as your Savior?*
> *With what moment of Peter's experience do you most identify?*
> *How do you think Peter's attitude towards Jesus changed because of this experience?*
> *The Good News of this passage is that God will save us even when we have "little faith" if we call out for Him. No matter what mess we are in, Jesus wants to be our Savior. What keeps people from calling out for the Lord's saving grace in their lives?*

It is significant that the Gospel tells us Jesus took time to pray while the disciples were in the boat. This is the first time in Matthew's Gospel that we read about Jesus praying. While we do not know the content of our Lord's prayer at this moment, it is apparent that His prayer prepares Him for what is about to take place. As we saw in the preceding reflections, Jesus is preparing to reveal Himself as the presence of God to the disciples. The Lord's prayer prepares Him for this revelation by establishing communion with the Father. The disciples were not at prayer, and so their absence of communion left them frightened, feeling alone, and doubting our Lord's revelation. The prayer of Jesus was not a brief experience. Rather, it was an extensive time that lasted all night until the fourth watch (between 3:00 and 6:00 a.m.). As the disciples are entering more deeply into fear, Jesus is entering more deeply into communion with the Father and clarity of His identity as the great I AM. This insight into the effect of prayer should inspire and motivate us as disciples to seek prolonged communion with God, especially when we feel distanced and facing the storms of life. Our Lord's prayer lasted for hours and that, too, is instructive for us that we should not expect immediate results for our efforts. Prayer is not so much about giving God our grocery list of needs as it is about being drawn into the Divine Presence and being conformed to the Divine Will. Ultimately, we are told the content of Jesus' prayer is when He prays in the Garden of Gethsemane (Mt 26:39–42). Our Lord makes it clear that prayer is not about convincing God to do our will but about motivating us to do the Father's will.

> *How differently do you think Peter would have responded to the situation of the storm and darkness had he spent the time in prayer like Jesus did?*
> *Who is experiencing storms in their life now, and how can you assist them with your prayer?*
> *Jesus prepared for His moment of profound self-revelation by immersing Himself in prayer. Before what moments do you pray most intensely?*
> *Why do you pray? What is the difference between prayers and prayer?*
> *How can you deepen your prayer life and learn to pray in new and more profound ways?*

The final part of this passage is the experience of the disciples paying homage to Jesus. Despite the reality of their little faith, the experience of the storm and our Lord's revelation has actually deepened their awareness. They have come to know Jesus in a new way because of His revelation in the midst of the storm and walking on the waters. Jesus is with them once again, and together they reach their destination in safety. The experience of finding God in the midst of adverse conditions and difficult situations is meant to change us as well. We are called to be people of deeper faith in Jesus who trust His presence regardless of our experience and who do not insist that His presence be manifested through a life of calm and smooth sailing. The great saints understood that the presence of God in their lives was not intended to preserve them from challenges but to accompany them in the midst of difficulties. A spiritual father of the fourth century wrote, "Do not pray for the fulfillment of your wishes, for they may not accord with the will of God. But pray as you have been taught, saying: Thy will be done in me (cf. Lk 22:42). Always entreat Him in this way—that His will be done. For He desires what is good and profitable for you, whereas you do not always ask for this." [46]

> *Who is someone you know that has grown deeper in faith because of a trial they have experienced?*
>
> *What are the significant experiences of your life that have helped you grow deeper in faith?*
>
> *What have you come to know about Jesus because of the trials you have experienced?*
>
> *How does it change your prayer to call Jesus your Savior after having passed through some of life's storms?*
>
> *The disciples gave homage to Jesus, which means that they submitted their lives to Him through the action of kneeling. How do you give homage to Jesus in your life?*
>
> *The voice of Satan tempted Jesus in desert with the words "If you are the Son of God..." Peter tempted Jesus on the sea with similar words when he said, "If it is you..." With what language do you find Satan trying to tempt you by questioning the presence or action of God in your life?*

---

46. Evagrius, "Prayer" in *The Philokalia*, Vol. 1, originally compiled by Nikodimos of the Holy Mountain and Makarios of Corinth, Ed. by G. Palmer, P. Sherrard, and K. Ware (London: Faber and Faber, 1979).

Twentieth Sunday in Ordinary Time

Our Scripture passage for this Sunday comes from the Gospel of Matthew 15:21–28. In this reading, we hear of Jesus encountering the Canaanite woman who seeks her daughter's healing. The discourse between Jesus and the woman may strike us as awkward and even offensive. However, at the end of the passage, the Lord proclaims her to be a person of "great faith". This is a distinction our Lord rarely gives, and we should pay close attention to this passage because it is an instruction for us in how we can be people of great faith as well.

It is interesting to note that sickness provided the motivation for the woman's encounter with Jesus. We may not often think about it, but sometimes in our lives it is a moment of tragedy or need that brings us to prayer as well. Every situation in life is an opportunity for prayer. The woman could have stayed at home and fostered anger and resentment at God for her daughter's affliction, but she didn't. Instead, she did something. She actively sought out Jesus and brought her request for healing before Him. The Lord wants us to see in our moments of distress an invitation to prayer and deepened relationship as well. When Jesus was in distress in the Garden of Gethsemane, He prayed to the Father, and in doing so, He gave us a model of faith to follow. There are various forms of prayer: praise, thanksgiving, adoration, intercession, expiation (seeking forgiveness), and petition. They can be communal (Liturgical) or personal. Different forms of prayer are appropriate for different moments in our lives, but some form of prayer is appropriate for every moment in our lives. Note, too, that the woman's request actually leads to a conversation (relationship) with Jesus in which both parties speak and both parties are changed by their exchange. The word "conversation" implies the "conversion" of those who participate and is different from a monologue, in which only one person speaks, or a debate in which two people speak, but neither is changed by the interaction. In order for prayer to be a true conversation that is the means of our conversion, we must participate by both our speaking and our listening. In fact, it is the act of listening that is often more important and powerful than the act of speaking. This insight has much to say about the way disciples pray.

> *What need do you currently have that the Lord is waiting for you to bring to prayer?*
> *Which form of prayer do you practice the least?*
> *Which form of prayer do you practice the most? What changed in the woman through this conversation of praying faith?*
> *What do you think changed in Jesus through this conversation of praying faith (if anything)?*
> *When you pray, is it a monologue, a debate, or a conversation?*
> *In your prayer, do you attempt to change God's mind or pray for God's will to be done?*
> *When do you find it most difficult to pray for God's will to be done?*

Next in the conversation with the woman, Jesus stresses that His mission is primarily to the lost sheep of the House of Israel as opposed to the Gentiles represented by the Canaanite woman. He then makes a striking statement when He says, "It is not right to take the food of children and give it to the dogs." That statement probably disturbs us because it appears to be a callous, indifferent and even insulting comment. There is another way to understand it, however, and this alternate interpretation helps to unlock the faith significance of this exchange. The word that Jesus uses for "dog" (Greek *kynarion*) refers more to a "puppy" or "household dog" in Gentile cultures as opposed to a wild or stray animal. Thus, Jesus is acknowledging that the woman is related to the House of Israel in some way but that His mission is first to the children of that house. Our Lord has given her a place in the House of Israel similar to that of the household pet. It is remarkable that the woman actually accepts whatever place the Lord gives her so long as she can be related to His ministry and a member of His household.

She then reminds the Lord that even the household dogs are fed from the scraps that fall from the table of the children. It is helpful to remember that in the verses immediately preceding this passage (Mt 15:1–20), Jesus' teaching and example were offered to the House of Israel but not accepted by the Pharisees. This means that the "food" (ministry) already offered to the children was not being eaten and was even being discarded. This is why the woman can now ask for the leftovers of our Lord's grace and favor. Jesus praised her response as an act of great faith. Sometimes it takes great faith for us to accept the place in life the Lord assigns for us. Sometimes we want to occupy a privileged place in God's plan rather than to accept a humble role. It is remarkable that the woman was happy to accept whatever place the Lord assigns to her so long as she could be recognized as part of God's plan. It is within her role in God's plan (the household dog) that she perseveres in her petition for God's blessing, her trust in God's goodness, and her faith in Jesus' power to heal her daughter. In this conversation, then, Jesus is acknowledging a place for Gentiles in God's plan of salvation.

> *Who do we consider to be "outsiders" to God's grace today?*
> *Who petitions you for your time, energy, or resources without a right for such a request?*
> *What are the scraps that fall from the table of your time, talent, and treasure that can help others?*
> *When have you felt like God has not given you the place in life you want?*
> *What qualities does a person need in order to faithfully and joyfully accept the place in life God gives them?*
> *How would you have responded to Jesus' words if you were the Canaanite woman?*
> *Why do you think the Canaanite woman persevered in her conversation?*
> *The woman in the story had no right to God's grace and favor, but she sought it with perseverance and faith nonetheless. What makes us think we deserve God's grace and favor?*

When Jesus proclaims the woman as having "great faith", we should realize that He is holding her up as an example for us to follow. You see, she stands in stark contrast to Peter who was identified as having "little faith" just a few verses before in Matthew 14:31. Peter showed his little faith by doubting the presence of God in the midst of his trial. The Canaanite woman showed great faith by her persistent struggle in prayer and her unwavering confidence in Jesus' ability to heal her daughter. Peter showed his little faith by questioning the reality of Jesus. The Canaanite woman showed her great faith by confessing Jesus with the title "Son of David". Peter was concerned for himself and his own safety. The Canaanite woman approached the Lord on behalf of her daughter and sought the wellbeing of another. Even in the face of seeming rejection, she continued to seek the Lord's grace and favor. Indeed, her faith was great, and based on that faith, Jesus granted her daughter's healing. As disciples, we are called to be like the Canaanite woman and come to the Lord day and night with petitions for those in need. So many situations in our world today require our prayers, and sometimes people have no one to pray for them except us. God wants us to acknowledge our need for Him and our dependence on Him; prayer is one important way in which we profess our faith in God and our love for others.

> *For whom do you pray?*
> *When do you pray for those who have no one else to pray for them?*
> *When have you stopped praying for a particular need, and why?*
> *Who has prayed for you in a time of need?*
> *How has your prayer been an expression of your faith in God and your love for others?*
> *Who do you refuse to pray for?*
> *It's interesting that the woman approached Jesus not for her own need but for that of another (her daughter). Why do you think faith becomes great when we look out for others' needs and not just our own?*

Prayer for Unity of Will with God (St Louise de Marillac)

O God, my spiritual and corporal existence is Yours since
You are my Creator.
But my will is mine because You have created it as free and
want it to remain such.
However, I am free to offer it in homage to You
and to make it a sacrifice of praise and honor to You.
Hence, I give my will entirely to You, so that it no longer
belongs to me.
Henceforth, I must be careful to let nothing proceed from
my heart
that would be unworthy of You.
I must exert constant vigilance over my will
to avoid taking away from You what is truly Yours.
Amen.

Twenty-First Sunday in Ordinary Time

O
ur Scripture passage for this Sunday comes from the Gospel of Matthew 16:13–20. This is the famous passage in which Peter professes the identity of Jesus and receives the commission to be the "Rock" on which the Church is founded. The dialogue between Jesus and Peter offers several points for our reflection as disciples who are called to profess our faith in Jesus as well.

It is interesting that Jesus first asks His disciples a question about popular opinion when He inquires, "Who do people say that the Son of Man is?" There are a variety of opinions about who Jesus might be, but none of them are necessarily true. Finally, Jesus poses the question as an address to the disciples themselves when He asks, "Who do you say that I am?" That is a personal and decisive moment of faith. It is no longer a matter of public opinion about what others are saying; now it is who the disciples themselves believe Jesus to be. It is in the midst of that confusion of faith and diverse opinions that Peter clarifies what is true and trustworthy as he confesses Jesus to be "the Christ, the Son of the Living God". Throughout the centuries disciples have continued to face moments when there have been questions of faith and Christian life (morals) as well. Certainly we experience such questions in our time. People today search for truth just as much as ever with the age-old questions, "What can I believe?" "What should I do?" and "What can I hope for?" When faced with such uncertainties, we should seek true faith by listening to the voice of Peter articulating for us the truth about Jesus even as he clarified it for the other disciples at Caesarea Philippi. One way in which Catholics (especially) hear the voice of Peter today is through the successor of Peter, the Bishop of Rome. An important role of the Holy Father (Pope) is to preserve the faith of the Church from error. Questions such as "Who is Jesus?" "What is the way to salvation?" "What should a disciple do?" and so forth, are constantly being raised in today's culture of secularism, relativism, and religious pluralism. Many of the common opinions on these issues are simply not true. For Christians, truth is not determined by public opinion but by divine revelation. When disciples allow their faith to be formed by public opinion, they have surrendered themselves to the whims of passing times.

> *Where do you go to find truth when you encounter questions of faith in your life?*
> *What is something the Holy Father, the Successor of Peter, has said or done today to bring clarity to the Christian faith for you?*
> *Why is it important to distinguish between the Holy Father speaking with the authority of faith as opposed to expressing his personal opinion?*
> *How do you draw that distinction?*
> *What are the current issues of faith or morals that need to be clarified through the voice of Peter in the Church today?*
> *How do you see erroneous popular opinion negatively influencing Christians today and eroding their faith?*

Peter's answer to Jesus' question wasn't the end of that conversation of faith. Rather, it was really the beginning. In response to that correct answer of faith, Jesus does two things. First, our Lord changes the name of "Simon" to "Peter" (Rock). Second, Jesus gives Peter a role in the life of the Church. This dynamic is teaching us important insights for our discipleship. The first insight teaches us that every conversation of faith in which we come to know and confess Jesus more clearly should change us as well. When we profess Jesus as Lord, we are acknowledging that we are His subjects and not the subjects of any temporal authority or worldly power. When we profess Jesus as Savior, we are acknowledging ourselves as sinners who need deliverance and redemption from the oppressive forces of sin that enslave and deceive us. When we profess Jesus as creator, we are acknowledging that everything we are is a gift from Him, even life itself, and that we are only stewards of the many blessings God has entrusted to us. When we profess Jesus to be the Good Shepherd, we are acknowledging that we are His sheep and that we willingly refuse to follow anyone else who tries to lead us astray. The important point is this—anything we say about Jesus changes us because of our relationship to Him. The beauty of prayer is that we come to know ourselves more clearly as we come to know Jesus more clearly.

> *How has your growth in Christian faith changed you?*
> *Which title of Jesus do you find most appealing and what does that say about you?*
> *Who has noticed a change in you as a result of your ongoing conversation with Christ in discipleship?*

The second insight is revealed when Jesus gives Peter a distinctive role (ministry) in the life of the Church. Specifically, Jesus assigns Peter the role of being the Chief Steward as the one who holds the keys to the Kingdom. He is also to be the one who "binds and looses", which was a rabbinical term used to describe the work of interpreting the Torah (Scriptures) and setting rules for the community. In short, Peter's confession of faith ended up giving Peter both a new identity and a new mission. The same commissioning is meant to happen for us as well every time we deepen our relationship of love and knowledge for the Lord. We all have a role to play in the ministry of the Church. If we are sitting on the sidelines watching "Church" happen but are not involved in it, we haven't been listening very well in our prayer. God has a mission for each of us in the work of the Gospel. To know Jesus is to work for Jesus. If our faith is only a matter of intellectual assent or emotional feeling but not active engagement in the work of the Gospel, we have not yet discovered the fullness of relationship to which Christ is calling us. It is when our faith motivates us to mission that we can be confident of the authenticity of our encounter with the Lord. This externally manifested change in both identity and ministry are signs of authentic religious experience.

> *How has your involvement in mission increased along with your growth in faith?*
> *How have you encountered the Lord by being involved in a particular work of ministry?*
> *What is a work of ministry you think God is calling you to, but you don't know how to respond?*

*Why is it that some people seem indifferent or deaf to hear-
ing the Lord's guidance in a conversation of faith?*

Finally, Jesus cautions Peter to not misunderstand the nature of
His Messiahship. The reality is that the Church will be caught up
in an ongoing struggle with the forces of evil (Hades). This struggle
will continue throughout history, and there will never be a perfect
time in this world when there are no forces opposing Christian
disciples. We may face this struggle constantly but always with the
assurance that the forces of evil will not prevail. The struggle may
endure, but the ultimate victory has already been accomplished
by Jesus in His triumph over the forces of sin and death through
the resurrection. As the common expression states, the war may
be won but the battles continue.

*When has the Church faced the greatest threat from the
powers of evil?*
How does the power of evil threaten the Church today?
What are the temptations Evil uses to erode people's faith?
*Why do you think Evil continues to attack the Church even
though Jesus accomplished a definitive victory through His
cross and resurrection?*
*How does our Lord's insight about the ongoing struggle
with Evil give you insight, hope, and encouragement as a
disciple?*

There are several quotes from C. S. Lewis' writing entitled *The
Screwtape Letters* that offer particular insights into this conversation between Peter and Jesus. This insightful writing explains how
Evil tries to lead us away from God. In order to understand these
quotes, it is important to remember that the statements are part
of an exchange between two agents of evil discussing how to lead
humans astray: the tempter, Wormwood, and his uncle, Screwtape.

[M]an has been accustomed, ever since he was a boy, to having
a dozen incompatible philosophies dancing about together
inside his head. He doesn't think of doctrines as primarily
"true" or "false," but as "academic" or "practical," "outworn"
or "contemporary," "conventional" or "ruthless." Jargon, not
argument, is your best ally in keeping him from the Church.
Don't waste time trying to make him think that materialism

is true! Make him think it is strong or stark or courageous—
that it is the philosophy of the future. That's the sort of thing
he cares about.

It is funny how mortals always picture us as putting things
into their minds: in reality our best work is done by keeping
things out.

It does not matter how small the sins are provided that their
cumulative effect is to edge the man away from the Light and
out into the Nothing. Murder is no better than cards if cards
can do the trick. Indeed the safest road to Hell is the gradual
one—the gentle slope, soft underfoot, without sudden turn-
ings, without milestones, without signposts.[47]

Which quote from C. S. Lewis' The Screwtape Letters *struck you in
a particular way, and why?*

---

47. C. S. Lewis, *The Screwtape Letters* (New York: Harper Collins,
2002), pp. 185–186.

TWENTY-SECOND SUNDAY IN ORDINARY TIME

Our Scripture passage for this Sunday comes from the Gospel of Matthew 16:21–27. In this reading, we hear of how Peter turns quickly and easily from thinking as God does to thinking as men do. In doing so, Peter tries to deter Jesus from embracing His passion in Jerusalem. Peter's statements of misguided faith and Jesus' corrective responses to Peter are instructive to us in our discipleship as well.

Jesus teaches His disciples that He must go to Jerusalem where He will undergo His passion and death. In using the word "must", Jesus is telling us that His passion is part of the Father's plan (divine necessity). Peter could not understand how God's plan could involve the suffering of the innocent, much less the death of the one whom he had just proclaimed to be the Christ. For Peter, such a statement was crazy, absurd, and even contrary to whom Peter thought God to be. Therefore, Peter tries to rebuke Jesus. The term "rebuke" is used primarily in the gospels to refer to the rebuking of evil spirits. If Peter doubted that Jesus' passion could be part of God's plan that means Peter thought our Lord's passion and death must be part of Satan's plan instead. Because of his mistaken understanding of the divine will, Peter actually wants to free Jesus of it! Jesus, in turn, reveals where Satan's will is really being promoted, and it is in Peter's mistaken efforts. Peter wanted Jesus to reject the experience of faithful suffering. Peter wanted to believe that following God's divine plan should result in happiness, wealth, success, and many other blessings but not the cross. In all of this, Peter was tempting Jesus to fulfill the earthly expectations of the Messiah. Peter, who had been the "rock" on which Jesus proclaimed His Church would be built, has now become little more than a "stumbling stone" on the path of discipleship. Peter, who once spoke what was revealed to him by the heavenly Father, now speaks what comes from human reasoning and earthly desires. It is sobering to see how quickly and easily Peter can change from expressing correct faith (Mt 16:18) to misguided faith (Mt 16:22). Certainly the same can happen to us when we lose sight of the necessity of the cross in Jesus' life and in the lives of all who would follow Him as His disciples. If we follow Jesus, we must accept the inevitable suffering that comes as a result of being a faithful Christian. Such moments of faithful suffering are not a sign of God's abandonment of us or of the triumph of evil, but rather of our following where the Lord has already led. Sometimes we can let our own worldly understanding of success and happiness actually deter us from following Jesus when faithfulness involves sacrifice. The rebuke of Jesus is a lasting reminder to all of us that we should be very careful about allowing the thoughts of men to determine and guide how we receive and respond to the thoughts of God.

> *How can the experience of suffering cause people to doubt the presence of God in their lives?*
> *When have you felt that God's will was calling you to embrace sacrifice and suffering as a consequence of your fidelity?*
> *What happens to a person's faith when they think that following Jesus will bring them health, wealth, success, and happiness each day?*

Jesus' response to Peter's rebuke is particularly instructive. When Jesus says, "Get behind me", He is not telling Peter to go away but rather to assume once again the role of a disciple (a disciple is one who follows). When Peter faithfully follows Jesus' lead, then he can be the foundation stone of the Church. But when Peter tries to be the one who leads Jesus, Peter stops being a disciple and becomes nothing but a stumbling stone. Jesus is pointing out to Peter what has gone astray in his faith; he is trying to lead God rather than follow God. Peter knows that a disciple will follow where the master goes, and Peter doesn't like where Jesus is going because our Lord has indicated His destiny involves suffering and death. Jesus then goes on to teach Peter that being a Christian disciple isn't just a matter of confessing the right faith. Being a Christian disciple also means accepting and facing the challenges, suffering, and persecution that come to us because of our confession of faith. Peter was happy to confess Jesus as the "Christ, the Son of the Living God" but not happy to follow where the Christ was now leading him. Our confession of faith is a necessary proclamation of whom we believe Jesus to be. However, that confession means little if we do not live it out in committed, obedient, and practical aspects of our lives. For this reason, Jesus states in Matthew 16:27 that every person will be repaid based on what they have done as opposed to what they have said. Thus, our judgment will be based not on our words but on our deeds. This is a consistent theme in Matthew's Gospel and challenges us to consider how well we are willing to embrace the cross with Jesus. Talk is cheap. Peter can profess the faith, but the more important question is whether he can carry the cross. That challenges all of us to ponder how well we live our Christian beliefs in practical daily life. Paul often taught the early Church about the necessity of living out their beliefs in daily life (Rom 14:12, 1 Cor 4:5, 2 Cor 5:10).

> *How do you see the temptation expressed today for people to separate what they believe from what they do?*
> *What are situations in which you find it difficult to let your faith guide your actions?*
> *How do people today try to lead God rather than follow God in their prayer?*
> *What might Peter's response to Jesus have been if he were speaking as a disciple rather than as someone who was trying to lead the Lord?*

One last thing to point out about this passage is that the disciples only learn about the sacrifice required of them after they have been following Jesus for some time and are already well on their way to Jerusalem. It's interesting that Jesus waits until this point in the Gospel to announce what awaits Him in Jerusalem and what following the Lord will really cost them as His disciples. That reality can be true for us as well. We don't always know what the commitment of our baptism means until it gradually unfolds and deepens in lived discipleship over the course of time. All too often we only realize the challenges that faith will present once we're well into the journey of Christian life. Such instances occur in the raising of a family or in taking a stand that opposes the culture of our time.

Had the disciples known from the beginning that Jesus would lead
them to the cross, many probably would not have followed the
Lord. Jesus reveals the necessity of the cross as the way to true life.
Indeed, those who willingly embrace the cross will find their life
while those who avoid it at all costs will end up losing their lives.
The disciples must have had a strong commitment to Jesus for them
to continue as His disciples once they knew where the Lord was
leading them. They are being presented to us as examples of perseverance to inspire and encourage us when we feel overwhelmed
or burdened by the sacrifices of faith we face. Once we make a
commitment to follow the Lord, we are giving God license to lead
us where He wants to go and not to pursue our own destinations.
Sometimes we only realize that God's ways are not our ways as we
grow in mature discipleship. This awareness can be, and is meant
to be, an important step in our spiritual development that can lead
us deeper in our commitment to Jesus by recognizing and rejecting
our false and earthly desires.

> *Why do you think the disciples were so committed to Jesus*
> *that they followed Him even after they heard of the necessity*
> *of the cross?*
> *When in your life have you made an irrevocable commit-*
> *ment to follow Jesus?*
> *When has your Christian faith led you to make some very*
> *difficult choices or undertake difficult actions?*
> *How have you experienced the life-giving reward of sacri-*
> *ficial love for others?*
> *What does the expression, "Whoever loses his life for my*
> *sake will find it", mean to you?*
> *How do people today try to find their life by "saving it"*
> *rather than giving it away?*
> *What is the greatest sacrifice you have made for God? What*
> *sacrifice do you fear most?*

Twenty-Third Sunday in Ordinary Time

Our Scripture passage for this Sunday comes from the Gospel of Matthew 18:15–20. In this reading, Jesus teaches us the importance of charitable correction for those who are harming themselves or the community. Disciples have the responsibility of helping others pursue a life of holiness, and sometimes that can require helping others turn away from serious and sinful actions. This passage is an important instruction for us on how we can seek the good of others in the most constructive and charitable way. The Lord knows that when we are offended we will respond. In this passage, Jesus is teaching disciples to respond in the right way.

For a Christian disciple, the experience of loving our neighbor means that we seek what is good for them in the eyes of God. God created each of us in the hope that we would live our lives in fulfillment of the Lord's will. Sin causes us to discard God's will in favor of our own misguided desires and disordered false values. Sin causes us to become less than the person God created us to be. God hates sin because sin wounds and destroys the human person whom God loves. Christian disciples understand the responsibility of helping one another recognize and overcome our misguided desires and false values so that we may become fully the person God intends. When someone wrongs us, our instinctive response is usually one of defense or aggression. Oftentimes this instinctive response can manifest itself in destructive ways such as gossip, slander, anger, antagonism and so forth. The reality is that sometimes we can make ourselves feel better about our own flawed lives by pointing out the seemingly greater faults of others. When this dynamic occurs, someone else's sin can actually lead us to sin even more. Jesus teaches us a different way to respond. Our Lord instructs us to pursue a supernatural way of responding to another's wrongful actions. First, we are to make the other person aware of how their actions have harmed us. This is necessary because sometimes people simply may not even realize that they have caused harm. Paradoxically, the initiative for reconciliation is presented as the responsibility of the one offended. Pointing out the harm that another has caused, then, is not a matter of attaching blame or guilt but of assisting them in understanding the negative impact their actions have on the wider community.

Second, we are to be motivated by love that seeks conversion, reconciliation, and growth in holiness rather than by anger or hurt that seeks revenge, punishment, or humiliation. Fraternal correction can be difficult because it risks misunderstanding, vulnerability, or even aggravating a situation, but it is a part of discipleship. What parent does not manifest their love for their children by helping them correct their faults? What friend doesn't help another friend by wanting to help them become a better person? Fraternal correction is one of the most loving things we can do for another person. It's also something the Lord expects of us. Ezekiel warns us that we are, indeed, the watchmen for our neighbor and that our silence will condemn us if we fail to warn them of the harmful nature of their actions (cf. Ez 3:18; 33:6). Mere knowledge of another's harmful actions imposes on us an obligation to help them.

> *How have you learned to overcome faults through the fraternal correction of another person?*
> *What are some of the instinctive ways you see people responding to the hurtful actions of others?*
> *With whom do you need to practice fraternal correction at this time?*
> *What action in your life is most harmful to others?*
> *What is the greatest example of fraternal correction you have ever witnessed?*
> *What qualities are necessary to engage in fraternal correction?*
> *What qualities are necessary to receive fraternal correction?*
> *How does the practice of fraternal correction go against our individualistic culture?*

Next, Jesus expands the scope of fraternal correction to address situations of reluctant repentance. Love requires that we never stop seeking the good of another even when our individual efforts for another's repentance fail. Rather, we are to enlist the help of others in a way that lovingly respects the privacy and dignity of those who have offended us. Sometimes people need to know that their actions affect the community and not just themselves or one other person. Any sin, any hurt inflicted on the Body of Christ, weakens and hurts the entire body. Thus, the individual offenses of one person, even through seemingly private sins, actually affect all of us. The goal of introducing others into the loving conversation of fraternal correction is not to create an intimidating situation or to alienate them but to help them realize the love of the Christian community. It is that community which seeks their change of heart and reconciliation. Only in the face of persistent lack of repentance is the issue to be brought before "the Church". While this term can mean the entire local community, it most likely refers to the leader(s) of the community, since that is how fraternal correction was practiced in the first century. Thus, respect for the privacy and dignity of those who have offended us remains important even after repeated refusals to repent. It is here that Jesus prescribes the disciplinary action of treating them as a Gentile or tax collector. That action is meant to remove them from communion with the Christian assembly for serious sins. Even in this extreme case, the goal of the action is not punishment, humiliation, or revenge but rather to elicit their conversion by awakening them to the seriousness of their actions and the damaging impact of their behavior on the community. Even the discipline of excommunication is intended for the ultimate purpose of reconciliation. Other New Testament Epistles confirm that the practice of excommunication occurred in the early Church as an effective discipline that brought about the conversion of others who had seriously sinned (1 Cor 5:1–5, 2 Thes 3:6–15, 2 Jn 10).

> *What are serious sins that the Christian community needs to guard against today so that our common life is not disrupted or corrupted by those sins?*
> *How does this explanation of excommunication change your understanding of the practice?*

How do you feel when someone goes over your head to address a situation rather than first speaking to you directly?

When are you tempted to go over someone else's head before speaking to them directly?

Why do you think Jesus was so concerned about preserving the privacy and dignity of people who had done sinful things?

How can you protect the privacy and dignity of people today when they do sinful or hurtful things?

How does it change your understanding of personal sin to see it in the context of affecting the entire Body of Christ?

What values do you think we need to most protect in the Christian community today during times of difficulty or disagreement?

The process of fraternal correction that Jesus outlines in this Gospel passage is not only for the conversion of one who sins but also for the protection of everyone involved in the situation. Because we are human, we will always be in danger of overstepping our bounds in our relationships with others. It's possible that our own judgment can become skewed by anger and prejudice. Additionally, individual zeal can lead us to ignore the wisdom and perspective of others. Situations of persistent serious sin can both harm the Christian community as well as give rise to simmering feelings of anger and distrust when conflicts remain unresolved. Fraternal correction, as taught by Jesus, is a practice intended to protect all parties involved. Certainly the one who offends is protected against being judged by only one other person, whether by the individual offended or a single leader of the Christian community. Also, the one who offends is protected from persisting in harmful behaviors that adversely affect themselves and others. The one who is responsible for calling others to repentance is protected from their own limited view, knowledge, or experience of the situation thanks to the counsel of two or three witnesses. The community is protected from the unaddressed presence of sinful actions that can cause confusion and end up leading others astray by bad example or by lack of confidence in community leaders. Jesus wanted the Church to experience justice and mercy in such moments. Saint Thomas

Aquinas taught about this necessary relationship between these two virtues when he said, "Mercy without justice is the mother of dissolution; and Justice without Mercy is cruelty."[48]

> *When have you seen someone practice justice without mercy?*
> *When have you seen mercy practiced without justice?*
> *How do you protect against your own prejudice and impulsiveness when you have to practice fraternal correction?*
> *What serious sin today has the potential to confuse, corrupt, or disrupt the communion of the Christian faithful?*
> *Why do you think Jesus considered fraternal correction so important that He gave a detailed teaching about it to the first disciples?*

One final note should be mentioned regarding Jesus' closing words to this instruction. Our Lord tells the disciples that whatever they bind or loose on earth will be bound or loosed in heaven. He also assures them that when two of them agree and ask the Father, it will be done for them. In closing, Jesus promises His presence to be with the disciples when two or three of them are gathered in His name. Each of these three closing statements is relevant for our lives as disciples and especially for the way in which we approach situations of serious sin in the lives of others. The first statement concerning binding and loosing promises divine recognition of the disciple's actions and of discipline from within the community. This recognition is not to give the disciples a sense of power by which they mistakenly think they control the Lord. Rather, it is to stress the seriousness of their decisions. Disciples must exercise caution when imposing disciplinary penalties. Such caution is warranted because their action of excommunication can have eternal consequences for those who are being disciplined. This caution is meant to restrain impulsive and punitive actions of Christian leaders lest they cause unnecessary spiritual suffering in the lives of others. Our Lord's promise to fulfill the request of disciples who agree must be kept in context in order to be properly understood. It is not intended to be a generic promise to grant us whatever we ask, whenever we

---

48. St Thomas Aquinas, *Super Evangelium S. Matthaei Lectura*, Chapter V, 1, 2.

ask it, no matter what. Rather, this promise is connected to the efforts for reconciliation and fraternal correction. Interpreted in this context, then, our Lord is promising to give divine assistance to our sincere efforts to reconcile and correct the seriously sinful behavior of others. It also reminds us that the first action in any effort of fraternal correction or Church discipline should be to pray for God's guidance and blessing on everyone involved. Lastly, our Lord's promise to be present where two or three are gathered in His name refers to more than just the liturgical context of prayer.

The presence of Jesus is promised even to the Church when it is gathered for administrative decisions for the good of the community. This promise is also a caution to leaders that their decisions are to always be made in the spirit of Christ who oversees their discussions. When we know that Jesus is with us and cares deeply about the decisions we make, then we tend to exercise caution, diligence, and mercy. As the Lord said in Matthew 7:2, the way in which we judge others is the way in which God will judge us. The promise of our Lord's presence is not an implicit approval or assurance of divine favor for any decision we make. Rather, it is a caution that all our judgments are carefully scrutinized by God, who knows our intentions and can discern whether our actions are undertaken in a spirit of love, reconciliation, and repentance or in a spirit of condemnation, vindictiveness, and punishment. Jesus is in our midst when we gather in His name; He is present in the Church leaders entrusted with the responsibility to care for the good of its members, and He is present even in the wayward sinner who is reluctant to repent. Indeed, our Lord will reveal that He is always present in the least of our brothers and sisters (Mt 25:31–46), and how we treat them in their moment of need (even repentance) can be the cause of either our salvation or condemnation.

> *How do these final statements of Jesus cause you to reconsider the way you approach decisions concerning others?*
> *When are you concerned that someone's eternal salvation may be affected by a decision you made concerning that person?*
> *What do you pray for when you see someone doing harm to themselves or others?*

How does Jesus' promise of His presence make you reconsider the motives for your actions especially when it involves how you respond to those who have hurt you?

TWENTY-FOURTH SUNDAY IN ORDINARY TIME

O ur Scripture passage for this Sunday comes from the Gospel of Matthew 18:21–35. In this reading we hear Jesus teaching His disciples about the need to forgive those who have offended them. Teachings on forgiveness occur frequently in the New Testament, and this passage provides us an excellent opportunity to consider what forgiveness might mean for our own lives as disciples, both as we receive it ourselves and as we give it to others.

Peter prompts Jesus' teaching with his question to the Lord, "How often must I forgive him? As many as seven times?" To this question, Jesus responds, "Not seven times but seventy-seven times." The Lord's response to Peter basically indicates that we are to forgive without limit. It is interesting to note that forgiveness is to be extended even when there is no indication that the offending party has repented. This is an important point that has beneficial implications on spiritual and emotional levels for us as disciples. Sometimes we need to forgive even when others aren't seeking our forgiveness. Oftentimes, forgiveness actually benefits the one who forgives more than the one who is forgiven. That might seem strange to us, but think about how lack of forgiveness can harm us. The Scriptures are full of warnings against anger and harboring resentment. We can certainly recall the teaching of Sirach 27:30 where it is written, "Wrath and anger, these also are abominations, yet a sinner holds on to them." We might also think of Saint Paul's letter to the Ephesians 4:26–27 when he said, "Do not let the sun set on your anger and do not leave room for the devil." These are only a few examples of the many teachings, which warn us against the destructive addictiveness of wrath and anger in the human heart. Jesus does not want His disciples to be corrupted by hatred or addicted to wrath and anger. Forgiveness is the only way to overcome these destructive influences even when others aren't asking for our forgiveness. To forgive does not mean that we approve of what the offending person has done or that we are willing to permit their actions to recur in the future. Rather, forgiveness is about not letting another person's wrongful actions dominate our thoughts and feelings any longer. When we don't forgive, we harbor ill feelings that end up corrupting our own ability to be happy and eroding our ability to love freely. Jesus certainly gives us an example of forgiveness in His own life and ministry, especially upon the cross, as He forgives those who are crucifying Him even though they don't ask for it. If God is love, then we cannot be living reflections of the image of God when we are harboring hatred and resentment.

> *When have you seen anger or resentment become addictive and erosive elements in people's lives?*
> *How is it possible to forgive someone who isn't seeking our forgiveness?*
> *How can the power of evil use our anger to "work on us", and what does evil try to do with our anger?*
> *Jesus teaches Peter that he is to forgive without limit (seventy-seven times). What are the typical limits we place on our forgiveness?*
> *What actions of others most cause you to become angry, resentful, or wrathful and why?*

Jesus then gives a parable that teaches about the absurdity of limiting our forgiveness. In short, if we place limits on our forgiveness of others, God will place limits on His forgiveness for us. In the parable, a contrast is given between the man who owes 10,000 Talents (analogous to a billion dollars) and the man who owes 100 Denarii (roughly three months wages). There is simply no comparison. When the man who received mercy and was "forgiven" his debt chose to not be merciful to someone else, then the mercy he had first received is revoked. The message is clear; if we are merciless in absolving people's debts to us (offenses), then God will respond accordingly and be merciless in resolving our debts (sins) to the Lord (compare with the similar instruction of Mt 6:14–15). We see this same teaching reflected in the Lord's Prayer (Mt 6:12) when we pray, "Forgive us our trespasses as we forgive those who trespass against us." When we close our hearts to forgive others (regardless of whether they want it or not), we close our hearts to receive God's forgiveness for us.

Our motivation to forgive others, then, should be prompted first and foremost by the awareness of our own need for forgiveness. That is why an important part of discipleship is the humble self-awareness of our sins and of our own need for God's mercy. It's easy for us to focus on the offenses we have suffered at the hands of others but rare for us to focus on how we have been the cause of offense to others. This parable reminds us that we should first be mindful of how great is our personal need for God's mercy and of our utter inability to earn it or pay our debt to the Lord. Only when we realize that God is gracious and merciful with us can we then become motivated to be a channel of that mercy to others. We all know the expression, "To err is human, to forgive is divine."[49] This saying takes on new meaning when we realize that forgiveness is a divine action that we can share with others only as we receive it ourselves. The key to becoming disciples who forgive others is to first be disciples who seek God's forgiveness in our own lives. The experience of Sacramental Confession is one important way in which we experience this enormous mercy of God for our own sins. Another way of remembering our need for God's mercy is through the daily examination of conscience, which is a prayerful review of the day so as to help a person recognize the wrongs they have committed.

> *How do you foster a healthy and humble awareness of the sins and offenses you have committed?*
> *How do you experience God's mercy for you? For whom are you denying mercy or forgiveness at this time?*
> *In the parable, there was no way the servant could repay the Master for his debt (10,000 Talents), but it would have been possible for the fellow servant to repay his lesser debt (100 Denarii). What does this comparison of debts mean*

---

49. A similar Latin expression attributed to Seneca says, "Errare humanum est, sed in errare (errore) perseverare diabolicum," that is, "To err is human, but to persist in error (out of pride) is diabolical."

*to you and your experience of forgiveness (both for yourself
and others)?*
What conditions do you place on forgiveness?

The experience of forgiveness offers us certain graces or gifts. These
gifts include peace, healing, freedom, integrity, and revelation. Let's
look at each of these for a moment to better understand them and
desire them for ourselves and others.

- Peace: Sin causes disharmony on a variety of levels. This disharmony can manifest itself as shame, sorrow, embarrassment,
  hurt, resentment, antagonism, anger, and so forth. All of these
  feelings cause us to lose our peace of mind and soul. Notice that
  this is true both for the offender as well as the one offended.
  The experience of forgiveness restores our peace by placing us
  in right relationship with God and ourselves. When forgiveness
  is shared and received with another person, then we experience
  an additional gift of peace by being in right relationship with
  others as well. Thus, forgiveness is the key to restoring the gift
  of spiritual peace in our lives.
- Healing: Sin wounds us. This is true for both the one who is
  offended as well as for the one who offends. When we sin, we
  are damaging our relationship with God and others. When we
  are sinned against, we know all too well the injury that occurs.
  Forgiveness is what allows us to heal the wounds of sin. To
  receive forgiveness is to receive a loving balm of mercy that
  lets us know we are no longer defined by the wrong we have
  committed. To give forgiveness is to stop licking our wounds
  and to willingly move on with our lives by choosing to leave
  behind our resentment and hurt.
- Freedom: a common word for "forgiveness" in Greek (either
  apoluo or *aphesis*) actually means to untie, release or dismiss.
  The experience of sin can actually be like a chain that binds
  us. We can find ourselves imprisoned by the wrongful experiences we have either suffered by others or committed against
  others. Forgiveness is the moment when we are set free from
  the burden of injury or the guilt of offense. Who doesn't want
  this freedom to move on with their lives? Sometimes we have

to realize how tired we are of carrying that burden or guilt before we have the grace to desire the freedom of forgiveness.

- Integrity: If we are truly created in the image of God, then we cannot authentically and truly become ourselves until we also reflect God's likeness. That likeness involves forgiveness because God's nature is to forgive. By forgiving others, we become a living channel of God's grace and action in the world as we manifest the Lord's mercy in a specific way. It is this spiritual integrity that allows us to move forward in our discipleship and to become more authentically a friend of God who acts as God acts and loves as God loves. Sometimes we can find ourselves stagnating in our spiritual lives because we have chosen either not to forgive or not to seek forgiveness. That stagnation and spiritual frustration can be the Lord's way of encouraging us to recognize and resolve the offensive obstacles that are preventing us from moving forward in our efforts to be more Christ-like. When we fail to practice forgiveness, we are fundamentally out-of-sync with the will of God.

- Revelation: Although it might seem strange to us, God reveals Himself through the events of our lives. All aspects of our lives, even our sin, can become a means of knowing, receiving, and responding to the presence of God. The great Spanish mystic Saint John of the Cross understood and articulated this spiritual insight when he prayed:

Lord God, my Beloved, if You remember still my sins in such wise that you do not do what I beg of You, do your will concerning them, my God, which is what I most desire, and exercise Your goodness and mercy, and You will be known through them. And if it is that you are waiting for my good works so as to hear my prayer through their means, grant them to me, and work them for me, and the sufferings You desire to accept, and let it be done. But if You are not waiting for my works, what is it that makes You wait, my most clement Lord? Why do You delay? For if, after all, I am to receive the grace and mercy which I entreat of You in Your Son, take my

mite, since You desire it, and grant me this blessing, since
You also desire that.[50]

This prayer of John of the Cross that God will be known through
our sins should encourage us to examine ourselves in a humble,
thoughtful, prayerful and reverent way. Even small sins can be a
means of God's self-revelation to us.

> *Which of these gifts of forgiveness do you most need at this
> time in your life?*
> *How does this list help you better understand the far-reach-
> ing benefits of forgiveness?*
> *What is a step you can take this week to give yourself the
> gift of forgiveness?*
> *In light of the above teaching on forgiveness, what reasons
> would a person have for not being willing to forgive?*
> *Who benefits most by our refusal to forgive others?*
> *How do you know when you have truly forgiven someone
> else, and what is the concrete sign for you that indicates
> forgiveness has taken place in your life?*

---

50. St John of the Cross, "Sayings of Light and Love, 26" in *The Collected
     Works of St John of the Cross* (Washington, D.C.: ICS Publications,
     1991), p. 87.

TWENTY-FIFTH SUNDAY IN ORDINARY TIME

Our Scripture passage for this Sunday comes from the Gospel of Matthew 20:1–16a. In this text, Jesus teaches us about the generosity of God by using the Parable of the Vineyard Owner. This parable gives us insights into the mind of God that challenge our commonly held notions of fairness and generosity. As disciples, we are called to take on the "mind of Christ" (1 Cor 2:16), and so this parable challenges us to think differently about how we exercise fairness and generosity in our lives. The process of thinking differently with its resultant practical change in life is more commonly known as repentance.

One of the first things to note is that the owner of the vineyard goes out several times to hire workers for his harvest. There could be two significant reasons for these multiple trips, and each of these reasons has something to say about our lives as disciples who are called to take on the mind of Christ and reflect the values of God in our actions.

First, the owner's multiple trips could indicate the importance of the harvest. It was the customary practice in the ancient world for day workers to gather in the town square and wait to be hired for work. The owner of the vineyard did what everyone else did: at the beginning of the day he went to hire workers for his harvest. However, those first people hired were not enough workers. He needed more workers, more people to help bring in the ripe grapes because the harvest couldn't wait another day. Any delay could mean the difference between a bumper crop and a lost crop. The harvest had to happen then when the moment was ripe. So the master of the vineyard invites other workers later, and again later in the day, because he doesn't want any of the harvest to be lost. The urgency of the harvest in this parable is an important reminder to us that the harvest of ministry is also just as time sensitive. The gathering of the harvest is an image that was already presented in various Old Testament texts and referred both to the gathering of God's people and the moment of judgment. For us today, the image of the harvest can refer to all the ways in which we bring people effectively to meet the Lord and receive His saving grace through the Sacraments and a life of committed discipleship. When we look at our world, we can see so many people who desire a more meaningful life and an encounter with the Living God. We are the workers the Lord sends out to bring in this harvest of souls to Him.

> *What's the harvest that's being lost in the Church today?*
> *It's possible that the first workers hired simply didn't do their jobs well and that necessitated the later hires. What could the Church do better in our time to bring in the harvest?*
> *When it comes to the harvest of the Gospel, how can you become more aware of ministry opportunities so as to be more involved?*
> *What are the common excuses people use for not accepting the invitation to be a worker in the vineyard who helps bring in the Master's harvest?*
> *What harvest is present in the secular world that is ripe for the Gospel, and who are the workers who can help bring it in?*

Second, the owner's multiple trips could reveal how much the Lord desires that everyone be given a place in the Kingdom (the image of the Vineyard was a well-established image for Israel as is evidenced by Is 5:1–7 and Jer 12:10). According to this second interpretation, the Master of the Vineyard brought in more and more people so that he could include as many people as possible. This second interpretation focuses not only on the importance of the harvest but also on the importance of inclusion and involvement in the work of the Gospel. The message is this: The Lord has a place for all peoples in the Kingdom, and each of us has our part to play. This individual role is our vocation in Christ. If we feel like we haven't found our place in the Church's mission or ministry, we are like the workers still standing around at noon or the ninth hour. There is a place for everyone in the work of the Church as Saint Paul taught in his epistles (Rom 12:5 and 1 Cor 12:12–22). Sometimes we have to ask the Lord to help us find our place and be willing to respond generously when He calls us to offer ourselves to Him so the work of the Gospel can continue. Whatever our talents may be, God gave them to us for a reason. Our gratitude for the gift of our lives and God-given talents and opportunities is expressed in how we place our lives in the Lord's service and use those gifts to build up the Kingdom of God.

> *When it comes to welcoming people and helping them find a place in the Church's life and ministry, do we look at them as strangers, or do we welcome them as brothers and sisters whose presence enriches our community?*
>
> *Many people may be seeking a deeper connection with God through involvement in a faith community, and they are like the people who are still standing in the town square late into the day. Who is someone you know whom you can invite to join you in the vineyard of your faith community? The Master had taken the initiative in reaching out and inviting the idle workers into his vineyard. How can we as a community be more welcoming and pro-active so as to create an inviting community for those who are idle in their faith?*

Next, this parable teaches us how much God wants everyone to have the basic necessities for life. The workers in the parable were not paid a lot. They were each given one Denarius, which was enough money to feed and care for one family for one day. That's it. To receive less than a Denarius meant that a family would go to bed hungry. God doesn't want that. We are told that the master of the vineyard gave everyone in the parable a wage that allowed them to sustain their families. This message reveals to us the heart of God who cares for the plight of the poor and the needs of families. Today in the United States alone there are millions of people living below the poverty line and many children who do not have adequate food and housing. It is a reality that we've almost become comfortable with, and that's in a first world country! Around the world there are hundreds of millions more living with inadequate food, water, shelter, and health care. In the Gospel, the master of the vineyard went out ceaselessly so such basic needs could be provided for every worker's family. Imagine the anxiety and fear of the workers who stood around all day not knowing how they would feed their families that night. Imagine, too, their joy at finally being given a daily wage that they could live on. God rejoices when needs are met and we pray for such a reality in the Lord's Prayer when we say, "Give us this day our daily bread." This aspect of the parable invites us to become more conscientious of our responsibility for others who struggle to survive and provide for their families. To take on the mind of Christ (1 Cor 2:16) requires that we begin to think with the same compassion and active social justice as exemplified in the master of the vineyard.

> *Who in your community cannot afford the basic necessities of life?*
> *When you see or read about people who live in poverty, are you moved to be generous and share with them the blessings God has given to you, or do you find it easier to turn away and absolve yourself of the Christian responsibility to care for others?*
> *When have you, or a loved one, been concerned that you could not provide for your family, and what event or opportunity in your life allowed you to alleviate that concern?*

The parable ends with the first workers grumbling at the master and saying, "You have made them equal to us." The ones who worked all day in the vineyard had no desire to be made equals with those who only worked one hour. It's important to note that no one was treated unfairly since those hired first received the wage for which they agreed. Those hired last received the same wage not out of justice but out of generosity (grace). Those hired first were upset because they did not want to be equal with the others. Instead, they wanted to be better than the others and have greater payment. Their complaints reveal their inner motivations that are focused on self-gain (reward) rather than the joy of working with the master (relationship). Because they were not motivated by joy and gratitude for the opportunity to work in the vineyard, they could not share in the master's joy and generosity by welcoming others even as the master had welcomed them. Sometimes it's difficult for us to accept others as equal heirs to the life of grace when we, too, are motivated by the desire to be better than others. The desire to be better than others can manifest itself as seeking greater prestige, greater position, greater attention, greater material wealth, and so forth. The same attitude can also manifest itself by seeing others as less than ourselves for whatever reason. Such exclusive attitudes make it difficult for us to rejoice when others are deemed equal to us. Perhaps others haven't done as much for the Church, or given as much to charity, or worked as much for the same causes for which we have worked. Whatever the measure of our labor, it can be easy to resent others when they are given the same standing we ourselves have worked hard to achieve. Thus, this parable can strike us as unfair just as it caused the workers to complain. In the parable, it is not a matter of some workers being treated better than others but of everyone being treated equally.

> *When have you resented being treated equal to others or having others treated as being equal to you?*
>
> *For which do you pray more, God's generosity in your life or God's justice in your life?*
>
> *The master questioned the workers to see if they are angry because he is generous. Has anyone's generosity ever caused you to be resentful?*
>
> *Those hired first were paid last so they could see everyone receiving the same wage. How do you think the master hoped the workers, who were paid last, might respond?*
>
> *The purpose of the parable is not about changing the mind of the master but about changing the minds of the workers. What part of this parable challenges you?*
>
> *In God's eyes we all have equal dignity as human beings created in His image and likeness whether we are rich or poor, sinner or saint, old-timer or new-comer, black or white, pastor or parishioner. With whom do you not want to see yourself as an equal?*
>
> *Indeed, as the first reading this Sunday states, "God's ways are not our ways" (Is 55:8). But they could be. Which aspect of this parable is most comforting for you?*
>
> *How might you imitate the qualities of the Master of the Harvest in the vineyard of your day?*

TWENTY-SIXTH SUNDAY IN ORDINARY TIME

O ur Scripture passage for this Sunday comes from the Gospel of Matthew 21:28–32. In this reading, we hear the story of the two brothers who respond differently to the request of the Father. One brother says what the father wants to hear while the other brother eventually does what the father wills. Ultimately it is the one who actually does the will of the father that Jesus esteems. These two practical examples emphasize the importance of actions over words when it comes to our lives of faith. Thus, this teaching offers important insights for the life of discipleship.

The first thing to note is how easily one can say "Yes" to the will of God without understanding what such a commitment entails, or even having the intention to fulfill it, in a person's daily life. We enter into commitments of faith sometimes without even realizing it. Such commitments are not a benefit to us unless we are prepared to fulfill them. For the Jewish leaders of Jesus' time, they had gone to hear the preaching of John the Baptist (Mt 3:5–7a), but they did not conform their lives to that preaching. Thus, they implicitly said "yes" on the one hand by going to hear him but then failed to respond to his teaching and ended up saying "no" to a life conformed to that teaching. For Christians, we enter into commitments of faith in our baptism, which oblige us to become a member of Christ's Body, a Temple of the Holy Spirit, a Child of God, an active member of the Church, and so forth. We also enter into a profound commitment of faith when we receive the Eucharist and are commissioned to become the Body of Christ in the world so as to allow the Lord's presence in the Eucharist to live in us and through us. Our commitments of faith continue when we acknowledge our sins and seek God's forgiveness while also resolving to avoid the occasions of sin and to amend our lives. The commitments of Christian marriage oblige us to give ourselves completely and irrevocably to our spouses even as Christ gave

Himself to the Church in complete self-giving unto death. Indeed, it can be easy for us to enter into commitments of faith without realizing what they mean or without intending to fulfill them just like the second son in this parable.

> *What happens when religious people don't witness the faith they profess in the lives they live?*
> *What are ways in which we can focus on exterior expressions of faith at the expense of active mission?*
> *What do you need to do each day to better fulfill your commitments of faith?*
> *The second son was interested in saying what the Father wanted to hear rather than doing what the Father asked him to do. When can we find ourselves saying prayers without intending to live them out in our lives?*
> *Some commitments of faith are listed above in the reflection. What are other unconscious commitments of faith people make (for example, the wearing of religious jewelry or clothing)?*

The second thing to focus on is the importance that Jesus gives to actually doing the will of God. There is a great saying that states, "People may not believe what you say, but they will believe what you do."[51] Matthew's Gospel previously reiterated this point when Jesus said, "Not everyone who says to me, 'Lord, Lord', will enter the Kingdom of heaven, but only the one who does the will of my Father in Heaven" (7:21–22). Actions always speak louder than words. In an ideal world, both our words and actions would conform to the will of God. It is the sad reality of human weakness that it is easier to say the right thing than to do the right thing. Thus, when it comes to our relationship with God, it is usually our actions that are lacking. An authentic relationship of faith asks for our complete and consistent response to God's will both in what we profess and in how we live. Sometimes we see unlikely people

---

51. Pope Paul VI taught, "Modern man listens more willingly to witnesses than to teachers, and if he does listen to teachers, it is because they are witnesses." Pope Paul VI, *Address to the Members of the Consilium de Laicis* (2 October 1974): *AAS* 66 (1974), 568; and *Evangelii Nuntiandi*, (8 December 1975), 41: *AAS* 68 (1976) 5–76.

responding to God's will in a way that inspires us and reminds us of what we should be doing. It's one thing when the person who inspires us is someone who has sat next to us in the pew every week for the past twenty years, but it's another thing when the exemplary action comes from someone who only recently joined the Church or comes from a troubled background. Certainly that was the case with the tax collectors and prostitutes to whom Jesus refers in this Gospel passage. They are the ones who were perceived as having rejected God's will in the Torah (Law of Moses) but were now conforming their lives to God's will as revealed in Jesus. The chief priests, on the other hand, said "yes" to the Torah but were not conforming their lives to the message of Jesus. The chief priests were concerned with the longevity of their religious standing more than the quality of their present and lived response of faith.

> *What are ways in which we can be tempted to value our religious standing (including membership in a congregation) more than, or in place of, our present lived response of faith to the will of God?*
> *The first son in this parable is the one who is praised for eventually doing the Father's will. How do you pray so as to know God's will and to do it?*
> *What are examples of people who have only recently started to embrace a life of faith but who are doing better than many people who have been sitting in church for years?*
> *How does this parable challenge you to learn from the good example of others when it comes to being responsive to the will of God? What good examples of others could we learn from today as a Church so to improve our ministry response and do the will of the Father?*
> *If actions do speak louder than words, what faith are we professing by the lives we live? If someone were to write a creed based on how they saw us live, what would that creed say?*
> *The younger son had time to repent of his negative response to the Father's will. What invitation of faith have you been resisting yet still have the opportunity to accept?*

Jesus tells this parable to the chief priests and elders of the people so that they would realize the mistake they were making by not accepting our Lord's teaching. The reality is that the chief priests and elders didn't want to become followers of Jesus in large part because of those who were already following Him. They considered such followers notorious sinners with whom they did not want to be associated. It was the chief priests' and elders' disdain for other disciples that actually led them to reject the invitation to discipleship. It is always easier to look around us and focus on other people's need to repent rather than our own need to repent. When it comes to opportunities for discipleship, the question we pose should not be, "Who else is responding?" but rather, "How can I grow closer to the Lord in this moment?" Sometimes we are only comfortable engaging in one opportunity of discipleship or another when we are assured that our friends or people like ourselves or people we respect will be part of it as well. Such a preoccupation with who else is involved can distract us and deter us from pursuing wonderful opportunities for spiritual growth and discipleship. It can also prevent us from encountering the goodness of others whom we may not currently know or have not already met. Jesus wants disciples who will respond to His teaching on their own initiative and without prejudice or preference for who else is responding. Sometimes we can be like the chief priests and elders who paid more attention to the disciples than they did to the Master. Disciples will always be flawed; if we are waiting to find the perfect community of Christians, we would do well to remember the statement, "When you find the perfect Church, join it! Then it won't be perfect anymore!"

> *Do you follow Jesus because of our Lord's message or because of the attraction or distraction of the others who are already following Him?*
>
> *What ministry opportunity have you been interested in but did not become a part of because of those who were or were not involved in it?*
>
> *What is the danger of conditioning our response of faith based on the example or presence of other people or how they respond?*
>
> *Who are the "sinners" with whom people don't want to be associated today?*

TWENTY-SEVENTH SUNDAY IN ORDINARY TIME

Our Scripture passage for this Sunday comes from the Gospel of Matthew 21:33–43. In this parable, Jesus continues to challenge the religious leadership of Jerusalem in an effort to motivate their positive response of faith to the message of the Gospel. While there are many good reasons that should motivate a person to accept the Gospel message, in this parable Jesus begins to also present the reality of negative judgment on those who reject His message. This teaching offers several challenging insights for us as disciples as well.

The first thing to note is how persistent and relentless is the master's desire to interact with the tenants of the vineyard. We are told that he sent two sets of messengers and then his own son. We are also told that the tenants became more and more hostile in their rejection of the master's interaction with them through the messengers. Scripture scholars interpret the two sets of messengers as possibly referring to the former and latter prophets (two prophetic groups in the Old Testament). The sending of the son is an obvious reference to Jesus. Thus, we see how persistent God is in His desire to engage us as His people. Even when we first reject the Lord's message or are resistant to His will, God tries to communicate His Word to us through other means. Eventually God's self-communication reaches its greatest clarity in the sending of the Son. The reality is that this parable speaks to us because we can be as resistant to God's message as were the tenants in the parable. There are many ways in which God persistently tries to motivate us to respond to His will. Perhaps it is in the comment of a friend, a homily at Mass, a reading from Scripture, a ministry invitation listed in the bulletin, something we read in the newspaper or hear on television, and so forth. When we recognize that there is a persistent and consistent message we are receiving from multiple venues, then we should probably consider it as a possible communication from the Lord.

> *When have you experienced a persistent and consistent faith message speaking to you, and through what venues did you experience that message?*
> *What are ways in which people can excuse or dismiss a message of faith when they experience it through various means?*
> *How can you cultivate a listening heart that is receptive and eager to hear the Lord's voice and do His will?*

Another thing to notice in the parable is that the messengers and the Son were sent at vintage time. A better translation says that it was the "season for fruit" rather than vintage time. In the Gospel of Matthew, the term "fruit" refers to the good works of justice God wants from His people (see Mt 3:8, 10, 7:16–20, 12:33, 13:8, 21:9, 21:18–22). The other thing to note is that the Master of the vineyard is seeking all the fruit and not just part of it. This is a challenging statement! This makes it clear that God has an absolute and total claim on our lives because our lives belong to the Lord. The response of the tenants can oftentimes be our response as well when we claim for ourselves what belongs to God. Yes, just think of how many times that sad dynamic is lived out. All our life is a gift from God, and the Lord has a right to a complete claim on our time, talent, and treasure. When we believe that our lives are our own, we perceive God's request, even through His messengers, as an intrusion and threat to what we falsely think is ours. This attitude can cause us to deceive ourselves into thinking we can rule our own lives while denying God's claim on us. When we give in to these thoughts, we are like the tenants in the parable who put to death the Master's request for that fruit which is His. The reality is that God expects us to produce the fruit of justice, mercy, and generosity. The Lord sends messengers to us in the form of charitable requests, those who need help securing their rights, and those who can benefit from our friendship and faith. The duty of the Church is to offer to the Master the fruit He so desires through the requests of His messengers. Oftentimes we find it easier to utterly ignore these requests than to respond to them.

That is because we can perceive requests for our generosity and time as an attempt to deprive us of what is ours. We can perceive requests for our solidarity and intervention as an inconvenience to our personal lives and schedules. We can even perceive inquiries into our faith as uncomfortable moments to be avoided rather than as opportune moments for witness. When we respond in such negative ways, we absolutely reject the requests being posed to us by the Master.

> *How does the Lord ask for a portion of your time, talent, or treasure in your life?*
> *Who are the messengers of the Lord whom you see regularly, and are seeking good fruit from your life?*
> *What fruit have you been blessed with but haven't yet found a way to use for the mission of the Gospel?*
> *The tenants in the parable believed that they could be the rulers of their own lives. What cultural values or factors can lead us to establish our own kingdoms and use our time, talent and treasure exclusively for our own will and purposes?*

The violent response of the tenants towards the son is both graphic and disturbing. Indeed, the tenants may have been able to secure a brief self-reign over the vineyard based on the rule of occupancy, but they were very short sighted in underestimating the response of the Master and believing that the Master would accept their self-claimed ownership. Instead, the Master responds by putting those wretched tenants to a miserable death. When we read this graphic exchange, we need to remember that Matthew is writing his Gospel after the Fall of Jerusalem in the year AD 70. The way in which the tenants treat the son is exactly the same way Jesus was put to death ("seized him, brought him outside the [city], and killed him"). Some Christians of the first century interpreted the destruction of Jerusalem and the miserable death of so many of its people as the Lord's judgment on the leaders for having rejected and crucified Jesus. The ways of humanity are not the ways of God, and we are always short sighted when we think we can make God conform to our will. Our expressions of self-claimed autonomy are always a rejection of God's rightful claim on our lives. Our acts of hostility towards Jesus' teachings on discipleship are always behaviors in which we reject the Son rather than surrender our lives to Him in loving and generous obedience. The Christians of the first century were very attuned to reading the signs of the times and interpreting them in a religious sense. Thus, even the destruction of Jerusalem was a cause for reflection and a motivation for deepened discipleship when interpreted as a sign of God's judgment on those who reject the Son.

> *What are the "signs of our times" that should move us to deeper reflection or motivate us to deeper discipleship?*
> *What are the ways in which we can expect God to conform to our way of life rather than surrendering to the Lord's way of discipleship?*
> *If we believe with the Christians of the first century that God acts in the events of history, what are we doing now as a society to reject the Son, and how do we see those actions of rejection bringing about negative consequences for us? Sometimes when people see events of great destruction and disaster, they can question how a good God could permit such things to occur. How would you answer such questions in light of this parable?*

Finally, the passage ends with Jesus cautioning disciples to read Scripture correctly when He asked, "Did you never read..."? Of course, they had read that passage, but they had not previously understood that passage in light of the person of Jesus. Thus, the challenge Jesus issues is for us to read Scripture through the lens of our Lord's person, ministry, passion, death, and resurrection. It is only by reading all Scripture through the lens of Jesus that we can come to correctly understand the Word of God (Scripture) through the Word of God (Jesus). Such an interpretive perspective will help us to deepen our appreciation for the Scriptures and to be protected against un-Christian interpretations. In this particular passage, Jesus reveals that He is the fulfillment of Psalm 118:22 and 23. As the "stone the builders rejected", Jesus has indeed become the cornerstone of the Church. A cornerstone in the ancient world had three primary functions. First, it gave stability to the house because the cornerstone was a large stone upon which the structural elements were placed with confidence. Second, it gave direction to the house because the cornerstone was oftentimes a naturally occurring stone around which a house was built and because of which the direction of the cornerstone determined the orientation of the house itself. Third, it was the focus of the house because it was the largest stone in the structure, and it could not be ignored or covered over as the most visible aspect of the building. When we apply these functional descriptions to Jesus in the life of the Church, we can see more clearly the role the Lord desires to have in our lives so that He can be the source of our stability, direction, and focus.

What forces or influences today try to take the place of Jesus by pretending to be the source of our stability, direction, or focus in life?

What passages of Scripture can you recall that have been interpreted in un-Christian ways because they were not read through the lens of Jesus?

What passage of the Old Testament or New Testament takes on new meaning for you when you read it through the lens of Jesus?

As disciples, we sometimes hear the words of Scripture over and over again each Sunday, yet they can fail to move us. What causes people to become indifferent to the Word of God in the Scriptures?

What can a faith community do to deepen people's appreciation of, and attentiveness to, the Scriptures when they are proclaimed in the Liturgy of the Word?

Twenty-Eighth Sunday in Ordinary Time

Our Scripture passage for this Sunday comes from the Gospel of Matthew 22:1–14. In this passage, we read the Parable of the Wedding Feast that contains several surprises and cautions for us as disciples. Some of the elements in this parable are similar to the Parable of the Vineyard, such as the violent response of the tenants towards the Son and the response of the Master. Also, this parable shares some similarities with the Parable of the Two Sons, such as initial commitment but subsequent rejection of the invitation. In addition to these similarities, there are also new elements in this week's passage that are distinctive to Matthew's account, so we will focus our reflection on these particular elements.

Two of the important elements to note are as follows: the event is a Wedding Banquet, and the summons to attend has been issued by the King. These distinctive elements intensify the theme of the parables presented during the past few weeks. This parable begins with messengers being dispatched to summon the invited guests. The practice for such events in the ancient world was to prepare a guest list in advance based on those who indicated their willingness to attend the celebration. Then, when the celebration was ready, those who were previously invited, and who accepted the invitation, would be notified that it was time to attend. This process involved two steps: the initial moment of notification for which people would indicate their willingness to attend, and then the moment of response to actually show up when the event was held. These two moments surface in our faith life as well. For example, in our baptism we are asked to reject evil and to profess our faith and trust in God. Yet that initial moment of commitment has to be lived out in specific moments when we do, in fact, choose to reject sin and to actively witness our faith and trust in God. The king in the parable had a legitimate expectation that those who said they would come to the wedding feast would actually fulfill their commitment, and the Lord has the same expectation of us.

> *When have you made a commitment that you regretted because you didn't wish to fulfill it?*
> *What are examples of faith commitments that are difficult to fulfill in daily life?*
> *When have you hosted an event and the guests who accepted the invitation did not actually attend?*
> *How does that experience help you understand the Lord's disappointment with us when we act similarly?*

Let us now look at what it is that the king (God) expects of us by our initial acceptance of His invitation.

First, God wants us to be part of the Wedding Banquet with His Son. The image of a wedding is used repeatedly in the New Testament to signify the relationship between Jesus and His disciples. In the Book of Revelation 19:7–10 we are told, "Blessed are they who are called to the wedding feast of the Lamb." In Ephesians 5:25–33 husbands and wives are instructed to love one another even as Christ loves the Church. In Mark 2:19, Luke 5:32, and Matthew 9:15, Jesus says with these or similar words, "How can the wedding guests fast while the bridegroom is still in their midst?" All of these passages indicate that the early Church understood discipleship as a deeply committed relationship with the Lord analogous to that of marriage. In fact, some of the great Christian saints and mystics spoke about their intense relationship with Jesus in terms of "spiritual marriage" including St Bernard of Clairvaux, St Catherine of Siena, Bl. Angela of Foligno, and St Teresa of Avila, just to name a few. That relationship is the Wedding Banquet to which the Lord has invited us and for which we have accepted the invitation through our baptism and the reception of other sacraments.

> *What similarities do you find between Christian discipleship and the relationship of human marriage?*
> *How can such a comparison guide you in your next step of discipleship?*
> *How do the Sacraments (Baptism, Reconciliation, Communion, and so forth) take on new meaning when they are*

understood through the image of Spiritual Marriage with Jesus?

Christian marriage, when lived fully as a Sacrament, is faithful, exclusive, permanent, and fruitful. How do these qualities apply to our spiritual relationship with Jesus?

Second, Jesus states in this parable that the summons comes from a King to his subjects. Thus, the meal in this parable is not an everyday event among friends but is actually an expression of our citizenship in the Kingdom of God. This aspect of the parable helps us to understand why the rejection of the summons evokes such violence: it is an act of disloyalty. To refuse the summons after having accepted the invitation would be an act of treason. We all know what the Pledge of Allegiance involves from our experience of growing up in the United States, and we have all made the Pledge of Allegiance. The challenge of being a good citizen is not so much to make the Pledge of Allegiance but to live it out with acts of loyalty each day. The same thing is true for our citizenship in the Kingdom of God. When we call Jesus "Lord", we are acknowledging Him as the King to whom we willingly surrender every aspect of our lives and from whom we willingly accept direction and guidance in everything we do. He is not only the Lord of our Sunday morning but of every morning, afternoon, and evening throughout the entire week as well. He is not only the Lord of our prayer life but also of our political, economic, and family life. Jesus issues a summons for us to be His loyal subjects and to let Him reign in our lives. We are called to live out our spiritual pledge of allegiance in the daily situations we face. It is much easier to claim citizenship in the Kingdom of Heaven than it is to live it. When the invited guests in the parable rejected the summons to the Wedding Banquet, they were rejecting the King himself.

What insights into discipleship do you gain through the image of citizenship in the Kingdom of God?

The two topics to be commonly avoided in social discussions are politics and religion, yet in this parable Jesus brings them together. What uncomfortable topic is Jesus prompting you to address as a disciple in your own life or the lives of others?

The invited guests in the parable had allowed something else in their lives to become more important than their allegiance to the King. When do you find yourself putting other things before God in your marriage, family, business, or social life?

Being a faithful citizen requires actions that promote, defend, protect, and support the good of the Kingdom. How can these various actions of good citizenship practically motivate you in your discipleship every day?

Next, the King in the parable sends his messengers to bring in others so that the Wedding Banquet may be filled. He specifically instructs them to go into the thoroughfares, which referred to the multitude of winding paths and roads that extended far into the countryside. They were to invite whomever they could find to the Wedding Banquet. That task required hard work! The outskirts of civilization were where the misfits, street people, prostitutes, and even criminals were to be found. These are not the pretty people of society. Imagine how much easier and more comfortable it would have been to lament those who did not attend rather than to exert the effort required to fill the empty spaces. That is actually what we do sometimes in our ministries today. We can find it easier to complain about who is not participating rather than exert the effort it takes to find new people who will participate. It takes work to make the invitation of the Gospel meaningful and relevant for people today, especially for those who are not in the mainstream of society. Jesus expects us to be like the messengers in this parable who are willing to do what is necessary so as to fill the King's banquet, and sometimes that means reaching out to those with whom we would not normally associate.

What are the ministries of your faith community that have "open seats" that need to be filled, and where are the "thoroughfares" that you can search to invite potential participants?

Who are people whom you would not want to invite to a ministry event?

*Some of Jesus' closest disciples were people He found on the
"thoroughfares" of society (Matthew the tax collector, Mary
Magdalene, and so forth).
Where would we look today for such unlikely disciples?*

Lastly, the parable ends with a surprising twist as the King encounters someone not appropriately dressed for a wedding feast and
throws him out of the celebration. We need to remember that
clothing in the ancient world was symbolic of the person's identity.
The experience of Christian conversion was sometimes described in
terms of wearing a new set of clothes. Even in our current Baptismal
Rite, we place a new garment on the baptized person as a symbol
of their change of life and identity. To wear a new garment, then,
was a sign that the person had left behind their former way of life
and that they were becoming a new creation in Christ Jesus. This
imagery is developed extensively in the New Testament and is a
consistent theme (see Rom 13:12–14, Gal 3:27, Eph 6:11, Col 3:12, Lk
15:22, Rev 3:4, 6:11, 19:8). This additional element of clothing and
its connection to a person's identity indicates that there is more
to Christian discipleship than just accepting to the invitation. The
need for a proper wedding garment means that a person must be
living a converted life in order to remain a part of the Wedding
Banquet. This is a very important message for all disciples because
it challenges us to cooperate with God's grace in everyday life so
that we can bear witness to the conversion that we have already
experienced. It is wonderful to be invited into a personal relationship with God in Jesus Christ, but it is something else to actually
conform our lives to that invitation so as to live out that relationship
in everything we say and do. Our ability to remain a part of the
eternal Wedding Banquet with the Lamb of God depends on our
willingness to be conformed each day into the likeness of Christ.
Otherwise, we are like the man in the parable who shows up without being prepared to remain one of God's chosen ones.

*How does this parable challenge you to take seriously your
commitments of faith?
How is it that people can be so happy to receive the invitation of faith, yet fail to respond with a life conformed to
faith?*

*How do you know when you are not "wearing the wedding
garment" of a converted life?*
*What kinds of obstacles typically prevent people from living
their true identity as Christians?*
What signs indicate that you are living a new life in Christ?

Pope Saint Leo the Great spoke of the necessary conformity of life
that must take place in Christian disciples when he proclaimed:

> Christian, remember your dignity, and now that you share
> in God's own nature, do not return by sin to your former
> base condition. Bear in mind who is your head and of whose
> body you are a member. Do not forget that you have been
> rescued from the power of darkness and brought into the light
> of God's kingdom. Through the Sacrament of Baptism you
> have become a temple of the Holy Spirit. Do not drive away
> so great a guest by evil conduct and become again a slave to
> the Devil, for your liberty was bought by the Blood of Christ.[52]

*How does this quote from Saint Leo the Great help you
understand the Parable of the Wedding Banquet?*

---

52. St Leo the Great, *Sermo 1 in Nativitate Domini*, 1-3: PI, 54, pp.
     190–193.

TWENTY-NINTH SUNDAY IN ORDINARY TIME

Our Scripture passage for this Sunday comes from the Gospel of Matthew 22:15–21. In this text we read of how the Pharisees conspire with the Herodians to trap Jesus with a question concerning the payment of tax to the Romans. Jesus turns their question into a greater challenge of discipleship.

The question posed to Jesus presented a serious dilemma for the Lord. Herod and his supporters presumably supported the payment of the census tax since they ruled under the auspices, and by the favor, of the Roman Empire. The Pharisees certainly managed to move about freely in Roman circles, and so they at least cooperated with Roman laws and tax requirements. Thus, it would appear that neither the Herodians nor the Pharisees were really opponents of the tax. As more people began to follow Jesus, the Pharisees and the Herodians were attempting to diminish our Lord's influence and power. If Jesus were to say that He opposed the tax, then the Pharisees and Herodians could turn Him in to the Roman authorities as a rebel or political insurrectionist. Such an accusation could easily result in His arrest as a revolutionary. If Jesus were to openly support the tax, then those followers who were looking for an earthly messiah to overthrow the Romans would mostly likely be disappointed and refuse to follow Him any longer. That is the dilemma of this question, and it is a direct threat to our Lord's mission. Disciples sometimes find themselves in the midst of a dilemma as well. Such situations can occur in marriages, families, friendships, and professional worlds. The Church today continues to face a variety of dilemmas in regards to certain questions. This is especially true when those who wish to diminish the mission and effectiveness of the Church seek ways in which to dissuade disciples, damage the credibility of Christianity, or impede the ability of the Church to function freely and readily.

What dilemmas have you faced and for which there were
no safe answers?
What decisions of the Church have been used by her oppo-
nents to discredit her mission?
What are the current issues in our society that present a
similar situation of dilemma for the Church today?
Jesus did not answer the question that was posed to Him.
How do you know when it is better to not answer a question?

Next, Jesus asked to see the coin used to pay the Roman census tax.
In order to understand the force of this request, it is important to
remember the setting in which the dialogue takes place. We were
told in Matthew 21:23 that Jesus entered the Temple area, and He
has remained in the Temple area while this discourse is taking
place. It is also important to remember that the Roman census
tax was paid with a Denarius and that this coin contained both an
image of the Emperor Tiberius Caesar as well as the inscription,
"Tiberius Caesar Vivi Augusti Filius Augustus Pontifex Maximus",
which is translated, "Tiberius Caesar, August Son of the Divine
Augustus, High Priest". To possess such a coin in the Temple area
that contained a graven image and an inscription attributing divine
status to a human person was both a sacrilege and an idolatrous
action. Note that Jesus Himself did not have such a coin on His
person and so had to request that someone else produce it! Thus,
the Lord revealed the hypocrisy of His opponents and the explicit
complacency of the Pharisees with the Roman Empire. Finally,
Jesus states that the coin already belongs to Tiberius Caesar and
that what belongs to the emperor should be returned to him as
his property. Therefore, paying the tax is not so much an issue of
violating the Law of Moses but of returning someone's property to
the rightful owner. There was little the Pharisees could say at this
point. By possessing the coin, they showed that they were willing
to participate in the Roman economic system. By possessing the
coin in the Temple area, the Pharisees were showing that they
themselves had already broken the religious rules of their time.
The Pharisees lost credibility for these two reasons, and that loss
of credibility prevented them from continuing the dialogue. It is
important for us as disciples to remember that we, too, can lose our
credibility when we choose to participate in systems or situations

that are contrary to our principles of faith. When we lose credibility, our ability to represent the Gospel is weakened by our poor example, and others can be turned away from Christ because of it.

What examples can you think of in which religious persons have lost credibility because of their participation in systems or settings that are contrary to their profession of faith? When has the Church's close alignment with any one government or political party undermined the credibility of the Gospel?

Jesus was not pointing out the Pharisees' fault as much as He was revealing their hypocrisy by accusing Jesus of something they themselves were already doing. Sometimes we find it easy to criticize others for things we are doing as well. How does this dialogue between Jesus and the Pharisees challenge you to reconsider your negative attitudes towards others?

The Catholic moral tradition recognizes that it is virtually impossible to function in the world without participating in some degree or another with systems or agencies that are committing evil acts (such as using Roman coins), but a distinction is made between "Formal Cooperation with Evil", in which we participate with the intention of supporting or assisting the evil action of an agency, and "Material Cooperation with Evil", in which we have little or no choice to participate but do not intend to support or assist the evil action of an agency.

How can this moral distinction help you navigate through the complex web of ethical decisions you must make? What are circumstances you face in which you have little choice but to participate in a system or setting with which you do not agree?

Jesus concludes this scene by issuing an important and profound instruction: Give to Caesar what is Caesar's but Give to God what is God's. That is an important statement given the fact that Jesus had just inquired about whose image was on the coin. If something bears the imprint of Caesar then it is Caesar's, and, according to the same logic, if something bears the imprint of God then it must be returned to God. This passage is sometimes understood as endorsing blind support for secular government. While early Christians did pay Roman tax (Rom 13:1–7, 1 Pt 2:13–17, Mt 17:24–27), there are certainly indications in Revelation 17–18 that they could also be very critical of the Roman Empire. Rather than interpreting this passage as supporting blind obedience to the state, the real thrust of the teaching is to give far greater obedience to God than we give to any secular authority. As Christians, we believe that we are created in God's image and likeness. Therefore, the whole of our life is imprinted with the image of God, and every blessing we have received is imprinted with the hand of God. The challenge of discipleship, then, is not to just give God a portion of what we have but rather to surrender everything to the Lord because it all bears His divine imprint. If we think that a part of our life doesn't bear God's imprint then we are denying the Lord's creative and redeeming power over us.

> *How does God collect His tax from you in regards to your time, talent, and treasure?*
>
> *How does the example of paying taxes inform and challenge your understanding of discipleship?*
>
> *What other analogies can you draw from the experience of paying taxes and discipleship?*
>
> *Caesar had a right to receive tax from those who participated in the Roman Empire. When in your relationship with God do you acknowledge that the Lord has a right to your life?*
>
> *The so-called "head tax" of the Roman Empire amounted to a flat rate of one Denarius per person and was paid by everyone regardless of economic status. What is the most basic tax that God can expect of every disciple, no matter who they are?*

THIRTIETH SUNDAY IN ORDINARY TIME

Our Scripture passage for this Sunday comes from the Gospel of Matthew 22:34–40. This text tells of the Lawyer's challenge for Jesus to identify the "greatest" commandment, to which the Lord responds by offering the joint instruction to love God and neighbor. This passage appears to be very simple on the surface, yet it offers some profound challenges for discipleship.

There were 613 commandments in the Jewish Law. Of these, 248 were positive instructions (what a person should do) and 365 were negative instructions (what a person shouldn't do). It was not always possible to observe so many commands in daily life, so the rabbis discussed ways in which the Law could be prioritized. For example, some commands were identified as being heavy and more important than those identified as being light. An example of prioritization would rank honoring a person's parents as heavier and more important than observing the rules governing the treatment of birds' nests in Deuteronomy 22:6–7. Another strategy was to establish summary statements of the Jewish Law that could help put it all in perspective. These summary statements served as a kind of organizing principal for all 613 commandments. An example of such a summary statement would be from the wise teacher Hillel who taught, "What is hateful to you do not do to your neighbor; that is the whole Torah while the rest is commentary; go and learn from it."[53] We all have life responsibilities and obligations that sometimes start to weigh on us. Maybe it is the long hours we spend in the office or the long drive each day. Perhaps, too, it is the obligation of taking care of children and the loss of freedom once experienced in our youthful years. Sometimes we ask ourselves the question "Why am I doing this?" As disciples, it is important that we be clear about our motivations for fulfilling the many obligations we face, or our

---

53. Hillel the Elder, *Shabbath 31ᵃ*, Trans. By H. Freedman (London: Soncino Press, s.d).

efforts can become meaningless burdens and our loving attitude can give in to resentment.

If someone asked you to state the greatest value in your life, how would you respond?

If you used your own answer to that question as a measure for how you have spent your time, energy, and resources this past week, how well would you be living that greatest value in practice?

What would you say is the summary statement of the Catholic experience of faith (by the way, we have many more than 613 rules in Canon Law!)?

What obligations in your personal, professional, or faith life have become burdensome or caused resentment in you because you have lost sight of your fundamental motivation for fulfilling them?

How do you re-focus and re-energize your discipleship when you lose perspective?

When Jesus answered the Lawyer's question, He did so by stating that love of neighbor is like love of God and that all the commandments hang (or "depend") on these two. In order for us to understand the significance of the word "hang" or "depend" used in this passage, we need to imagine a rod suspended by two strings with a weight hanging in the middle of the rod. If one string fails then the weight comes crashing to the ground. That is the necessary image that helps us understand the meaning of our Lord's explanation. Every action of our Christian lives must be motivated and directed by both Love of God and Love of Neighbor. If we fail in one, we fail in both because they are intrinsically connected as is clearly stated in 1 John 4:20, "Whoever claims to love God yet hates his brother is a liar. For whoever does not love their brother and sister, whom they have seen, cannot love God, whom they have not seen." Our discipleship can only be sustained when we are fully responsive in love to both God and neighbor in all our decisions and actions. Sometimes we like to separate these two commands and exempt ourselves from fulfilling one while claiming to fulfill the other. This separation occurs when a person dedicates extensive energy and resource to religious practices but does not give of themselves in charity for others. It also happens when a person is deeply immersed in social services or humanitarian efforts but does not have a living relationship with God. Jesus' statement prevents such an disconnected approach; discipleship "depends" on both commands and never just one. That is why love of neighbor is "like" love of God; one is not possible without the other.

> *What happens when a person emphasizes love of God at the expense of love of neighbor?*
> *What happens when a person emphasizes love of neighbor at the expense of love of God?*
> *When can our love of God and neighbor legitimately call us to act in a way that our neighbor may not want or like?*
> *How do we express love of God and love of neighbor in our local community of faith?*
> *If someone looked at your life from the outside, how would they know that you love both God and others?*

Our Lord also wants us to choose carefully our fundamental reason for following Him and His way of life. Jesus knows that there can be lots of reasons which can motivate us to follow rules and laws; our Lord wants us to be motivated by love when we seek to do His will. Some people are obedient out of fear of punishment or guilt. Others are obedient because they want to be rewarded for doing the right thing. Some can be obedient out of self-righteousness and a desire to see themselves as "better" than those who aren't as faithful in fulfilling their responsibilities of life and faith, whatever those that might be. Still others can be motivated to follow rules and laws more out of ideological, sociological, or nationalistic passions. Many people are even motivated by the emotional desire for respect, acceptance, praise, or the approval of others especially from those in positions of authority. Still others can be motivated by something as simple as cultural conformity. In our American culture we have a saying that states, "The Law is the Law", and implies that rules are to be followed simply because they are imposed by the governing authority. This motivation may lead us to be good citizens, but it cannot make us good Christians. For Christians, we follow Jesus' way of life not out of fear, desire for reward, ideology, self-righteousness and so on. Rather, Christians must be motivated by the law of love in all that we do. Love is not only the motivation for our obedience; it is also the very reason why God reveals Himself to us through the writings of Scripture, so we can love the Lord and our neighbor more readily. That is why Jesus says that even the writings of the Prophets "hang" on love of God and neighbor.

> *How do you know when you are motivated by something other than love of God and Neighbor in your practice of faith?*
> *How does the motivation of love for both God and Neighbor change the way you read and understand Scripture?*
> *Who is someone you know who is motivated only by love?*
> *What makes a person want to love?*
> *How has your motivation for following God's law changed with your growth in discipleship?*

Finally, it is worth noting that when Jesus speaks about loving God and Neighbor, our Lord has something very specific in mind. Love in the Scriptures is never presented as an emotional feeling of affection or attraction. Rather, love is always a motivation for action and a commitment of life. You see, we have lots of ways in which we understand the term "love" in our contemporary society, but the real definition of Christian love is in the very life and ministry of Jesus. He shows us what love of God and our neighbor looks like. Jesus loved the Father by fulfilling His will even on the cross. He prayed regularly and praised the Father for His love and presence. He offered the Father His whole life to be used by Him for the salvation of the world. Jesus also loved those who followed Him as well as those who wouldn't follow Him. He loved those who washed His feet with their tears and those who drove the nails in His hands (see Mt 5:21–48 for teachings on the need to love enemies). He loved the religious leaders who rejected Him and the sinners who came to Him. He cared for others in their weakness, forgave them in their sins, and offered Himself for them in His sacrifice on Calvary and in His Eucharist at the Last Supper. That's something very different from what today's media tells us "love" means!

> *When people talk about "love" in today's world, what do they generally mean?*

How does the lived example of Jesus challenge you in your understanding of what it means to love God and Neighbor?
What loving action of Jesus would you find most difficult to live out in your life?
How can we as a faith community help people want to love God more like Jesus did?
How can we help people love their neighbor more like Jesus did?

One of the great quotes from the story of Saint Thomas Becket is this: "The last temptation is the greatest treason: To do the right deed for the wrong reason."[54]

How do you think this quote relates to the Christian life and the law of love?

---

54. T. S. Eliot, *Murder in the Cathedral* (New York: Harcourt, 1963), First Act.

Thirty-First Sunday in Ordinary Time

Our Scripture passage for this Sunday comes from the Gospel of Matthew 23:1–12. In this text, we hear Jesus instructing His disciples on certain pitfalls to be avoided both in their roles as religious followers and religious leaders. These cautions offer a timeless counsel for us as well because we can face many of the same pitfalls that sometimes arise from human weakness in any organization.

The first caution issued to the disciples is that they should not be deterred from following the truth of a message despite the flawed witness of the messenger. This is an important reminder for Christians of all time. When Jesus instructed the disciples to "Do what they tell you but do not follow their example", our Lord was emphasizing that the human weaknesses of religious leaders should never prevent us from hearing the truth of what they teach. The reality is that we are all flawed because of the corruption of sin, but that doesn't mean we are incapable of recognizing, accepting, and communicating the truth of God's Word. It is a sign of mature discipleship when a Christian can accept the truth of the message despite the weakness of the messenger, and that is the discipleship to which Jesus calls us. There can be a tendency in all of us to exempt ourselves from the challenge of discipleship. For a disciple who lacks spiritual maturity, the flawed witness of others, especially those who are in positions of authority, can be an easy way to justify such an exemption. The truth is the truth whether it is spoken by a sinner or by a saint, and we need to remember that. Disciples who are attuned to the voice of the Lord can recognize His Word in the most surprising of circumstances. If we are waiting to meet the perfect person before we listen to what they have to say, we will be waiting a very long time and we will be missing lots of opportunities for spiritual growth.

When can an experience of human weakness actually help
someone understand more clearly the truth of the Gospel?
How has the message of Christianity been diminished
because of the poor witness of Christians?
When do you find it easy to dismiss the message because
of the poor, lived example of the messenger?
How does this teaching of Jesus challenge you to reconsider
the way in which you have approached your faith life?
When have you heard truth spoken from the most unlikely
of sources?
What helps someone to not be deterred in their discipleship
because of another person's weakness?

Next, Jesus focuses on three particular pitfalls He observed in the religious people of His time. Each of these pitfalls has something to say to us because the Lord wants us to specifically avoid these misguided and self-centered tendencies of human nature. It would be a mistake to misread these pitfalls as only existing in the Pharisees and Scribes of ancient Judaism. These same tendencies have tempted Christians as well. The practice of religion is meant to lead us closer into communion with the Lord and others. Anytime we use religion as a tool for some other reason, especially self-gain, then we distort its meaning and purpose. Let's reflect on each one of these three cautions and see how they might apply to our lived experience.

First, Jesus says that the Pharisees and Scribes bind heavy burdens for other people to carry but are not willing to lift a finger to help them. This caution most likely refers to the imposition of religious obligations or expectations that are difficult for the average person to fulfill. In such a situation, it can be easy for religious observance to become a weapon with which to afflict others. Jesus does not want us to use religious observance as a way of putting others down by pointing out how incapable they are of fulfilling religious obligations. Neither does the Lord want religious practices to inflate our pride by making us feel more righteous than others. The reality is that the Christian life is very challenging, but it is a challenge that is always offered with love. Truth without charity can be a harsh reality that can bruise the human spirit rather than help others live out their faith. Charity is reflected in our desire to help others become the best person they can be in the eyes of God. This desire takes proper form in the realization and communication of God's vision for our lives and in our willingness to help others personalize this vision in their own realities. Religion is meant to bring us into closer communion with God and others, and when religion becomes a means of disassociating ourselves from others, it has become misguided. When we recognize the need to communicate a message of faith to someone else, we must also recognize the obligation to help that person as they apply that message of faith to their lives. Telling people what they should do isn't being a Christian witness; helping others to actually do what they should is being a true disciple. In no way does Jesus want disciples to water down the challenging nature of His message. Rather, our Lord wants us to understand that an important part of sharing the Good News is to help others live it and not to lay it on them like a crushing burden that might make us feel better but makes them feel worse.

> *To whom do you need to speak the truth with charity as described above?*
> *When has someone challenged you with the message of faith and offered to help you live it?*
> *What teachings of faith today represent heavy burdens for people?*
> *How can a faith community help others with the burdens they bear because of their discipleship?*

Next, Jesus cautions against the use of visible religious signs as a way of attracting public attention to oneself rather than helping people focus their attention on God. The two primary examples used are those of the Phylactery and the tassel. The Phylactery was a small leather box worn on the forehead and the forearm during special times of prayer. It is not the box that was important but rather the text of Scripture written on a small scroll and placed inside the box that was of value. The box became a sign of a person's commitment to, and love for, the Word of God. By increasing the size of the box (Phylactery), people could draw more attention to themselves and give the impression that they had greater devotion to the Word of God. The tassels on a person's outer garment were a symbol of that person's commitment to the Law (Torah). The use of longer and more visible tassels was to make sure others knew of their devotion to the Law. Thus, these two actions of enhancing the visible manifestations of an individual's practice of faith were more for the purpose of drawing public attention than for helping that person focus their prayer. When religious symbols become a decoration or just a piece of jewelry rather than an inspiration and motivation for prayer, then we have fallen into the same temptation. Religious symbols such as clothing, art, bumper stickers, and so forth can be helpful so long as they serve to raise our thoughts and attention to God. Religious symbols can be detrimental to our faith when we use them to promote our own status, gain the attention of others, or as a substitute for real conversion of heart.

> *How does this teaching challenge you?*
> *What are symbols of faith that help you in your prayer and Christian life?*
> *What symbols of faith are being cheapened today by their misuse as mere decoration or for self-serving purposes?*
> *What are ways today in which we can be tempted to make our religious observance more visible for the sake of gaining the respect and admiration of others?*

Lastly, Jesus criticizes those people who use their religious standing in order to secure privileged positions and titles of public honor. These practices reveal an excessive desire for status in the eyes of others. Certainly this desire is as alive and well in our world today as it was in the world of Jesus. The need for affection and esteem is normal and is even identified as one of the three basic human drives (the other two basic human drives are security/survival and power/control). Who doesn't want to be honored and respected by their peers or to be given a privileged place when they attend an event? We need to be honest with ourselves in order to realize how much these desires actually do influence our lives. However, the pursuit of these desires can lead us to focus more on the respect, affirmation, and approval of others than that of God. When that happens, we begin to use our religious standing as one more tool to gain the attention and respect of others rather than as an encouragement to greater discipleship. Jesus wanted the Christian community to find greatness in their service for others. Rather than seeking a privileged life, Christian disciples are called to live a more profoundly committed, sacrificial, and humble life in which we serve others as brothers and sisters. Rather than seeking titles of honor that distinguish us from the rest of humanity, Christian disciples are called to seek greater communion with the rest of humanity. When a person expects to be respected, honored, or rewarded because of their faith standing, they have given in to the temptation of religious superiority and arrogance. Jesus addresses His final caution to that temptation. Religious observance is not about improving our standing in society; it's about improving our standing with God and that never leads us to be exclusive or judgmental towards others. For Christians, titles should exist to denote roles of service rather than privilege.

> *When have you encountered people who want the title but are not willing to fulfill the role?*
> *What are the titles you have that are difficult to live out in your personal, professional, faith, and family life?*
> *Jesus addressed the use of titles that were common in His society. If Jesus were to speak to us today, what titles do you think He would address and why?*
> *How can people today use their religious standing to secure privileged positions or titles of public honor?*

THIRTY-SECOND SUNDAY IN ORDINARY TIME

Our Scripture passage for this Sunday comes from the Gospel of Matthew 25:1–13. In this text we read the story of the ten maidens who await the return of the bridegroom with varying degrees of preparedness. The response of the bridegroom may seem strange and even harsh. Our Lord told this parable so as to encourage disciples to use wisely and timely the opportunities for faithful preparation while they are available. This passage offers us important reflections to guide our own spiritual preparation to meet the Lord as well.

One of the important keys needed to unlock the meaning of this passage is to understand the symbol of oil. The reference to oil most likely indicated olive oil, which had many uses in the ancient world and was a prized commodity because of its usefulness and endurance. It was used as fuel in lamps to give light, in cooking to enhance flavor, placed on the skin for medicinal use, and so forth. Oil was so highly regarded in the ancient world that Jewish tradition equated it with "good works" and even with the Torah (Law). The implied connection between the importance of oil as a symbol for good works is reinforced by the connection between this parable and the subsequent text of Matthew 23:31–46 in which individual good works form the basis of divine judgment. We need to also remember that oil in this parable served to provide light. The image of light as a symbol for a life of faith that bears good works was previously used in Matthew 5:16 when Jesus said, "Your light must shine before others, that they may see your good deeds and glorify your heavenly Father." This interpretation of oil helps us understand why it could not be shared. It is not a matter of the wise maidens' lack of generosity but of the inability for someone else to claim for themselves the manifest good deeds, living faith, and Christian decisions of another person's life. Our oil is that gift of divine life within us and expressions of our faith that prepare us to meet God. With this understanding we can properly appreciate how important it is to possess and treasure that gift.

> *How does this interpretation of "oil" enrich your understanding of this passage?*
> *What are ways in which a person can falsely rely on the good decisions, living faith, and deeds of others rather than working on their own life of faith and relationship with God?*
> *How do you know whether you have enough "oil" or not?*
> *In the Rite of Baptism, a candle is passed to the newly baptized as they are given the commission: "Keep the flame of faith alive in your heart. When the Lord comes, may you go out to meet Him with all the saints in the heavenly Kingdom." What spiritual practices, good works of charity, or personal study manifest and nurture the flame of faith and keep it burning brightly in your life?*

The other important thing to note about this parable is that five of the maidens are identified as being foolish while the other five are identified as being wise. It is worth studying the qualities that denoted each group so that we can learn from both their good and their bad example.

The foolish maidens failed to consider the reality that the bridegroom could be delayed and so they were not prepared for the extended time of waiting. In addition to their prior lack of preparation, they even failed to undertake actions of preparation, when they actually did have time to do so, during the bridegroom's delay. Perhaps they really didn't think the bridegroom would come back or that he would not care if they had no oil (or light) for their lamps. Maybe they thought they would be able to calculate the arrival time of the bridegroom so as to prepare at the last minute. Finally, perhaps the foolish maidens thought that someone else would take care of them at that moment, or they could just borrow from others. All of these factors surface elsewhere in Matthew's Gospel as examples of people who are mistaken concerning the preparation needed to faithfully and personally meet the Lord.

The wise maidens, on the other hand, were prepared with more than enough oil. They reasonably anticipated the delay in the bridegroom's return yet remained confident that he would come back. They had no need to frantically pursue futile efforts at the last minute or to carefully decipher the exact hour of the bridegroom's return; they could sleep peacefully knowing they were prepared for his arrival. They also knew that the decision to be a disciple is a deeply personal one that no other person can make for them, and they took responsibility for their own lives, decisions, and actions of faith. Matthew's Gospel has also touched on all of these themes.

> *As you think about the different qualities that made one group of maidens wise and the other group of maidens foolish, what insight strikes you as most meaningful and relevant for your own discipleship?*
> *What does our secular culture teach us it means to be wise? What does our secular culture teach us it means to be foolish?*
> *What does a wise person look like today when they act according to the example of the wise maidens in this parable?*
> *How do people typically prepare to meet the Lord, and how does this parable challenge their previous methods of preparation?*

Lastly, the parable ends with a scene of judgment as the bridegroom returns, and those who are prepared (wise maidens) are welcomed inside while those who are not prepared (foolish maidens) are excluded. When the foolish maidens come to the door and realize they have been locked out, they begin to cry, saying, "Lord, Lord, open to us." But the bridegroom responds saying, "I do not know you." In Matthew's Gospel, Jesus had previously issued a warning in 7:21–22 that it requires more than just saying "Lord, Lord" to enter the Kingdom of Heaven. Rather, entrance requires that a person "do the will of my Father who is in heaven". Now we see an illustration of what happens to those who have all the right confession of faith in what they say but do not have a life that corresponds to that faith (symbolized by lack of oil). Jesus ends the parable with the challenge to "watch". The watchfulness He calls for is not that which avoids the sleep that comes to all people (an image for death) but to prevent the lack of attentiveness that causes us to fall asleep in our faith lives (spiritual sloth). Watchfulness, not cleverness or last minute planning, is what denotes a wise disciple. The watchfulness we seek is that which recognizes every opportunity to grow in virtue and holiness by manifesting our faith in good deeds, hope, and love and acts on those opportunities without hesitation. An example of such watchfulness can be found in the life of Mother Teresa who, when presented with an unforeseen change in her schedule such as an airline delay, canceled meeting, waiting at a bus stop, and so forth, would say to her Sisters, "God has given us this gift of time; let us use it to do good." She would then begin to lead others in prayer, reach out to others in need, or share a message of good news with a stranger.

> *What do you typically do when you have an unexpected change in your schedule that provides the gift of time (is it a "wise" use of time or a "foolish" use of time)?*
> *In what ways can people reduce faith today to mere sentiment or religious profession rather than a conviction that is manifested in lived expression?*
> *What is the difference between the situation presented in this parable and the scene of the Good Thief on the Cross who calls out for Jesus' mercy in His last moment and receives it (Lk 23:40–43)?*
> *What tempts you to procrastinate doing good works of faith, hope, and love?*
> *What are the excuses you use to not take advantage of opportunities you have to grow in your faith through various ministries?*

THIRTY-THIRD SUNDAY IN
ORDINARY TIME

Our Scripture passage for this Sunday comes from the Gospel of Matthew 25:14–30. This teaching is commonly known as the Parable of the Talents. In the parable we hear of a master who entrusted a large sum of money (five talents was worth fifteen years' wages) to each of his three servants and of how each servant responded to such responsibility while they awaited the master's return. While this passage is often used to encourage the development of human skills or to praise industrious efforts, Scripture scholars agree that the real commission to which Jesus is referring is that of multiplying the gift of Christian faith itself. This teaching has much to offer us as disciples and challenges us to reflect on how well we have multiplied the gift of faith and the message of the Gospel we have received.

The Parable of the Talents indicates that there were two reasons why the master entrusted his funds to the servants. The first reason was so that the master could find out which servants were capable of taking on even greater responsibilities. Of interesting note, it is because of this parable that the English word "talent" has come to mean "capability". Sometimes we do not discover our capabilities until we are faced with a challenge. After gaining self-confidence with smaller responsibilities, we are ready and willing to take on greater ones. One message for discipleship, then, is that we should be courageous in accepting challenges that take us beyond our comfort zone when it comes to witnessing our faith and sharing the message of the Gospel with others. In doing so, we will multiply the gift of faith we ourselves have received.

The second reason why the master entrusted his funds to his servants was to find out which ones would share his joy. This, too, is a challenging message for discipleship. God created us to know Him, love Him, and serve Him in this life and to be with Him forever in eternal life. Those servants in the parable who knew the master and served him worked diligently to multiply the treasure they received so as to return it with manifold increase. Such responsiveness allowed them to share in the master's lasting joy. When we share our faith and communicate the message of the Gospel to others, we are expressing our knowledge, love, and service of God as well. In doing so, we are also demonstrating our desire to share in the Master's eternal joy. God does not present us with opportunities to witness and share our faith in an effort to burden our lives but as an invitation to be His faithful co-worker in this world and His eternal companion in the next. When we see such opportunities as a blessed invitation of faithful servant-hood, we will respond with eagerness, creativity, gratitude, and industriousness.

> *What are some of the challenges you have faced that have helped you discover your talents?*
> *What is a step of discipleship for which you feel poorly equipped or not well prepared?*
> *When are you comfortable sharing your faith? When are you uncomfortable sharing your faith?*
> *How do you express your desire to spend eternity with God?*
> *Who is someone you know with whom you could share the gift of faith so as to become a spiritual multiplier?*

Another aspect of this parable that is worthy of our reflection is how well the servants used their time while they waited for the master's return. The theme of waiting was present in the Parable of the Ten Maidens as well (see last week's Gospel reflection). For Christians of the 1st century, the return of Jesus was something they anticipated and for which they longed. Other sections of the New Testament address the Christian question about the purpose of Jesus' delayed return by interpreting the period of waiting as providing graced opportunities for salvation on both personal (repentance) and communal (spread of the Gospel) levels. It specifically states in 2 Peter 3:15–16 that the delayed return of Jesus is not to be understood in a negative way but as a blessing when we are told, "Consider the patience of our Lord as salvation." Accordingly, Christians are not to spend their time passively sitting around while we wait for Jesus' return but we are to use well the time we have so as to do the Master's will while we can. Such will is personal for each disciple.[55] Jesus did not leave us a detailed program of life for every single human person to follow. Rather, the Lord gave us the gift of the Gospel, the Holy Spirit, the example of Christian life in the Apostolic Tradition, and the human capacity for reason, prayer and judgment so we might discern God's will and do it. Such an approach to our faith calls for spiritual maturity that is not content with mere obedience to basic rules. Instead, mature faith calls us to interpret and apply the Gospel with responsibility and accountability in every situation we face. This challenge calls us to a discipleship that is not content with only theological correctness but is also manifested in industrious faithful servant-hood. This connection between theological correctness and servant-hood is illustrated in the parable by the good servants who both knew the Master's will and who fulfilled that will.

> *What practices help you to know God's will for your life?*
> *How are you challenged and inspired in your life by the good servants in this parable who demonstrate a discipleship that goes beyond mere obedience to rules and was manifested in mature faith?*
> *Who is a good example of someone who is preparing well for the Lord's return?*

Lastly, it is worth studying the figure of the third servant who failed to multiply the master's treasure. This servant received the Talent but then buried it. He returned it to the master exactly as he had received it. He may have preserved it, but he didn't multiply it. That action of burying the gift of God is something we can do as well. Faith is deeply personal, but it is not intended to remain only a private experience. When we bury the Lord's grace we have received, we are acting like the third servant in the parable. We can bury God's gift when we receive the Sacraments but fail to live our life fully in Christ. We can bury God's gift when we fail to invite others into the life of faith and discipleship with which we have

---

55. St Thomas Aquinas reminds us of the proactive ministry of the virtue of patience when he says, "Patience is said to be the root and safeguard of all the virtues, not as though it caused and preserved them directly, but merely because it removes their obstacles." *Summa Theologia*, II–IIae, q. 136, a. 2, r. 3.

been blessed. We can even bury God's gift when we gain insights into Scripture and the mysteries of faith but keep those insights only to ourselves rather than sharing them with others so that their lives can be enriched as well. There are lots of erroneous thoughts that can lead us to fail in our Christian responsibility. In the Parable of the Talents, the third servant considered the master a hard man and said that he was afraid. His false perception of the master and his lack of courage led him to hide the money. Sometimes our misconception of God can lead us to act as immature disciples as well. If we have a faith that is based on fear or desire for reward, we will never come to know God as a generous, trusting, loving Father who invites us to be His instruments and co-workers in the world. It is also worth noting that the master identifies the true reason for the third servant's lack of creative and industrious discipleship: The master says he was "wicked and lazy". The wickedness of the servant is demonstrated in how he knew his master's expectation to "reap where he did not sow and gather where he did not plant", yet that servant did nothing to increase the master's gift. God has given us the gift of faith because the Lord wants to establish His Kingdom in us and in others through us. We know that is God's will. When we are afraid to share our faith, we are acting wickedly in the eyes of God. The second negative quality the master identifies is that of laziness. The servant found it easier to bury the money than to figure out the best way to invest it and multiply it. It does take persistence, ingenuity, creativity, problem solving, and risk to share our faith with others. Sometimes it may seem like it's not worth the effort, but that is spiritual laziness. Jesus summarized the moral of this parable when He said, "To him who has, more will be given; from him who has not, the little he has will be taken away." Faith doesn't survive in a person who buries it! Faith multiplies only in those who share it with others.

> *Do you want greater faith? How do people typically "bury" their faith today?*
> *What insights have you received in prayer or study that other people could find useful in their lives, and how could you share those?*

What are examples of mistaken images of God that can prevent people from serving the Lord with eagerness, love, and freedom?

What image of God is important for you to keep in mind in order to become a disciple who shares the gift of faith with eagerness, creativity, industriousness, risk and persistence?

How can the wickedness of knowing God's will but failing to do it be manifested in our lives?

It takes work and risk to effectively multiply the gift of faith with others. What are some of the typical excuses we can use to exempt ourselves from the responsibility of sharing our faith with others?

Jesus ends the parable with the observation, "To those who have, more will be given; but from those who have not, even the little they have will be taken away." How have you experienced this dynamic occurring in your life?

SOLEMNITY OF CHRIST THE KING

Our Scripture passage for the Solemnity of our Lord Jesus Christ, King of the Universe, comes from the Gospel of Matthew 25:31–46. This weekend we celebrate the final Sunday in our liturgical year. This is the well-known parable of divine judgment commonly called the Parable of the Sheep and the Goats. It tells us that judgment will be based on the actions of charity commonly known as the Corporal Works of Mercy. This passage is particularly important since it is the final public teaching of Jesus in Matthew's Gospel, and the fourth and final in a series of parables concerning divine judgment. There are some interesting aspects of this parable that make it especially challenging for us as disciples.

On the surface the parable offers two important points for our consideration. First, Jesus reveals that every charitable encounter is actually an encounter with the Lord Himself. It is this encounter with God through works of mercy and charity that distinguishes holy Christian service from merely humanitarian good efforts. When we reach out to the less fortunate, we are doing more than just a secular act of kindness. Rather, we are entering the sacred arena of divine encounter. In this parable, Jesus opens our eyes so we can recognize His presence in the "distressing disguise of the poor",[56] as Mother Teresa described it, and know Him, love Him, and serve Him there. Such awareness should motivate us to readily demonstrate heroic and faithful generosity and compassion for others. The second thing Jesus reveals is that there are privileged places of encounter where we meet the Lord more immediately, intensely, and readily than other places. Some of those privileged places of encounter are found in charitable service to the poor, the marginalized, and the suffering. The Lord is demonstrating a certain preferential option for the poor through His identification

---

56. Mother Teresa, *In the Heart of the World* (Novato, CA: New World, 1997), p. 55.

with such groups. When we choose to minister to these groups, we can encounter the Lord with an intensity and immediacy.

> *When have you had a religious experience of God while serving the poor, marginalized or suffering?*
> *How do you reach out to the poor, marginalized, and suffering in our world?*
> *When you seek a divine encounter, where do you go?*
> *What is a practical way that you can open yourself to meet Jesus in a new way this week by reaching out to someone who is poor, marginalized, or suffering?*
> *When have you been frustrated because you have not experienced the presence of God where you expected it?*
> *How does it challenge you to know that judgment will be based on our ability to show mercy and charity in situations where we do not recognize the presence of Christ?*
> *Pope Francis challenged the Church with his own gestures to let ourselves be evangelized by the poor whom we serve. How does this insight challenge your discipleship to realize that in serving the poor we are the ones actually being evangelized by Christ in them?*

There is a deeper level on which we can read this parable so as to be challenged in an even far greater way. We usually read this parable as an instruction to Christian disciples, and so we perceive the challenge to be that of practical charity. However, it is important to note that this parable is significantly different from the previous teachings on divine judgment, which we have studied for the past three weeks. In each of the previous parables, judgment took place upon someone who was already an "insider" and associated with the House of God as a Steward, Maiden, or Servant. In this final parable the subjects of judgment are the "Nations". The term "Nations" referred to the Gentiles and those who were not already associated with the House of God. Thus, this parable most probably deals with the judgment of those who are non-believers in Jesus (those who do not know God). That insight gives this parable a new twist. You see, Disciples should have already known that Jesus is present in others because our Lord instructed them as such in Matthew 10:40 when He said, "Whoever receives you receives me."

This teaching about the hidden presence of Christ in the least of His brothers and sisters should not be anything new at all to someone who has read Matthew's Gospel or who has been following Jesus. Jesus presumes that His disciples will serve Him in one another. This parable is most probably intended as the basis for divine judgment for those who are not His disciples! That insight has serious implications for us as His followers. It means that disciples are held to a much higher standard than non-disciples. It is not enough for us to aspire to the lowest possible standard. Rather, we must strive to fulfill the Father's will as revealed in Jesus and taught in the Gospels. If we are challenged by the commission to do works of mercy for the less fortunate, we have not been listening very well to the Lord's teaching for this past year. Jesus holds disciples to a much higher standard than the Nations in this passage. He expects us to not only do good for the less fortunate but to even love our enemies (Mt 5:43–48). He expects us to not only clothe the naked but to give our cloak to the oppressor (Mt 5:38–42). He expects us to practice a chastity of heart (Mt 5:27–30), control of anger (Mt 5:21–26), and desire for perfection (Mt 5:17–20) that goes beyond the ordinary. Simply put, the Lord expects more of us than just works of charity. We cannot appeal to the standard of a non-believer and exempt ourselves from the more demanding challenges of discipleship.

> *As you have read the Gospel of Matthew this past year, what have been some of the most challenging teachings for you?*
>
> *How does it challenge your discipleship to realize that you will be held to a higher standard than the Nations in this parable?*
>
> *Who are people who have demonstrated that higher standard in their lives?*
>
> *Who are people who are not currently disciples but are manifesting their cooperation with the Holy Spirit through works of charity and mercy?*
>
> *How can a faith community help people to experience and respond to the challenge of discipleship at all levels?*
>
> *Sometimes in our moral lives we like to appeal to the least common denominator and compare ourselves with exam-*

ples of lesser discipleship, but this interpretation of the
parable doesn't allow us such a comfortable self-exemption.
When are you tempted to search for the least common
denominator in your faith life, and how does this interpre-
tation challenge your basis of comparison?

Finally, this Sunday is a good opportunity to consider the many biblical images of the Last Things (Death, Judgment, Heaven, and Hell)
that have emerged in recent weeks. These parables of judgment
reveal the awesome and terrible reality that our temporal choices
can have eternal consequences. The consequences of judgment
are expressed in terms of two possibilities commonly known as
heaven and hell. It is becoming somewhat culturally unacceptable
to speak about the reality of hell, but it is a part of the Gospel message and disciples need to beware that such an option does exist
for those who turn away from God. Our Catholic faith teaches us
that God desires for all people to be saved (1 Tm 2:4) and that the
Holy Spirit can even work in the hearts of those who, through no
fault of their own, do not explicitly know Christ in order to lead
them to salvation.[57] While we hope and pray that God's mercy will
grant us all a share in eternal life, we must also be aware that our
human free will and our attachment to sin can lead us away from
God and cause us to reject the gift of eternal life.

The biblical images that have been presented in these parables
indicate that our judgment will be based upon our acceptance of
the invitation to faith and our subsequent willingness to conform
our lives to Christ (Mt 22:1–14), how well we have prepared to meet
the Son of Man and have used wisely the gift of time to acquire
the oil of faithful works (Mt 25:1–13), and whether or not we have
carried out the will of God revealed to us in Jesus and become
spiritual multipliers (Mt 25:14–30). The biblical images of heaven
include the following aspects: recognition, increased responsibilities, and lasting joy (Mt 25:21); acceptance, inclusion, warmth,
and feasting (Mt 25:10); honor and friendship (Mt 24:45–47). The
biblical images of hell include the following aspects: darkness,
sadness, loss (Mt 25:30); exclusion, alienation, cold, and rejection

---

57. Congregation for the Doctrine of the Faith, *Declaration Dominus
    Iesus,* (6 August, 2000), 21: *AAS* 92, (2000), pp. 759–761.

(Mt 25:12); punishment and humiliation (Mt 24:51). These images are worthy of our reflection.

> *Which aspect of heaven do you find most appealing?*
> *Which aspect of hell do you find most discomforting?*
> *Do you believe that your temporal decisions have eternal consequences, and how does that awareness change the way you will approach your life decisions?*
> *Which of the criterion for Judgment challenges you the most?*

As a last note, we should consider what it means to celebrate this Solemnity of our Lord Jesus Christ, King of the Universe. This Solemnity was established by Pope Pius XI in 1925. His declaration came in the midst of various secular movements, all of which laid absolute claim as the guiding principle for the lives of peoples and nations. Such movements include the following: capitalism, Nazism, Communism, Fascism, and secularism. While the immediate context on the Italian peninsula was that of Mussolini and his claim to power, the Pope considered it an opportune time to remind all people of all nations that only one person has the right to absolute claim on our lives, and that is Jesus Christ. In his encyclical we read:

> Nations will be reminded by the annual celebration of this feast that not only private individuals but also rulers and princes are bound to give public honor and obedience to Christ. It will call to their minds the thought of the last judgment, wherein Christ, Who has been cast out of public life, despised, neglected and ignored, will most severely avenge these insults; for His kingly dignity demands that the State should take account of the commandments of God and of Christian principles, both in making laws and in administering justice, and also in providing for the young a sound moral education.[58]

> *Why do you think this Solemnity is appropriate for our own time and circumstance?*

---

58. Pius XI, *Quas Primas*, (11 December, 1925), p. 32: *AAS* XVI (1925), pp. 633–646.

As you look back on the past century since the establishment of this Solemnity, how do you think history might have been different if the Kingship of Christ had been accepted by world powers?
What challenges do you experience when it comes to allowing the Kingship of Christ to reign in your life?

Bibliography

Barron, R. WordonFire.org. Retrieved October 2015–March 2016 from WordonFire.org Website: http://www.wordonfire.org/resources/homily/.

Bernard of Clairvaux, St. *De Diligendo Deo.* 7.22, (3:137.18-138.2), quoted by B. McGinn, *The Growth of Mysticism*, vol. II, New York: Crossroad, 1994.

Bonaventure, St. *Vita di S. Francesco d'Assisi.* Assisi: Edizioni Porziuncola, 2008.

Brown, R. *The Gospel According to John I-XII Anchor Bible Volume 29.* New York: Doubleday, 1966.

Brown, R. *The Gospel According to John XIII-XXI Anchor Bible Volume 29.* New York: Doubleday, 1970.

Cantalamessa, R. *The Eucharist, Our Sanctification,* Collegeville: The Liturgical Press, 1995.

Catechism of the Catholic Church. New York: Image, Doubleday, 1995.

Chromatius, St. "Tractate on Matthew, 14.5" in *Ancient Christian Commentary on Scripture,* New Testament, Ia, Matthew 1-13, Downers Grove: Inter Varsity Press, 2001.

Claude de la Colombière, St. "Act of Hope and Confidence in God" in *Hearts on Fire,* Ed. By M. Harter, Chicago: Loyola Press, 2004.

Congregation for the Doctrine of the Faith, *Declaration Dominus Iesus,* (6 August, 2000), 5: *AAS* 92, (2000).

Cornelius a Lapide. *The Great Commentary of Cornelius a Lapide.* Four volumes. Translated Thomas W. Mossman, revised and completed Michael J Miller. Fitzwilliam: Loreto Publications, 2008.

Eliot, T. S. "The Dry Salvages" in *Four Quartets,* Orlando: Harcourt, Inc., 1943.

Eliot, T. S. *Murder in the Cathedral,* New York: Harcourt, 1963, First Act.

Ephrem the Syrian, St. *Sermo IV in Hebdomadam Sanctam.* CSCO 413/Syr. 182, 55, quoted by John Paul II, *Ecclesia de Eucharistia,* (17 April, 2003), 17: *AAS* 95 (2003).

Evagrius. "Prayer" in *The Philokalia,* Vol. 1, originally compiled by Nikodimos of the Holy Mountain and Makarios of Corinth, Ed. by G. Palmer, P. Sherrard, and K. Ware, London: Faber and Faber, 1979.

Evagrius of Pontus. *Praktikos* and *On Prayer,* Oxford: Faculty of Theology, 1987.

Fitzmyer, J. *The Gospel According to Luke I-IX* Anchor *Bible Volume 28.* New York: Doubleday, 1981.

Fitzmyer, J. *The Gospel According to Luke X-XXIV Anchor Bible Volume 28A.* New York: Doubleday, 1985.

Gregory of Nyssa, *The Life of Moses,* New York: Paulist Press, 1978.

Harrington, D. *The Gospel of Matthew Sacra Pagina Series Volume 1.* "A Michael Glazier Book." Collegeville: The Liturgical Press, 1991.

Hillel the Elder, *Shabbath 31ᵃ,* Trans. By H. Freedman, London: Soncino Press, s.d.

Hilton, Walter. *The Scale of Perfection,* Book 1, 63. New York: Paulist Press. 1991.

Hopkins, Gerard M. "God's Grandeur" in *Poems and Prose,* London: Penguins Classics, 1985.

Ignatius of Antioch. *Epistle to the Magnesians.* Lightfoot & Harmer, 1891 translation.

Ignatius of Loyola, St. *Spiritual Exercises,* New York: Image, Doubleday, 1964.

John Chrysostom, St. "The Gospel of Matthew: Homily 4.4" in *Ancient Christian Commentary on Scripture,* New Testament, Ia, Matthew 1-13, Downers Grove: Inter Varsity Press, 2001.

John Chrysostom, St. "The Gospel of Matthew, Homily 89.2." in *Ancient Christian Commentary on Scripture,* NT 1b, Matthew 14-28, Downers Grove,: Varsity Press, 2002.

John of the Cross, St. *Ascent of Mt. Carmel,* prol. 5-6, Washington: ICS Publications, 1991.

John of the Cross, St. *Dark Night, Book 1.* Washington, D.C.: ICS Publ., 1991.

John of the Cross, St. *Spiritual Canticle,* XXVIII, 1 and Diego de Estella, *Meditaciones devotísimas del amor de Dios,* vol. I, Barcelona: Subirana, 1886.

John of the Cross, St. "Spiritual Canticle, Stanza 3" in *The Collected Works,* Washington, D.C: ICS Publications, 1991.

John Paul II, Apostolic Letter *Dies Domini,* (31 May, 1998), 21: *AAS* 90 [1998].

Johnson, T. *The Gospel of Luke Sacra Pagina Series Volume 3,* "A Michael Glazier Book." Collegeville: The Liturgical Press, 1991.

Leibowitz, D. *The Ironic Defense of Socrates: Plato's Apology,* Cambridge: Cambridge University Press, 2010.

Leo the Great, St. *Sermo 12.*

Leo the Great, St. *Sermo 1 in Nativitate Domini.*

Lewis, C. S. *The Screwtape Letters,* New York: Harper Collins, 2002.

Maloney, F. *The Gospel of John Sacra Pagina Series Volume 4.* "A Michael Glazier Book." Collegeville: The Liturgical Press, 1998.

Merton, T. *Contemplation in a World of Action,* South Bend: Notre Dame University Press, 1999.

Mother Teresa, *In the Heart of the World,* Novato: New World, 1997.

Mother Teresa, "Nobel Prize Lecture" in *Nobel Lectures,* Peace 1971-1980, Editor-in-Charge Tore Frängsmyr, Editor Irwin Abrams, Singapore: World Scientific Publishing Co., 1997.

The New Interpreter's Bible Volume VIII. Nashville: Abingdon Press, 1995.

The New Interpreter's Bible Volume IX. Nashville: Abingdon Press, 1995.

The New American Bible Revised Edition. Wichita: Fireside Catholic Publishing, 2010.

Nietzsche, F. *On the Genealogy of Morality,* II Essay, 8, Cambridge: Cambridge University Press, 2006.

Noffke, S. *Letters of Catherine of Siena,* vols. 1-3, Arizona Center for Religious Studies, 2007.

Nouwen, H. *Discernment,* London: SPCK, 2013.

Plato, "Phedrus" in *Dialogues* [244], Chicago: Encyclopaedia Britannica, Inc., 1952.

Pliny the Elder, *Natural History.* See the edition of Baldwin and Cradock, London, 1928.

Pope Paul VI. *Address to the Members of the Consilium de Laicis* (2 October 1974): *AAS* 66 (1974), 568; and *Evangelii Nuntiandi,* (8 December 1975), 41: *AAS* 68 (1976) pp. 5-76.

Pseudo Dionysius. "Divine Names" in *Complete Works,* New York: Paulist Press, 1987.

Pseudo Dionysius, "The Mystical Theology" in *Complete Works,* New York: Paulist Press, 1987.

Rich, A. D. *Discernment in the Desert Fathers,* Milton Keynes: Paternoster, 2007.

The Roman Missal. Translated by The International Commission on English in the Liturgy. 3rd typical ed. Washington D.C.: United States Catholic Conference of Bishops, 2011.

Sacrum Commercium sancti Francisci cum domina Paupertate, Ed. Stefano Brufani, Assisi: Edizioni Porziuncola, 1990.

Teresa of Avila, St. "Oh Hermosura" in *Complete Works,* Vol. III, Trans. By A. Peers, London: Burns and Oates, 1946 (2002).

Thérèse de Lisieux, St. "Manuscript B, 1r" in *Oeuvres completes.*

Thomas Aquinas, St. *Summa Theologia.*

Thomas Aquinas, St. *Super Evangelium S. Matthaei Lectura.*

Scupoli, L. *The Spiritual Combat,* Mesa: Scriptoria, 2012.

Stein, E. "Le Mystère de Noël (Ger: *Das Weihnachtsgeheimnis*)" in *La Crèche et la Croix,* Paris: Ad Solem Editions S.A., 2007.

Suso, H. "Little Book of Eternal Wisdom" in *The Exemplar,* New York: Paulist Press, 1989.

Tillich, P. *Dynamics of Faith,* Introductory Remarks, New York: Harper & Row, 1957.

USCCB Liturgy Committee. "Order of Blessing for a Catechetical Meeting" in *Book of Blessings,* Collegeville: The Liturgical Press, 1992.

CPSIA information can be obtained
at www.ICGtesting.com
Printed in the USA
LVOW10s0049091116

511953LV00001BA/1/P